MADNESS, CHAOS, AND VIOLENCE

THE AUTHORS

———

John Brendler, A.C.S.W.
Associate Clinical Director, Child and Family Inpatient Service
Philadelphia Child Guidance Clinic

Michael Silver, M.D.
Medical Director, Child and Family Inpatient Service
Philadelphia Child Guidance Clinic

Madlynn Haber, A.C.S.W
Clinical Director, Child and Family Outpatient Clinic
Franklin/Hampshire Community Mental Health Center,
    Northampton, Mass.

John Sargent, M.D.
Director, Child and Adolescent Psychiatric Training
Philadelphia Child Guidance Clinic

MADNESS, CHAOS, AND VIOLENCE

Therapy with Families at the Brink

JOHN BRENDLER, A.C.S.W.

MICHAEL SILVER, M.D.

MADLYNN HABER, A.C.S.W.

JOHN SARGENT, M.D.

BasicBooks

A Division of HarperCollins*Publishers*

The excerpt on page vii from *The Little Prince* by Antoine de Saint-Exupéry, copyright 1943 and renewed 1971 by Harcourt Brace Jovanovich, Inc., is reprinted by permission of the publisher.

The excerpt on page 16 from *Axe Handles*, copyright 1983 by Gary Snyder, published by North Point Press, is reprinted by permission.

Library of Congress Cataloging-in-Publication Data
Madness, chaos, and violence: therapy with families at the brink/
John Brendler. . . [et al.].
    p. cm.
    Includes bibliographical references and index.
    ISBN 0-465-04310-0
    1. Family psychotherapy.   2. Family psychotherapy—Case
    studies.
    I. Brendler, John.
    RC488.5.M33   1990
    616.89' 156—dc20   90-55664
                                         CIP

The boredom of insanity was a great desert, so great that anyone's violence or agony seemed an oasis, and the brief simple moments of companionship seemed like a rain in the desert that was numbered and counted and remembered long after it was gone.

—Joanne Greenberg (Hannah Green),
I Never Promised You a Rose Garden

"Come and play with me," proposed the little prince. "I am so unhappy."

"I cannot play with you," the fox said. "I am not tamed."

"Ah! Please excuse me," said the little prince. But after some thought, he added, "What does that mean—tame?" . . .

"It is an act too often neglected," said the fox. "It means to establish ties."

"To establish 'ties'?"

"Just that," said the fox . . . "if you tame me, then we shall need each other. To me, you will be unique in all the world. To you, I shall be unique in all the world."

. . . "One only understands the things that one tames," said the fox. "Men have no more time to understand anything. They buy things all ready made at the shops. But there is no shop anywhere where one can buy friendship, and so men have no friends anymore. If you want a friend, tame me . . ."

"What must I do, to tame you?" asked the little prince.

"You must be very patient," replied the fox. "First you will sit down at a little distance from me—like that—in the grass. I shall look at you out of the corner of my eye, and you will say nothing. Words are the source of misunderstandings. But you will sit a little closer to me, every day . . ."

—Antoine de Saint-Exupéry, *The Little Prince*

CONTENTS

FOREWORD

M *ADNESS, CHAOS, AND VIOLENCE* is about therapy with overwhelmed and hopeless families that seem impervious to change and keep baffling and debilitating mental health professionals. It deals with families who live at the brink of disaster, entangled in life-threatening problems such as suicide, sexual abuse, physical violence, substance abuse, and psychosis.

With clarity, compassion, and respect, the authors first describe the unique dilemmas these families bring to therapists and then offer a model for inducing crisis and capitalizing on it to disrupt the cycles of abandonment and violence in which the families are caught.

This is a sobering and instructive book about promoting transformations that seldom come about quickly. It offers realistic guidelines on how to facilitate "de-fusion," moments of discovery of independence in very inflexible relationships. A unique contribution of the book is the way it highlights how bringing about change requires a great deal of repetition and constant challenge. As this hard-hitting book amply demonstrates, unleashing the growth process that creates corrective interaction can be fostered and facilitated, but seldom forced. The eroding of dysfunctional patterns and the establishing of new ones cannot come about by the force of clever strategy. This is not just because of insufficiencies in the therapist's goals and tactics, as current myths would have us believe, but because of the tenacity of the patterns that characterize rigid and overwhelmed family systems as they try to reor-

ganize. The authors show that the slippery patterns must be rediscov-
ered in different interpersonal sectors and vigorously addressed over
and over by the therapists.

Madness, Chaos, and Violence will inspire clinicians, particularly the new
breed of method-driven therapists, to develop among their creative
affective resources, the patience, humanity, and humor that tame the
chaos of relationships within families at the brink.

—Braulio Montalvo
Family Institute of New Mexico

ACKNOWLEDGMENTS

TRANSFORMING ONESELF into a therapist is necessarily intertwined with maturing as a person. We learned much about both from our teachers, colleagues, and students, and from our patients and their families. We are grateful for their guidance and companionship during our personal and therapeutic journeys. Special recognition goes to the families who courageously left their homes to move into the hospital apartments and who shared their lives with us so intimately.

We are especially indebted to the members of the inpatient apartment team for their participation in the development of the model of crisis induction. Without their openness to experimenting with different, more intimate ways of relating to families at the brink, and their willingness to put their guts on the line in very difficult situations, this book would never have been possible. Brenda Pemberton, as the program coordinator of the team, deserves special mention for her personal devotion to the team and to the families, and for her unique ability to rally the team around her in a spirit of collaboration and commitment.

We would like to thank Dennis Piermattei, Alberto Serrano, and Connell O'Brien, the president and chief executive officer, medical director, and vice-president for inpatient services, respectively, of the Philadelphia Child Guidance Clinic, and Jim Reis, director of children and family services, Franklin/Hampshire Community Mental Health Center, for their appreciation of our struggles in attempting to write a book while carrying out the responsibilities of our full-time jobs. Special thanks go to Dennis for introducing us to the Macintosh computer.

Bernice Rosman, director of education at the Philadelphia Child Guidance Clinic, facilitated a vital connection by introducing us to Jo Ann Miller, our editor at Basic Books. We are grateful for Jo Ann's commitment to making the book a reality, and for the time she devoted to editing the book. Her emphasis on brevity and simplicity, and her keen eye for what was relevant and what was not, were particularly helpful.

The comprehensive fine tuning of the manuscript performed by the copy editor, Nola Lynch, and the coordination of the final phases by Susan Zurn, the project editor, were thorough and much appreciated. We also thank Rona Rosenberg for giving her time so generously to type numerous drafts of the manuscript.

Three of the leading therapists and thinkers in the field were instrumental in inspiring our thinking and in shaping the final version of the book. Braulio Montalvo urged us to put our therapy and ideas about working with hospitalized families into print, and graciously contributed the Foreword. We are deeply appreciative of his willingness to read the original text and offer many detailed comments that served to sharpen our focus on the key principles of the model. Salvador Minuchin read the entire manuscript and spent hours on the phone sharing his impressions and helping us define what was at the heart of our work. The respectful and spirited manner with which he cut through to the essence of things was an invaluable source of support. We are also grateful for Kalman Flomenhaft's ongoing encouragement for the writing of the book during the past five years, and for the humanity and pragmatism that he brought to his critique of the manuscript.

We thank several of our colleagues, Fran Henkel, Cathy Nevins, Wendy Shumway, Mike Hart, and Judy Davis, for reading portions of the manuscript and providing constructive criticism and encouragement throughout the process of writing. Paul Youngs and Sam Scott read the entire manuscript and offered affirming and thoughtful suggestions that helped us to formulate and express our thinking more clearly. Joe Micucci's incisive comments, particularly about the concepts of conditional and unconditional acceptance in relationships, helped us to clarify a number of essential ideas.

In the early stages of planning for the book, two brainstorming sessions with Donald Langsley helped us to think through the process of organizing and writing the book. Lee Combrinck-Graham was also helpful in encouraging us to emphasize practical applications of the lessons learned from our experiences working with hospitalized families. Ann Itzkowitz's collaboration in workshops during the past several years has inspired us to refine our thinking about the practice and teaching of crisis induction.

I want to express my deep appreciation and respect for my most loyal comrade in this project—my wife, Jeanine. Her patience, encouragement, and understanding freed me to focus on writing during the past two and one-half years, and her loving spirit nurtured the family and kept it going. My children, Michael, Cara, and Rebecca, I thank for being so understanding and supportive of my intense involvement in this book, for being so alive and caring about their relationships, and for always reminding me about what is important in life. I also want to thank my mother and father for instilling in me a love of life, people, and relationships, and for being so accepting and trusting of me. And to my grandparents, Ray Ray and Max, I am grateful for their interesting me in contexts and in writing a book. —John Brendler

I thank Genie for her love and for sustaining me through the writing of this book despite the many demands of her own work. I have learned much from her about dedication, perseverance, and commitment. Dan was always generous with his love, and he is the best son I could ever wish for. I am also grateful to my parents for bringing me up in a way that was right for me. —Michael Silver

I am grateful to my colleagues at the Franklin/Hampshire Community Mental Health Center—Marge Barnett, Margaret Tomasko, Jennifer Parker, Jane Curran, Michael Katz, Sharon Dombeck, Alex Chesner, and Heather Hornik—for their willingness to experiment with applications of this model and for sharing with me the day-to-day joys and struggles of clinical work. I thank Judith Fox and Joseph Canevello for the hospitality, nurturance, wisdom, and encouragement that they provided during my many trips to Philadelphia, and Susan Kahn and Sandy Mandel for their support at home. I especially appreciate Donald Benjamin for his love and understanding and for helping me stay true to my own values. Growing up in Brooklyn with my grandmother Ruth, mother Laura, sister Susan, and a house full of aunts, uncles, and cousins who encouraged my sense of humor, compassion, stamina, and appreciation for intensity, prepared me well for the challenges of doing therapy and writing this book. —Madlynn Haber

Meri, your faith in me and your consistent support have taught me daily about the transforming power of relationships. Thank you from my heart. My children—Erin, Jonathan, and Patrick—through their love for me, have strengthened and given personal meaning to my commitment to children and their families. I honor always—and my contribution to this book honors—my parents, Margaret and Jack, for their belief in me and their encouragement that I be all that I can be. I also want to thank John, Michael, and Madlynn for the opportunity to collaborate with them on this book. It has been a truly special experience. I have grown through this work and been enriched through their friendship.   —John Sargent

INTRODUCTION

—————

THIS IS A BOOK about psychotherapy with families in serious trouble, and about the critical nature of the therapist's relationship with the family as the source of healing and growth. It is not a technical manual. Techniques are important, but only insofar as they are extensions of the therapist, not discrete interventions separate from his person. When the therapist views techniques as his primary tools, he loses the strength of his own healing power—that is, the power emanating from his own integrity and the integrity of the relationships he cultivates with family members.

The clinical material from which our model of treatment is derived is drawn primarily from our work as members of an interdisciplinary team that treated approximately two hundred families who were hospitalized in the inpatient apartment program of the Philadelphia Child Guidance Clinic between 1980 and 1985. The apartment program is part of the clinic's Child and Family Inpatient Service, a short-term psychiatric hospital for children, adolescents, young adults, and their families. While there is no longer a treatment team dedicated to working primarily with hospitalized families, the inpatient apartments continue to be actively utilized by the four treatment teams that currently comprise the inpatient service.

During the years 1980–1985, John Brendler was the director of the apartment team and was largely responsible for developing the conceptualization of its treatment approach. In 1987 he initiated and directed the collaborative effort of writing this book. He and Madlynn Haber were the primary therapists working with hospitalized families. Michael Silver was closely involved with the team as a cotherapist on a number of cases and as a supervisor of therapists who worked on the team. John Sargent also supervised therapists working with hospitalized families and was involved in several cases as a cotherapist.

All of the case material in the book is based on our clinical work with actual families. When referring to therapists in general, we have alternated masculine and feminine pronouns from chapter to chapter. Names, identifying characteristics, and other details of the cases have been changed in the interest of protecting confidentiality, without sacrificing the actual progression and highlights of treatment.

The book is divided into two parts. Part 1 (chapters 1–3) describes the conceptual framework of crisis induction and the essential ingredients of the therapeutic process. Chapter 1 introduces the reader to severely symptomatic families and to the idea of crisis induction, and then describes the historical and clinical context in which the model of treatment developed. In chapter 2, we describe the theoretical model and provide an overview of the four phases of treatment (madness, chaos, violence, and transformation), illustrated by the case of a nineteen-year-old woman who was bulimic and was unable to individuate from her family despite years of outpatient and inpatient treatment. Chapter 3 describes the critical qualities of the therapist that guide the therapeutic process; clinical vignettes illustrate each of these principles.

Part 2 (chapters 4–7) illustrates the clinical application of the model through a detailed presentation of the four phases of crisis induction with the three families described at the beginning of chapter 1: the Cabrinis, the Harmons, and the Monroes. An overview of each phase, highlighting its essential components, precedes a description of the treatment with each of the families in the particular phase being described.

The Epilogue (chapter 8) describes implications of our model for therapists and their work with severely symptomatic families.

PART ONE

CONTEXT, THEORY, AND TECHNIQUE

Going against the Grain: The Development of a Model

There are only two or three human stories, and they go on repeating themselves as fiercely as if they had never happened before.
— Willa Cather

Snapshots from the Family Album

MARIA Cabrini, eighteen years old, lived with her two siblings, her mother, and her stepfather. Her stepfather frequently stormed out of the house, staying away for days at a time after fighting with his wife. Maria's sixteen-year-old brother, Bruno, and her thirteen-year-old half sister, Anita, attended school only sporadically. Bruno and Mr. Cabrini often fought violently.

Maria was admitted to a psychiatric hospital after she began to hear voices and attempted suicide. Shortly before her admission, her three-year-old son, Nicholas, had been removed from his home by the child protective service agency after allegations of neglect and abuse. Maria had been hospitalized several times previously for suicide attempts, depression, and psychotic behavior. Her parents had repeatedly refused to participate in therapy in the past, saying that Maria's problems were too difficult for them to handle. The family's hopelessness, fear, and distrust of one another were compounded by their distrust of professionals.

Josh Harmon, thirteen years old, felt alienated and trapped. His drug use and explosive outbursts at home were becoming more frequent, and recently he took an overdose of Tylenol after an argument with his father. He had had academic and behavioral problems in school since the first grade, and was labeled a "screw up" by his peers. During the past six months he was suspended from school several times for fighting with other students and being disruptive in class. Suzanne, Josh's seventeen-year-old sister, had been using marijuana and alcohol regularly for several years.

Outpatient therapy had begun with several therapists, but the parents had always stopped treatment. The family was currently working with its fourth therapist in three years. A wide variety of agencies and professionals had become involved in the family's life, including Josh's teachers and school counselors, the local police, and Suzanne's drug counselor. Input from all these professionals, none of whom had any contact with the others, left the family feeling even more confused and overwhelmed.

Jennifer Monroe's difficulties began two years ago, when she was twenty, a sophomore in college. She came home on winter break to find her parents arguing continuously, her father drinking heavily, and the family saddled with financial problems. Jennifer became severely depressed, cut her wrists repeatedly, and was hospitalized in a psychiatric institution for six months. While in the hospital she began abusing laxatives and starving herself. Following discharge, she continued to lose weight, and the family was referred to a therapist with special expertise in the treatment of eating disorders. The therapist tried working with Jennifer and her parents, but there was no significant progress and he ended treatment. Later, Jennifer returned to individual psychotherapy, but her weight continued to drop and her laxative abuse intensified, necessitating five medical hospitalizations for dehydration and dangerously low levels of serum electrolytes. Everyone, including her therapist, felt terrified and helpless.

Challenges of the Severely Symptomatic Family

Stories like those of the Cabrinis, Harmons, and Monroes are familiar to most mental health professionals. These families become embroiled with professionals in a repetitive and ineffective battle over a symptom that threatens the life of one or more of its members, such as suicide attempts, physical violence, sexual abuse, psychosis, substance abuse, and psychosomatic problems. The family tries to gain control of the symptom, but the more the family struggles, the more entangled with the symptom it becomes. Nothing seems to work. More and more of the family's time and energy are consumed, until the symptom affects every facet of its life. The family turns to experts, yet their advice, guidance, and direction only aggravate the situation. The family goes from one professional to another, as if on a quest for a magic cure, yet believes that nothing can change.

This book describes a model for promoting transformations in the most hard to reach, severely symptomatic families. These families are trapped in a cycle of escalating entanglements with a symptom that leads to a logjam, an impasse in the developmental process, whereby the ability of individual family members and the family as a system to grow and meet their own needs is thwarted. These entanglements constitute a symptomatic system. That is, the symptom has organized a complex pattern of relationships involving the symptomatic person, family members, friends, therapists, and members of social and legal agencies. External intervention is required to dissolve the blockade and permit the natural flow to resume.

The model of treatment we use to break up the logjam is *crisis induction.* The model evolved from our work with hospitalized families in the inpatient apartment program at the Philadelphia Child Guidance Clinic between 1980 and 1985. Though the inpatient apartments, which are described later in this chapter, constitute a specialized setting for treating families who have exhausted conventional inpatient and outpatient resources, we have found through our own clinical work in varied settings as therapists, supervisors, consultants, and teachers that the principles of crisis induction are widely applicable to work with severely symptomatic families in such settings as psychiatric hospitals, residential and day treatment facilities, partial hospital programs, consultation and liaison services to schools and medical hospitals, and outpatient practice, both agency-based and private.

In spite of the overwhelming suffering and stress that come from living with life-threatening behaviors, these families live on the brink of disaster and expect to go on living there indefinitely. Because they experience their circumstances as ongoing and relatively stable, they are not literally in crisis, not at a turning point. Consider the family of a seventeen-year-old girl with severe anorexia nervosa, who had continued to starve herself and lose weight to a medically dangerous level at home, despite intensive outpatient psychotherapy and antidepressant medication. Based on the referral information, we were concerned enough about her physical condition to have added the chief nurse and the medical director to the usual therapy team observing the initial session behind the one-way mirror; we had also alerted the emergency room staff at Children's Hospital, which is adjacent to the Philadelphia Child Guidance Clinic. Upon being informed of our preparations, the mother expressed surprise: "We've been living with this for the last three years! There's no cause for alarm."

Severely symptomatic families are so rigidly entrenched in their patterns and absorbed by the compelling nature of their symptoms that they seem impervious to therapists' efforts to effect change, as if they are in a symptomatic trance. The therapist must generate a high degree of intensity to disturb the family's equilibrium enough for the family to reach a crisis point, where it is most open to new ideas and ready to experiment with alternatives. Crisis induction is a process of amplifying stress in the family by repetitively challenging family members to modify their perceptions, beliefs, and behaviors, while simultaneously inviting new patterns of interaction. In the context of a trusting relationship between the family and the therapist, these challenges create the dynamic tension necessary to catalyze transformation. The integrity of the therapeutic relationship is essential to promote change, allowing family members to feel safe enough to tolerate the stress of crisis induction and to become free to take risks.

As the therapist engages a family, he challenges its organization around the symptom. He questions the family's rules, traditions, and myths; probes and exacerbates conflicts; exposes hidden coalitions and the toxic secrets that accompany them; and attacks destructive entanglements. He often takes an immovable position when proposing a treatment contract, mobilizing the family to reorganize around him instead of around the symptom or symptomatic person; for example, the treatment team was willing to admit Maria Cabrini to the inpatient unit only after her parents had demonstrated competence in managing her behavior for three days at home. When family members break the treatment contract and run from each other and the therapist, the therapist must pursue them. When there is imminent danger, such as physical, sexual, or psychological abuse, the therapist may enforce separations. For example, when a father's efforts to discipline his psychotic son consistently lead to violence between them, the therapist may insist that the father move out of the house and have no further contact with the boy until the boy's mother is convinced that the father will control himself. If family members retreat from each other to their own separate worlds, forcing conflicts underground, the therapist may compress the symptomatic system, increasing proximity among family members until the conflicts are out in the open. Throughout the therapeutic process, the therapist must closely monitor the family and himself for retreats into symptomatic patterns and be prepared to repeat interventions over and over again.

In addition, the therapist creates scenarios that draw upon the family's strengths, activating its members to explore and experiment with their own untapped resources and those of the community. He musters all the available interpersonal and physical resources, including the family's social network and the educational, medical, and legal systems.

The Nature of the Severely Symptomatic Family: Isolation and Disconnection

Though severely symptomatic families have different symptoms, different styles of interacting, and different backgrounds, beneath the surface there are important similarities. Each member suffers from a sense of isolation and alienation exacerbated by the anticipation, occurrence, or recollection of a traumatic event. Whether it be the death of a family member, the placement or threat of placement of a child, a divorce, physical or sexual abuse, or loss of employment, the family experiences a massive discontinuity in the flow of its everyday life. The usual boundaries of the family, the family's sense of identity, the composition and coherence of the family, are stretched and dislocated. A sense of death permeates these families. They are haunted with the fear of losing the symptomatic person through death, suicide or homicide, or long-term institutionalization. Lifeless expressions, murderous looks and threats, and suicidal fantasies and behavior paralyze their lives, leaving them feeling cut off emotionally from one another and from their own sense of vitality.

The symptom reflects a profound lack of connectedness and a breakdown in the integrity of family relationships. People who are symptomatic sail rudderless in chaotic, turbulent straits, feeling profoundly alone and powerless to contend with the exigencies of everyday life. Having no control over events or other people, they see themselves as inadequate and unworthy of being taken care of. This self-image is reinforced by their intimate relationships, in which they routinely experience only conditional acceptance. That is, there is always the explicit or implicit message from others that "I will accept and value you *if* or *until* or *provided that* certain conditions hold." Ultimately there is a sense of violation and physical or psychological abandonment, and symptomatic persons cry out through their symptoms to be accepted, respected, and heard. In response to their experience of ruptured relationships and betrayal, they may lash out in intensely destructive ways.

The family appears to be held hostage by its own symptoms. While the symptoms are difficult to manage, they are also impossible to ignore. Knives may be hidden to protect the suicidal adolescent. Mealtimes may last several hours, with parents coaxing and cajoling their starving daughter to eat. The symptomatic person assumes such a position of importance that other members appear invisible and other aspects of the family's life are neglected. A major consequence of the family's entanglement with the symptom is a derailment of the developmental process.

Behind the protectiveness and appearance of overinvolvement lies a deep fear of being alone. Adult family members have not individuated from their own families of origin, and they are threatened by the natural processes of growth and change in themselves and their children. So stressful are these processes that it is often easier to live with the daily horrors than to change. The family lives in a state of suspended animation, frightened of living differently because of the pain and suffering that change might bring.

Although family members may appear to be overinvolved with and protective of one another, in fact there are thick, rigid walls between them. Family members seem deaf and blind to each other's needs; no one knows who the other is, what the other likes, needs, or feels. As the father of a family with an anorectic daughter said: "We keep our emotions inside of us. We don't let them out, we don't tell each other how we really feel about things. We try to be nice all the time. We just don't let each other know how we feel or what we really think."

These families come for therapy, having absorbed the interventions of previous therapists into their routines. At any moment a therapist's comments might be disqualified by reference to Dr. So-and-so, "who made the same suggestion and it didn't work." Family members are prepared to analyze and evaluate therapeutic techniques using the diagnostic and clinical language they have picked up along the way. In this way they distance themselves from their pain and attempt to hide its reality from the therapist. Their experiences of defeat lead to mistrust of professionals and support their expectation that the next therapist, too, will fail them. Stimulating the family to reawaken the other dimensions in its life is a crucial part of effective therapy. Attending to the needs of siblings, spouses, extended family, and friends allows the therapist to revitalize dormant or atrophied parts of the family's universe.

The Shark-Infested Waters of Treatment

In working with severely symptomatic families, the therapist can easily become overwhelmed by the anguish and fear with which family members live. He is likely to brand the family resistant and manipulative, or to see it as a shark or a barracuda that nourishes itself by capturing and devouring therapists (Bergman 1985). These responses reflect the therapist's emotional withdrawal and disconnection from the family. They connote the presence of a therapeutic impasse, which reflects deterioration in the therapeutic relationship.

The most dangerous sharks are the *ideas* therapists hold about families and the process of change. More often than not, the waters are not shark infested until the therapist jumps in. One of the more common sharks is the view that severely symptomatic families are as helpless, defeated, and unmotivated as they appear. Although these families are adept at demonstrating their limitations, they have an enormous resilience and tolerance for emotional and behavioral extremes that allows them to stay together in the worst situations. Consider the family of a fourteen-year-old psychotic boy who, in the course of the session, started a fight with his father, threw a chair at him, and ended up being physically restrained. When asked about this session in a follow-up visit five years later, the father remembered it vividly. "Yes," he said, "that was the time Larry got physical in the session. But you know, we'd been living with that type of thing for years, wondering when it ever was going to end."

One could interpret such monumental accommodation to symptomatic behavior as evidence of massive denial and weakness; it is also accurate, however, and considerably more useful, to view it as an unusual capacity to tolerate overwhelming circumstances when no other options seem available.

The most vicious shark is the belief that the therapist can be more powerful than the family and can control how the family lives its life. The therapist can become so absorbed in trying to rescue families from symptomatic behaviors that he sees neither the family's strengths nor how his own behavior can replicate the family's dysfunctional patterns. Therapists must avoid the temptation to camouflage their feelings, deceiving themselves and the families, in the name of trying to be supportive. The therapist's reluctance to disturb or agitate the family because it is suffering and fragile is really a way of shielding himself. The alternative is to actively engage the family, facing and accepting the feelings of vulnerability, impotence, and rage that he experiences in response to family members who treat each other, and sometimes him, in a dismissive, disqualifying, and cruel manner.

We thus developed a model for treatment that would encourage the therapist to embrace his own pain and that of the family while simultaneously finding and activating their strengths, thereby keeping the sharks at bay. While it is a model that grew from our particular treatment context, it did not develop in a vacuum.

The Heritage of the Model

The Philadelphia Child Guidance Clinic's Apartment Program evolved from a lineage of clinicians who had experimented with approaches to treating severely symptomatic families on an outpatient and inpatient basis. They challenged the therapeutic efficacy of the custodial mental hospital, in which the symptomatic person is isolated from his or her family, work, and community, and is viewed as the locus of pathology. They questioned the wisdom of the paternalistic attitude characterized by the professionals assuming responsibility for the patient; such an attitude implies that symptomatic people and their families are too fragile, incompetent, or irresponsible to manage their own problems and participate in a meaningful way in their own healing process.

In the 1960s and 1970s, when the new community mental health movement inspired unbridled optimism about the treatment of severe mental disorders, there was great concern about the debilitating effects of long-term psychiatric institutionalization, such as induced dependency, stigmatization, and the breakdown of social functioning (Goldberg 1966; Gruenberg 1967; Herz et al. 1977; Langsley and Kaplan 1968; Ruesch 1966; Silverstein 1968; Test and Stein 1975). In an effort to address these problems, innovative projects were established to work with severely symptomatic people and their families at home and in the community, such as in halfway houses, partial programs, or "psychosocial rehabilitation centers" (Bowen 1961; Davis, Dinitz, and Pasamanick 1974; Glasscote et al. 1971; Langsley and Kaplan 1968). Experimental projects were also developed to treat families in hospital settings (Abroms, Fellner, and Whitaker 1971; Bowen 1966; Grunebaum and Weiss 1963; Lynch, Steinberg, and Ounstead 1975; Main 1958; Nakhla, Flokart, and Webster 1969).

While experimentation with family hospitalization was occurring in Great Britain and the United States, intensive family participation in hospital treatment was considered a matter of course in many other parts of the world. Often, this was due to the lack of sophisticated technology, the limited numbers of professional staff available to attend to the patients, and a strong sense of kinship ties. In *The Family in the Hospital* (1971), John Bell describes his observations at Central Hospital in Cameroon:

During the whole time a patient is in the hospital he is virtually never separated, either day or night, from at least one member of his family. He is never isolated from a familiar voice, from a hand pressing himself, from food he usually eats, prepared in ways he prefers and by relatives or friends he trusts. Those who have a special stake in his recovery are right there at his side all the time, no matter what reordering of their lives was necessary to make this possible. (Pp.7–8)

Bell also describes the strong sense of attachment family members had to one another at a psychiatric hospital in India, which became known as the Outdoor Hospital, after tents were erected on the grounds to house family members:

Many patients and relatives travel by buses that pass the doors every fifteen minutes. Others arrive by pony cart, oxcart, pedicab, bicycle, taxi, private auto, or on foot. As they come they may bring bedrolls, firewood, primus stoves, brass cooking pots, water pots, suitcases, and food. Many, particularly those from a distance, expect to stay, even if only for a few days. Usually one or more relatives accompany the patient, but if no relatives can manage to come (very unusual, although the relatives may not be close) a friend, neighbor, or servant may come. The staff takes the attitude with the relatives that "You can take your patient back any time you like; you can visit any time you want; you can make suggestions not only for your own patient but for others"—and the hospital takes the suggestions. (1971, 39)

Against this backdrop Salvador Minuchin led the Philadelphia Child Guidance Clinic to its new campus in 1974. Although Minuchin held an anti-institutional bias, he did not agree with those who urged against including an inpatient unit in the new site as a solution to the "problem" of psychiatric hospitalization. Rather, he envisioned a "noninstitutional hospital" to provide short-term inpatient treatment for families of children, adolescents, and young adults with severe symptomatology.

From the late 1970s through the mid-1980s, in weekly consultations with Salvador Minuchin and later with Carl Whitaker, and in ongoing seminars and supervision with Braulio Montalvo, Lee Combrinck-Graham, Marianne Walters, Sam Scott, Harry Aponte, and Ronald Leibman, among others, we heard voices encouraging us to challenge ourselves. Their relentless focus on competence and the search for alternatives created a spirit of optimism, an atmosphere of exploration and experimentation. In spite of their differences in theory and technique, each one of our teachers taught us that it is the therapist as a person, not as a technician, who is the key to helping families change.

Our team thus entered into the venture of hospitalizing families with a set of beliefs about families and the process of change that developed in the context of our exposure to a culture of exceptional clinicians and teachers at the Philadelphia Child Guidance Clinic. Their influence challenged us to go beyond facile formulations about the antithetical nature of family therapy and institutional psychiatry.

Instead of the traditional goals of hospitalization—to stabilize symptoms, protect the patient and others during periods of acute stress, and provide respite for an exhausted and overwhelmed family—our goal was to use hospitalization to induce crises and escalate stress in the family system in order to promote a therapeutic transformation (Minuchin and Barcai 1969; Minuchin, Rosman, and Baker 1978). Rather than to assume responsibility for the family, the goal was to help the family assume responsibility for itself.

The Apartment Program

There were two inpatient family apartments adjacent to a more traditional inpatient area for children, adolescents, and young adults. Each apartment had a large living area, a bedroom, and one bathroom. The living room had a kitchen and dining area and a sofabed. The living area also included a one-way mirror through which staff could observe, though only with the family's knowledge and permission. The apartment had enough space to comfortably sleep six, although families with as many as ten members were admitted on occasion.

The hospital billed the relevant insurance carrier or other third-party payer for each registered patient, according to the established per diem rate; often several family members, both children and adults, were registered.

The apartment program had no set treatment protocols. Treatment consisted of using all available materials to construct a new context in which conflicts could be resolved and functional ways of relating could emerge. One building block was the inpatient unit proper. The permeable physical and conceptual boundary between the apartment and the rest of the inpatient unit allowed a family whose child had been hospitalized individually on the inpatient unit to move into an apartment with its child prior to the child's discharge. This allowed family members to become more intimately engaged in treatment and to practice taking more responsibility for themselves in a staff-intensive and supportive context (Combrinck-Graham, Gursky, and Brendler 1982). Other building blocks used by the team included the day treatment program, the apartment, the treatment team, other patients and their families, and families who had previously been hospitalized in the program. The team also worked with other systems in which the family had been entangled, such as the child's school, the family's neighborhood, the referral source or outpatient therapist, and the medical, legal, and welfare systems.

The principles underlying the treatment process did not vary. Each family was engaged in creating its own treatment program, weaving with the team a therapeutic tapestry in its own style, texture, and design. The treatment plan was devised in family therapy sessions and was elaborated on in team meetings. These meetings took place as often as necessary—two or more times a day—and the family would often be invited.

Although the treatment team represented the standard professional disciplines, roles were flexible and negotiated, according to the particular goals for each family and the strengths and interests of team members, rather than rigidly defined by professional training (Auerswald 1972). For example, a psychiatrist who was also a parent might assume a peerlike position with a single mother who was feeling overwhelmed and isolated, while another team member might spend time in the gym playing basketball with a father and son. By sharing interests and life experiences, a rich and complex network of relationships between each family and the team was established.

Much more than family therapy took place. The aim was to create a total ecosystem. The inpatient apartments provided the testing ground for generating and refining knowledge about difficult-to-treat, multi-problem families and facilitated systematic experimentation with a variety of interventions and contexts in a controlled environment. The primary question was always the following: What combination of physical and interpersonal resources would be most influential in disrupting the existing interactional patterns in the family and in facilitating the emergence of new ones? For example, with a family with socially isolated and disruptive children, the inpatient unit's residential living area could be defined as a neighborhood center, where the children could be rewarded for good behavior by having opportunities to play with kids their own age. For a family terrorized by an adolescent's physically violent or threatening behavior, the same area could become a "cooler" to temporarily relieve the parents and contain the acting-out teenager.

The day treatment classrooms could be used in different ways as well. A child in one family might participate in the psychoeducational program all day long without seeing a parent. A child of the same age in another family might participate in selected peer group activities in the classroom while a parent observed from behind the one-way mirror. Alternatively, that parent might be in the classroom working directly with his or her child, working with another child in the unit from a different family, or helping the team conduct a therapeutic activity based on the parent's own area of expertise.

At close range, the team shared the myriad tasks and routines of the family's everyday life, becoming intimately acquainted with its language and style, its particular rhythm and tempo. We participated in each family's unique rituals and culture. We saw aspects of family life not often visible in the therapist's office, the "trivia of everyday life" (Henry 1973, xix) generally hidden from outsiders. We knew what the family members ate for breakfast and what time they went to bed, how their leisure time was spent, how their conflicts got ignited and settled, how they fought, how they played together and enjoyed each other, how they managed cooperative tasks, and how alliances and coalitions were reflected in the normal course of family life.

The hypotheses developed from our observations and interactions were evaluated through various interventions and tasks and modified in response to the family's feedback. Through this process, we learned a great deal about what severely symptomatic families are like, what keeps them entangled with symptoms, and what makes them change.

The setting also permitted us to observe and modify our own interactional dynamics with the family in response to the feedback generated by the system of family plus team. We learned from and changed in response to the families in a process complementary to the one by which they learned from and changed in response to us.

Just as family members were expected to take risks and try alternatives, team members took risks as they expanded their clinical repertoire. The culture was continually enriched by the excitement of exploration and discovery.

CHAPTER 2

The Symptomatic Cycle and Crisis Induction

Through mud, fouled nuts, black grime
it opens, a gleam of spotless steel
machined-fit perfect
swirl of intake and output
relentless clarity
at the heart
of work

—Gary Snyder
"Removing the Plate of the Pump on the
Hydraulic System of the Backhoe" from *Axe Handles*

Theory is not just another gadget which can be used without
understanding.

—Gregory Bateson
quoted in Berger, *Beyond the Double Bind*

The Symptomatic Cycle
How Symptoms Beget Systems

THE TERM *symptomatic cycle* denotes the repetitive pattern of behaviors that develops within the family and between the family and professionals who have become involved with the symptomatic person. The development of the cycle in which the symptom generates the symptomatic system (Hoffman 1985) occurs in the following way.

The cycle begins when a person's behavior is defined as symptomatic either by the person or by an observer. In response to this definition, someone—typically someone in the person's family—attempts to control or change the symptom. If such attempts alleviate or eradicate the symptom, the matter ends there. However, if the behavior persists or escalates, the boundaries of the symptomatic system begin to expand beyond the person and the family to incorporate therapists and other professionals who, in their effort to respond to the family's request for help, attempt to control the family and thus become part of the cycle. The cycle is especially likely to develop if family members convey only conditional acceptance of each other and if people try to solve interpersonal problems unilaterally. In such situations, imbalances in power are worsened and mistrust and disconnection are accentuated. The system enlarges like the concentric ripples from a stone thrown into a pond.

PITFALLS FOR THE THERAPIST

Viewing symptomatic behavior as part of a symptomatic cycle has two major pitfalls of which the therapist must beware. The first pitfall is the belief that severe symptoms, in particular violence, are merely a punctuation of an interactional sequence. A dangerous implication of this belief is the assertion that one person cannot have power over another. When therapists disparage designations of victim and perpetrator as examples of linear thinking, they inadvertently collude with the person committing violent behavior by allowing him or her to evade responsibility. Physical or sexual violence and abuse should be viewed not as systemic constructs but as matters of life and death. Therapists should treat these matters with a strong conviction that people are responsible for their own behavior and should insist that families do the same with their own members.

The second pitfall lies in overlooking the diagnosis of the symptomatic person. Schizophrenia, for example, clearly has significant genetic, anatomical, biochemical, and physiological correlates. Saying that schizophrenia merely represents a developmental impasse would be not only inaccurate but clinically irresponsible. However, there are pathways of functional developmental progression for families with schizophrenic members. When such families repeatedly encounter impasses in their internal relationships and their relationships with mental health professionals, this progression is stalled. At that point, the therapist needs to address the problem at the level of the symptomatic cycle by working with the relationships among patient, family, and treating professionals, while also paying attention to the levels of individual biology and psychology.

ILLUSTRATION: A CASE OF BULIMIA

The case of Susan Jepsen and her family demonstrates a way of formulating the symptomatic cycle based on information gathered from the referral and the initial session. Susan was nineteen years old, living with her parents, and had recently completed a training program as a lab technician subsequent to high school graduation. She had a five-year history of anorexia nervosa, which had evolved in the last several years into bulimia. Because she at times had episodes where she lost consciousness following protracted vomiting, there was much medical concern that she might choke on her vomit and suffer severe physical consequences. She had also been caught stealing money from a co-worker in order to purchase food for binging. A host of therapeutic approaches, including individual and family therapy, psychiatric hospitalization, day treatment programs, and various medications had failed to help Susan separate from her parents in a healthy way. At the time of her referral to the inpatient unit at the Philadelphia Child Guidance Clinic, she was a patient in a state mental hospital.

During the first session with Susan and her parents upon their arrival at our inpatient unit, the therapist explored the nature of the relationships among the symptom, Susan, her family, and the medical-psychiatric system. Susan said that she would like to be living in her own apartment, working and associating with people her own age. Her parents also wanted this. But each time Susan attempted to move out, her binging and vomiting intensified. A pattern had developed whereby Susan would vomit in secret, leaving clues for her parents, who, upon finding the evidence, would become angry and engage in ineffective attempts to monitor and prevent her behavior. Susan would then make greater attempts at self-control, which would usually lead her to become more out of control. She would then redouble her attempts at concealment, which would increase her parents' suspicions and anxieties, leading them to look for new ways to monitor her behavior covertly. Each time her parents found her weak or passed out, they would call her therapist or take her to the local emergency room, which resulted in hospitalization. Separation from her parents was thus organized by Susan's symptoms and the professionals. During each hospitalization, Susan's binging and vomiting remitted rapidly, and the doctors would discharge her to home. At some point thereafter, she would become severely symptomatic again and be readmitted.

The symptomatic cycle abstracted from this information is depicted in figure 1. Susan's symptomatic behavior can be seen as embedded in

Figure 1   The Symptomatic Cycle

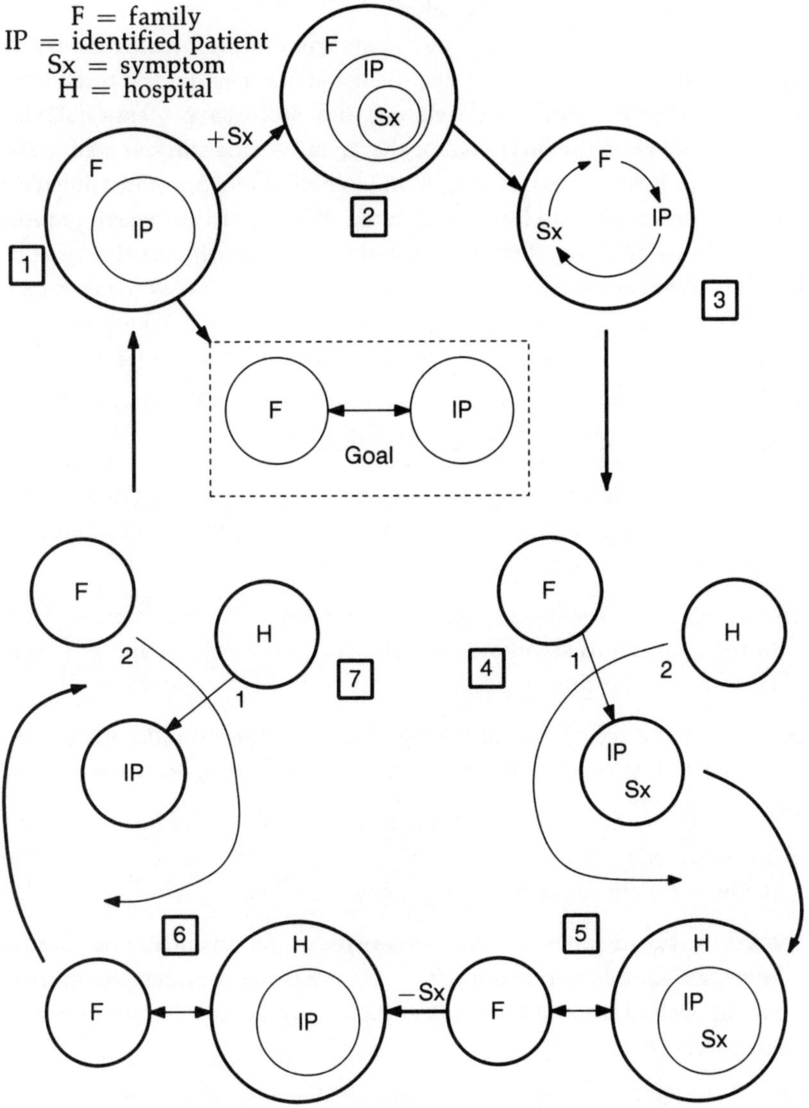

systems of conflict on at least two levels, in addition to the level of her own internal struggle of individuation. One level was that of the family (condensed in step 3), in which her struggle to separate from her parents was intimately intertwined with the bulimia. On a broader level, the symptoms were the focal point of an implicit conflict between the family and the medical-mental health system (steps 4 through 7), in which responsibility for and ownership of Susan's symptomatic behavior oscillated from one to the other.

Impasses in the cycle (that is, circumstances of unresolved, stalemated conflict) were responded to by the inclusion of a new person or institution. When the family felt helpless and stuck, a professional was brought in. When the physician or therapist became stuck, a medical or psychiatric hospital was brought in. When the community hospital became stuck, the state hospital entered. With each successive request for help outside the system, the system became larger and the cycle of helplessness continued.

Steps in the Symptomatic Cycle

Goal: For Susan to live apart from her family while maintaining a reasonable equilibrium in her relationship with them.

Step 1: We can arbitrarily designate any point as the beginning of the cycle. Here Susan is living at home with her parents, in a state of relative calm.

Step 2: Efforts at separation, initiated by Susan or by her parents, result in the addition of symptomatic behavior to the system. Initially, this is contained by Susan and is a secret from her parents.

Step 3: As the recurrence of the symptom becomes public, the family enters into its own patterned sequence of symptomatic interactions.

Step 4: When a certain threshold is exceeded, Susan and her symptoms are extruded from the family and incorporated into some aspect of the medical-psychiatric system, typically a hospital.

Step 5: As the hospital assumes responsibility for Susan and her symptoms, an equilibrium is temporarily established between the professional custodians and the family, occupying nonintersecting spheres of influence.

Step 6: Soon after hospital admission, Susan becomes asymptomatic.

Step 7: In many ways this step is the mirror image of step 4. Susan's symptomatic remission exceeds the hospital's threshold for keeping her, and she is discharged back into the care of her family. The cycle has wound its way back to step 1.

Yet at any point of impasse, the cycle can be interrupted and modified. Successful therapy requires the recognition that the symptom is a characteristic property of the system as a whole, not just of the symptomatic person or the family. A primary goal of crisis induction is to disengage the symptomatic behavior from the family and larger system and return it as a private matter to its rightful owner. In this case, the inpatient therapist would need to find a way to return responsibility and ownership of the vomiting to Susan in order to help her and her parents find a developmentally appropriate way of disengaging from each other.

Crisis Induction

Crisis induction is not a single intervention that is used to solve a problem or create change. It is the entire process by which the therapist catalyzes the dissolution of the developmental impasse and fosters transformation in the family. Because severely symptomatic families frequently present to therapists in a state of emergency, it is easy to assume they are also in a state of crisis. Actually, this is not the case.

DIFFERENCES FROM EMERGENCY MANAGEMENT

A crisis is a turning point, a decisive or crucial time, whereas an emergency is a sudden or unforeseen situation requiring immediate action. In an emergency what is most salient is the emergent event, not its context. In emergency management, also known as crisis intervention, the therapist responds to the family's presentation of a problem by focusing on the removal of the symptom and alleviation of the family's immediate source of stress. In crisis induction, the therapist responds to the family's presentation of the problem by exposing the underlying conflicts in which the symptom and the acute stress are embedded, molding them in a way that triggers a transformation.

In crisis induction the emphasis and the steps are different from those of managing an emergency. In emergency management the first step is to take charge of the emergent event, for example, by breaking up a fight in the midst of a session or calling for help to stop it. In crisis induction the first step is to take charge of the context in which the symptom is occurring, for example, by establishing that violence will not be permitted in or out of sessions, and that if violence does occur, the therapist may report it to the police and refuse to continue to work with the family.

In the second step of emergency management, the objective is to stabilize the event and decrease its intensity. In crisis induction, the

therapist aims to destabilize the symptomatic cycle and increase intensity. This can occur only after the therapist has cultivated relationships
of influence and respect vis-à-vis the family and other significant members of the symptomatic system, including other therapists, physicians,
courts, welfare agencies, and so on.

The goal of emergency management is to return the system to the
normal state of functioning that obtained before the emergency,
whereas the goal of crisis induction is to catalyze a transformation of
the system to a new level of functioning. For example, the therapist
needs to go beyond stopping a fight in the session to creating the
conditions under which family members can settle potentially destructive conflicts without resorting to violence or abandonment.

PHASES OF CRISIS INDUCTION

Crisis induction has four principal phases. This section offers an
overview of the phases; each will be described in more detail in the
second part of the book. Although there is a typical chronological order
to their occurrence, there may or may not be a clear demarcation of the
progression. Phases may overlap with one another, and the critical
components in any one phase can also be seen in each of the others (see
figure 2). Also, the pace and relative length of phases can vary substantially from case to case. For this reason, the four phases of treatment
serve as a general orientation rather than a recipe; in crisis induction, as
elsewhere, the map is not the territory.

In the first phase, madness, the therapist becomes entangled in the
drama of the family's current situation, which, for these families, embodies all of the passion and frenzy that madness connotes. The therapist explores how relationships within the family and between the
family and professionals maintain, and are maintained by, the existence
of the problem. In her search to understand the nature of the symptom,
the therapist is interested in the context in which the symptomatic
behavior is embedded and thus obtains a biopsy of the symptomatic
cycle. There are two primary goals of this phase: to assess the nature of
the symptomatic cycle and to establish a therapeutic context, defined by
the creation of a treatment contract to which both therapist and family
agree.

In the second phase, called chaos, the family's symptomatic patterns
reemerge in response to the disorientation and destabilization engendered by the therapist in the first phase. Disorder and turmoil arise and
are manifested in an escalation or *runaway,* in which both therapist and

Figure 2   Phases of Crisis Induction

Although the overall progression leads from the first phase toward the fourth, there can be considerable back-and-forth motion between phases. Elements of several phases may be present simultaneously. Also, phase four does not necessarily represent the termination; the process may loop back to phase one on a new level.

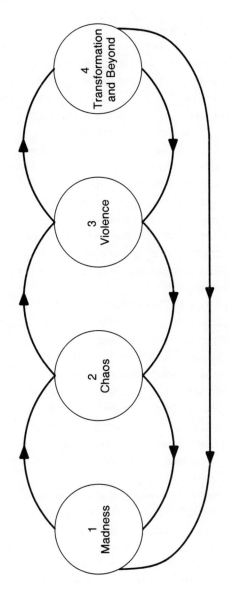

family will experience an urge to flee from each other. The goal of this phase is for the therapist to embrace the runaway; that is, to accept family members' ambivalence about changing, while pursuing them and providing hope that change is possible. A successful reengagement marks the establishment of a therapeutic system, in which a commitment to mutual accountability and integrity in relationships is demonstrated not only in words but in actions.

The third phase, violence, is the climax of crisis induction. Here *violence* refers to the therapist's relentless attack on the family's destructive patterns and to the intense struggle to develop new patterns that ensues among family members and between the family and the therapist. It may seem that generating the intensity required is dangerous, like playing with dynamite. However, in the context of the trusting therapeutic relationship established in the previous stage, the family can safely work through conflicts that were previously expressed through violent means.

The outcome of the crisis induction results in the birth of a significant relationship change within the family that heralds the dissolution of the developmental blockade. This change, punctuating the beginning of the fourth phase, called transformation and beyond, is marked by new perceptions of symptomatic behavior and is often accompanied by the disappearance of the symptom. If the original symptom persists, it loses its compelling hold on members of the symptomatic system, and the family lets go of the pressure to control it. This disengagement frees family members to develop more mutually enriching relationships both inside and outside the family, simultaneously promoting differentiation and affiliation.

Consider, for example, the mother mentioned in chapter 1, page 6, who expressed surprise at the treatment team's degree of concern for her anorectic daughter's physical well-being. She could not envision any way in which she could contribute to the solution of her daughter's problem. That, she said, was precisely why the family had left its home in Wyoming to come to Philadelphia. She was apathetic and despairing, and seemed paralyzed.

The family was admitted to the inpatient apartment program, and there followed four days of crisis induction in which the mother's sense of incompetence was repeatedly challenged. On the fifth day, she came to the therapy session animated and enthusiastic. Her daughter had eaten and gained weight for the first time in months. "What happened?" we asked. The mother related that she had had a revelation the preceding evening. "I was so confused before!" she said. "I thought that everyone was telling me that it was up to me to cure my daughter, and I figured that if it was my responsibility to cure her, we might as well go back home, for all the good being here was going to do. Then, all of a sudden it came to me that you weren't telling me that I had to *cure* her—all I had to do was *feed* her! And it was simple after that." Though much work remained to be done, the mother's perception of the problem had changed dramatically. Despite the intensity of the struggle she would now face, it was a struggle in which she felt empowered to make a significant difference in her daughter's life. Curing was for the experts, but feeding was something she could do.

The goal of this phase of treatment is to help the family experiment with new patterns of interaction, incorporating new approaches to individuation and attachment. The family finds itself free of the prison constituted by the rigid system of interactions of the symptomatic cycle. With increased freedom comes the need for responsibility and choice, a state usually accompanied by the uncertainty of a life-cycle transition. This state of uncertainty is captured in the following vignette. A family from a rural farming community had entered treatment to deal with the psychotic behavior of a teenage son. As the father's attention had moved from his son's unusual speech and sleeping habits to his wife's chronic preoccupation with suicide, the father began meeting individually with the therapist to discuss how to help his wife. Soon after, he told the therapist the following dream: "I've moved my family to a large apartment building where there are many people dressed in strange clothing and speaking foreign languages. I feel very confused, because I know that something of tremendous importance is about to happen, and I can't figure out whether it is a funeral or a wedding."

Crisis Induction with the Jepsen Family

As a clinical overview of the therapeutic process, it will be useful to sketch briefly the phases of crisis induction in the Jepsen case.

MADNESS: ESTABLISHING A TREATMENT CONTEXT

We have outlined the symptomatic cycle in the case of the Jepsen family. The primary goal of crisis induction was to disentangle the bulimic behavior from the family and the medical-psychiatric system in order to allow Susan and her parents to separate and to enable Susan to be in charge of her own body. The therapist assumed that the problem was not the presence of the symptom, but the covert conflicts over who was responsible for it.

Using these considerations, the therapist developed the following treatment contract with the family: the goal of therapy would be for Susan to separate successfully from her parents, evidenced by her living apart from them, holding a job, and interacting with a peer group. Since this would require the parents to observe and monitor her carefully, and since she binged and vomited only at home, the family would need to agree to temporarily make the hospital its home by moving into an inpatient apartment. The family's agreement with this contract established a context in which the family was part of the hospital setting, rather than outside of and in opposition to it (figure 3).

Using an inpatient apartment is not the only option. Another possibility would be to make the hospital part of the family by teaching the parents about fluid and electrolyte metabolism, how to assess their daughter's medical status by checking her pulse and blood pressure, how to insert an intravenous catheter to rehydrate her when she became fluid-depleted, and when to call the paramedics—in effect, by setting up a home care program for bulimia, as is done with diabetes, asthma, and many other disorders of physical functions.

CHAOS: EMBRACING THE RUNAWAY

As its history would predict, once the family moved into the hospital, Susan's symptoms abated, and the therapist worked with the family on other issues related to the goal of disentanglement. Soon, however, the runaway struck in two ways: Susan's symptoms returned, and her parents professed hopelessness and helplessness each time they heard or suspected that Susan was vomiting or binging.

The first step in embracing the runaway was to acknowledge the parents' dilemma and accept their distress. As a second step, the therapist solicited their agreement that Susan's binging and vomiting was unhealthy and disgusting, and that if they found her doing it, they would not allow her to continue it under their roof (in this case, the hospital apartment). The parents agreed on a plan to take equal shifts to monitor Susan for every minute of the day she was in the apartment, including when she went to the bathroom.

This arrangement effectively prevented Susan from binging or vomiting, since she could no longer do it in secrecy. More important, it accepted the parents' position and pushed it to an extreme, increasing

Figure 3   The Treatment Contract

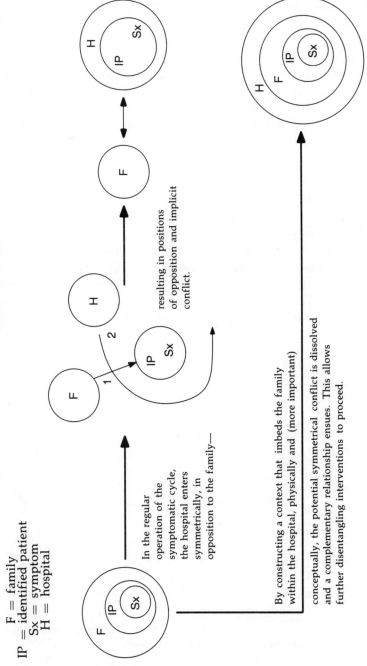

F = family
IP = identified patient
Sx = symptom
H = hospital

In the regular operation of the symptomatic cycle, the hospital enters symmetrically, in opposition to the family—

resulting in positions of opposition and implicit conflict.

By constructing a context that imbeds the family within the hospital, physically and (more important) conceptually, the potential symmetrical conflict is dissolved and a complementary relationship ensues. This allows further disentangling interventions to proceed.

the level of intensity in the system through compression. The family was able to continue its overinvolved dance, but its focal point now was the *absence* of bulimia, rather than its occurrence. It would be easier to help the parents and Susan move toward disengagement once Mr. and Mrs. Jepsen had experienced themselves as competent in relation to their daughter's symptoms (figure 4). The gaps or dislocations in intrafamilial relationships previously filled by symptomatic behavior had begun to be spanned by relationships of mutual responsibility.

VIOLENCE: PRECIPITATING A CRISIS

Although the threatened runaway had been successfully dealt with, no developmental transformation had yet taken place. That is to say, although the parents had successfully banished the symptom through their constant shadowing of their daughter, Susan and her parents were still entangled over the symptom and Susan was not yet in charge of her own body. To foster individuation and disentanglement, the therapist would need to increase the intensity. She chose to do this by reintroducing the symptom into the system.

Figure 4   Embracing the Runaway: Compression

F = family
IP = identified patient
Sx = symptom
H = hospital

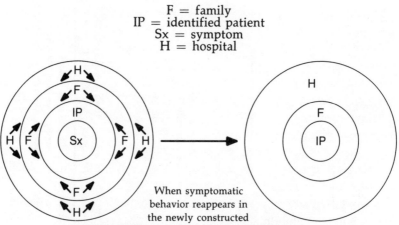

When symptomatic
behavior reappears in
the newly constructed
therapeutic context, the therapist's challenge
is to respond with understanding and acceptance,
rather than to abandon the treatment contract and the family.
The next phase of treatment can then propose reinstalling
symptomatic behavior, but in a way that allows
its continued disentanglement from the
larger system.

The therapist proposed to the family that since Susan had demon-strated that she could handle the urge to binge or vomit given the proper supervision, she should have the opportunity to practice vomiting in order to develop ways of controlling it herself. To establish a boundary between Susan and her parents, the therapist emphasized that this new vomiting should occur only when Susan was *out* of the apartment. She added that since Susan had been vomiting for years, it was unreasonable to expect her to stop completely right then and there. It was perfectly reasonable, however, to expect her not to vomit in her parents' apart-ment. The family saw the logic of this and agreed.

Defining a boundary in this manner made Susan's vomiting an issue of privacy, with connotations of autonomy and differentiation, rather than one of secrecy. Once Susan had staked out her own territory, separate from that of her parents, she could decide whether she wanted to use it for vomiting or for other purposes, such as for talking with the staff about ways of beginning to build a social network for herself (figure 5).

The therapist pressed Mr. and Mrs. Jepsen to agree not to permit Susan to live with them if they discovered her throwing up in their apartment. Over the next three days a number of heated discussions took place between the parents about their hopes and fears of their daughter's growing up and leaving home, and about their own develop-mental transitions. On the fourth day, a crucial event occurred.

That evening after dinner, Susan told her parents that she was going out for a walk. Her father half-jokingly said he figured she needed to vomit by now, but Susan vehemently denied that this was her intention. As Mr. Jepsen said later, "I could tell by the look on her face that something was up, so I followed her to spy on what she was doing, even though I knew we weren't supposed to do that any more. I couldn't find her anywhere, but one of the staff told me they saw her going into a bathroom. When she came back about eight o'clock, my wife and I asked her where she had gone to vomit. Susan got all angry, started cursing and shouting, and said we didn't trust her. Finally, though, she admitted having done it."

What happened next represented a major shift in Mr. Jepsen's percep-tion of Susan's symptomatic behavior, and consequently in his relation-ships with his daughter and wife. Mr. Jepsen became furious with his daughter for having lied to him, not for vomiting, and took her to the inpatient unit where he chewed her out in front of the staff and the other patients. Susan was dumbfounded. Mr. Jepsen and his wife told Susan to stay on the unit for the rest of the evening and said that if they

Figure 5   Disentangling the Symptom

F = family
IP = identified patient
Sx = symptom
H = hospital
? = patient's choice
----- = boundary between apartment
and rest of hospital

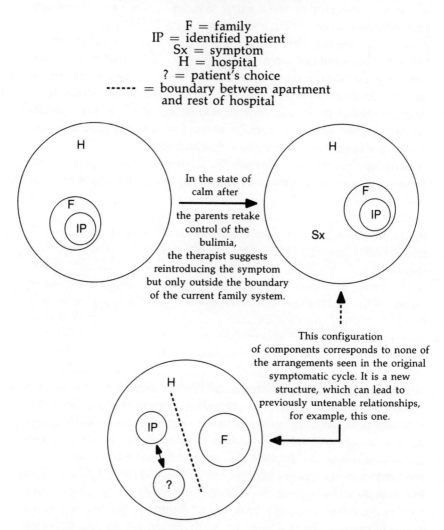

In the state of calm after the parents retake control of the bulimia, the therapist suggests reintroducing the symptom but only outside the boundary of the current family system.

This configuration of components corresponds to none of the arrangements seen in the original symptomatic cycle. It is a new structure, which can lead to previously untenable relationships, for example, this one.

ever caught her lying to them again she would have to leave the house for good.

TRANSFORMATION AND BEYOND

A transformation had occurred in the symptomatic cycle. Rather than responding to Susan's vomiting with helplessness, her parents acted out of their growing sense of confidence in their relationship with each other, with the therapist, and with the treatment team. Furthermore, rather than responding to the *content* of the symptomatic behavior, by taking her to a doctor for help, they responded to its *context,* by addressing the effect it had on their relationship with her.

To consolidate this transformation and further the process of disengagement, the family's dysfunctional way of relating to the medical system had to change. Previously when Susan had been vomiting, her parents, usually Mrs. Jepsen alone, would rush her to the hospital emergency room. They often ended up helplessly watching Susan being admitted to an inpatient unit at the direction of the professionals. Now the therapist told the parents that if they discovered that Susan was lying to them, they could insist that Susan live for one to three days in a bedroom with the other patients on the inpatient unit as a disciplinary measure and not return to the apartment unless they allowed it. In this way, the parents would be in charge of the context in which the symptom occurred, rather than feeling controlled by the symptom.

By directing Susan's inpatient stays, the parents were able to view the doctors, nurses, and other hospital staff as resources to their daughter in *her* struggle to overcome *her* bulimia. The new arrangement replaced the hidden competition between the parents and professionals about who was responsible for stopping the vomiting. Once the parents became disentangled from the symptom, Susan could explore more freely the details of her life as a bulimic, and whether and how she might want to change it (figure 6).

As discharge approached, the therapist relentlessly pursued the theme of Susan's leaving home: when would it happen, who would initiate it, what the circumstances would be, over and over again. After three weeks of hospitalization, Susan and her parents returned home. They were not interested in pursuing continued treatment with anyone in their hometown, but they did have several outpatient appointments with the hospital therapist.

Five years later, a follow-up visit was held at the therapist's request. Susan had had no subsequent hospitalizations, either medical or psychiatric, and no psychotherapy. She had gotten a part-time job immediately upon returning home, and three months later moved in with a cousin who lived about seventy miles from her parents. While at the job, she met a young man whom she married eighteen months later. At the time of the follow-up, she had a two-and-a-half-year-old daughter and was five months pregnant with her second child. She was working full time as a lab technician in a local hospital.

With regard to her bulimia, she said that at first she vomited regularly at home after discharge, but that she went to great pains to hide all

Figure 6   Consolidating Change, Creating Choices

F = family
IP = identified patient
Sx = symptom
H = hospital
H* = inpatient unit
? = patient's choice

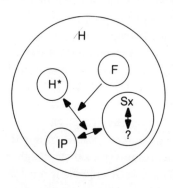

The new set of relationships obtaining in the system offers much more variety and options than the rigid structure of the symptomatic cycle. Although the system is still imbedded in the institutional context, there are dynamic equilibria between Susan and options for spending her time, including getting a job, making friends, or indulging in symptomatic behavior. This equilibrium is itself in equilibrium with the inpatient unit, according to the choices Susan makes, and this latter equilibrium is under the direction of her parents, rather than determined by the presence or absence of her symptoms.

traces of her behavior from her parents, which she had not done before. She could not satisfactorily explain why she did this, since she repeatedly stated that "I know they never would have kicked me out," although every time she said this she asked her parents, "Would you?" Finding no traces of vomiting, her parents said, "We figured she must have been cured," and eventually they stopped worrying about it. Susan reported that now she might vomit once or twice a year, just to prove to herself that she could still do it if she wanted.

Mr. Jepsen said that he remembered the stay in the apartment as "nothing special, just sitting around and talking." Mrs. Jepsen said that what had helped Susan the most was "getting out of the house, and having a baby. She didn't have any time for vomiting after that and couldn't be so involved with herself." Susan attributed the changes in her life to her having made a decision that "it was time to grow up."

CHAPTER 3

The Therapist as Key

IN A STORY by the ancient Taoist sage Chuang-tse (cited in Hoff 1982), an old man remains whole in the face of violent forces that threaten to overwhelm him. Years of practice jumping into the pool at the bottom of a huge waterfall have transformed him into one who can enter a chaotic system and still maintain his integrity. Rather than struggling against the water's superior power, he actively merges himself with its churning turbulence. If he attempted to survive by trying to gain control over the water, by rigidly attempting to resist its impact, or by passively yielding to its force, the outcome would likely be death by drowning. Although the goal in therapy is to stretch beyond survival to transformation, therapists working with severely symptomatic families can learn much about survival from this old man.

As Paul Dell describes the process of change: "The individual's behavioral coherence is the lock—and the therapist's intervention is the key. It does not matter how many jeweled, ornately scrolled, gold, silver, and platinum intricate keys the therapist has. It is always the lock which determines which keys will work" (1982, 35). Dell correctly emphasizes that the family's coherence determines how it is influenced by the therapist's interventions. However, the keys to the therapeutic process are *within* the therapist, not in his interventions. Catalyzing a transformation in the family hinges on the therapist's use of himself to generate a balanced interrelationship of the following critical elements of treatment:

1. Taking charge of the therapeutic context
2. Using symptoms as hooks and levers
3. Focusing on competence
4. Generating intensity
5. Using play and humor
6. Maintaining integrity

This chapter will describe these six critical elements in more detail, illustrated with stories from the treatment with various families. These elements are themselves expressions of two overarching and complementary themes that are interwoven throughout the course of the therapeutic process: acceptance and disorientation.

Acceptance is not a strategy or a technique, such as positive connotation; it is not mere tolerance of a family's pathology. Rather, acceptance is an attitude that conveys wholehearted, unconditional embracing of the madness, chaos, and violence that pervade symptomatic relationships. The therapist's acceptance arises out of his appreciation for family members' struggles with themselves and each other in relation to the symptom and from a conviction that symptoms develop logically from processes (biological, familial, and societal) that are understandable, even if they are not yet understood. The same attitude of respect and acceptance should be conveyed to professionals who are members of the symptomatic system, regardless of the outcome of their interventions thus far.

Accepting families as they are includes recognizing their ambivalence about changing. Even though the family sincerely desires an amelioration of the symptoms, it also wants certain longstanding elements of its usual repertoire to be respected. The therapist's job is to accept both wishes simultaneously and to develop an approach that integrates the two. Accepting this duality and connecting with the family's underlying spark of hope for a better future are essential.

Yet acceptance alone is not sufficient. Since most people are accustomed to clutching onto what is familiar, even if it is intensely painful, the therapist must induce *disorientation* to what is familiar to them so that they can construct new realities. The disorientation is aimed at changing not only the family's way of viewing and interacting with the symptom, but also its interaction with its own members and professionals.

Disorientation springs from several sources. The therapist's unconditional acceptance of a family, accompanied by his willingness to remain connected and close at hand, is disorienting to people accustomed to distancing others with symptomatic behavior. The most powerful disorientation results, however, from the therapist's active and purposeful disruption of the family's equilibrium. This occurs as he begins to explore the context of the symptom, rather than analyze the symptom itself. For example, instead of asking a parent to describe the child's behavior, the therapist asks how the child's behavior influences the relationships in the family. The therapist may ask a family whose daughter is starving to death, "How does the anorexia paralyze the family?" rather than, "Could you tell me about your daughter's eating habits?" A clash of cultures ensues between the therapist and the family, whereby the therapist questions much of what the family takes for granted and continually blocks the family from playing by the rules of the symptomatic cycle.

Crisis induction requires that the therapist work in proximity to the family to provide the degree of acceptance and disorientation necessary to disrupt rigid and repetitive patterns and to promote transformation. To make a difference, the therapist has to become an integral part of the family's life. His voice needs to be heard as coming from inside the family, and he has to become an ever-present irritant under the family's skin, a spur to change.

Taking Charge of the Therapeutic Context

Safety is a critical consideration in doing therapy with families who present with life-threatening symptoms. In an atmosphere where people fear physical or psychological abuse, it is difficult, if not impossible, to form relationships of integrity. Therefore, it is essential that the therapist establish himself from the beginning as in charge of therapy, unwilling to tolerate any threats or acts of violence during or outside of sessions for as long as he is working with the family. At any point that the family exhibits abusive behavior, he must be prepared to end therapy or to make drastic changes in the treatment contract. The therapist will need to be alert throughout the therapeutic process for the emergence of psychological or physical violence, especially during the intensification of the crisis induction in the third phase of treatment and its aftermath.

Having a clear map of the direction in which he plans to go helps the therapist tolerate the uncertainty and intensity generated in crisis induction and allows him to take charge of the context. The map orients him to the dynamics and entanglements of the symptomatic cycle through which he must travel and alerts him to the directions in which runaways may go. The map also defines the perimeters of the therapy— that is, who the players in the therapeutic system should be, where the treatment will take place, how long sessions will last, and how situations should be defined. Time and space are critical factors that can be used in different ways to build therapeutic leverage.

One of the pitfalls in working with families who are battering one another physically and emotionally is to act on their request for external control by attempting to supply it. The therapist must understand what he can and cannot control. He cannot control anyone's behavior but his own, nor can he control feelings, his or anyone else's, as they come and go involuntarily; however, he can control how he responds to behaviors and feelings. He can create the conditions in which alternative courses of action are available, but he cannot determine whether and how family members will explore those alternatives.

One of the ways the therapist takes charge of the context is by creating it, that is, by building and organizing interpersonal networks. Assigning the family tasks that involve work with extended family members, neighbors, and other community resources is one way of engineering new contexts within which relationship shifts can occur. In addition, if the therapist works with a team of colleagues in an inpatient or residential setting, the team can join with family members to create an expanded therapeutic family. The team can model a structure with a clear hierarchy, mutual support for competence, effective conflict resolution, and the sharing of responsibility. For example, the team can act as grandparents to the family. One team member can cross generational boundaries and ally with the symptomatic child against his parents, as an intrusive grandparent might do. In this case, a second team member can assist the parents in challenging the first's intrusiveness, exploring ways in which the first team member can be helpful without taking over for them. Or the team can act as children to the parents as a way of promoting an atmosphere of playfulness and challenging the parents' heavy-handedness. In families where children seem incapable of playing cooperatively and continually pull their parents into their conflicts, a team member can join the sibling system and instigate a conflict with one of the children. He can then help that child resolve the conflict directly with him, while another team member joins the parents behind the one-way mirror to observe and comment on this interaction.

The following vignette illustrates how the therapist and apartment team constructed an interpersonal context to induce change in a family whose single-parent mother was completely overwhelmed and isolated in the community.

Mrs. Bryant was the mother of thirteen-year-old twin daughters, Ruth and Mary, each of whom was retarded and obese. Neither girl had attended school in over two years, and several attempts at outpatient therapy, in which therapists had attempted to help the mother gain control of her oppositional children, had failed miserably. The family was admitted to an inpatient apartment after Mary had thrown a butcher knife at her mother.

On the first day of hospitalization the twins refused to leave their mother's side. By the end of the day, with considerable support from the staff, Mrs. Bryant was able to leave her daughters with their peer group for thirty minutes. The therapist recommended that the following day the twins should attend the day treatment program by themselves, and their mother agreed. The next morning, the twins barricaded the door to the apartment, holding their mother hostage, and took refuge in their bedroom. Mrs. Bryant's frantic efforts to coax them out were met with loud cursing and threats.

The team considered having several staff members break down the door and carry the girls off to the classroom. The team, however, was concerned that for the staff to succeed where the mother had failed would simply reinforce the mother's sense of defeat. As an alternative to physically taking control of Ruth and Mary, the therapist decided to enlist the twins' peer group to entice them away from their mother, allowing the team to support mother in letting go of her daughters, rather than taking over for her.

In preparing a strategy, the team presented the problem to the other adolescents in the day treatment unit. Collaborating with Mrs. Bryant over the telephone, the team organized the peer group to pursue its classroom activities in the Bryant's living room. After the maintenance crew took the hinges off the front door of the apartment, a group of eight teenagers and two staff members entered the apartment to carry on with the morning routine. Eventually, curiosity got the best of the twins, and they peered out the bedroom door. Several of their peers then moved into their bedroom and began talking with them. Soon Mary and Ruth were part of the group. As lunchtime approached, the entire group, including the twins, moved back to the classroom.

Over the next few days, Mrs. Bryant became more assertive in pushing her daughters to separate, and the twins negotiated time away from her to be with their friends and team members. By refusing the temptation to control the twins' behavior, accepting it instead as an invitation to construct a different therapeutic context, the team dissolved the impasse and introduced new possibilities to the family.

Using Symptoms as Hooks and Levers

The most effective hook by which to engage a severely symptomatic family in therapy and maintain sufficient therapeutic traction is the presenting symptom. Symptoms bring the family to therapy and invite a handshake, introducing the family to the therapist. To the extent that the symptom is a hand outstretched, reaching for help, the therapist's ability to engage with it provides a critical avenue into and out of the world of the family. Therapists who ignore the proferred hand run the risk of missing the opportunity to form a relationship altogether; refusing to let go of it will compromise their own and the family's maneuverability.

The presenting symptoms can also be used as levers to build and maintain intensity throughout treatment. When a stalemate or impasse occurs in the therapeutic process, the therapist can reinvoke the presenting symptoms to add intensity and get the juices flowing in the therapeutic system, as when the Jepsen's therapist suggested that Susan begin to practice vomiting outside of the family's apartment.

The case of Maurice illustrates another way the presenting symptom can be used for therapeutic traction. The family was referred because Maurice had recently set three large fires. He lived with his mother and two younger siblings, his mother's boyfriend, and his mother's sister. The therapist initially defined Maurice's fire setting as out-of-control behavior, and focused the mother on the need to provide her son with more effective limits and nurturance. After several sessions, she had begun to supervise Maurice more closely, and he responded with a decrease in his acting-out behaviors, yet he still seemed very lonely and sad.

In an effort to understand the problem more fully, the therapist resurrected the presenting symptom by questioning Maurice in painstaking detail about the circumstances surrounding the fires. Eventually Maurice revealed that he set fires after he had misbehaved and was fearful that his mother would beat him and lock him out of the house, which she admitted to having done several times. He described having a recurrent nightmare in which his mother was being hit in the face and bloodied by her boyfriend. When asked why he had not previously revealed this information, Maurice said cautiously, "I'm afraid my mother might get so upset that she'll go crazy and run away, and no one would take care of me."

The therapist commented that Maurice's fire setting seemed to be a statement about how angry and fearful he was about the possibility that his mother would abandon him. Maurice's mother, who had been listening attentively, disclosed that in fact she often contemplated suicide. She revealed that she had been exploited and victimized by her sister for many years, starting at age thirteen, when her sister forced her to become a prostitute to provide income for her sister's drug addiction. She confessed that this secret had been a source of ongoing anguish and despair, which had been distracting her from parenting her children and working out her conflicts with her boyfriend.

As the mother worked with the therapist to free herself from the shackles of her past with her sister, she became more responsive to Maurice's emotional and developmental needs and more intimately connected in her own relationships.

Focusing on Competence

Carol Anderson writes that "the psychiatric system's preoccupation with deficits, coupled with a lack of attention to assets, often leads already upset families to believe that professionals seek to establish family responsibility for the patient's problems. With this impression, it is not surprising that family members give their information and their 'patient' to the hospital system and quickly leave" (Anderson, Reiss, and Hogarty 1986, 27). To move toward the goal of transforming the symptomatic cycle, the therapist must believe that family members have the ability to change; and to ensure their active collaboration in treatment, he must persistently search for hidden strengths.

The lure to take over for the parents in working with severely symptomatic families is strong. Yet the therapist must resist it and convey at all times his conviction that the family is more competent than it appears and that it is responsible for itself. By expecting family members to accomplish tasks that seem just slightly out of their reach, the therapist will frequently be surprised and delighted to discover that the family will rise to the occasion, mastering the challenge with satisfaction, competence, and creativity. Consider the case of Sonny Williams, a sixteen-year-old referred for psychiatric hospitalization by the rehabilitation center that had provided his care since he had suffered severe head injuries in an automobile accident four years previously. The rehab staff reported that in their center, Sonny maintained bowel and bladder control, fed himself, and got around with a walker, whereas at home he was in a wheelchair and diapers, often refused to eat, and ruminated about suicide.

In the preadmission assessment session, it was apparent that Sonny's mother and brothers felt helpless. They feared that Sonny would have to be permanently institutionalized, as the social worker at the rehab center had intimated to them. Toward the end of the session, the therapist told Mrs. Williams that he was impressed with her persistence and her commitment to Sonny. He said that he and his team wanted to help the family, but the mother would also have to help the team, as it was less experienced than she in working with people who had suffered brain injuries.

To further activate the mother's competence, the team offered the family a treatment contract stipulating that prior to Sonny's admission, Mrs. Williams and her other sons needed to spend several days observing Sonny's treatment in the rehabilitation hospital. The family would then conduct one training session for the team and one for the other adolescents in the classroom unit where Sonny would be assigned. During Sonny's hospitalization, his mother would supervise his participation in the classroom and determine which activities would be appropriate for him. In collaboration with the team's nurse, she would be the contact person with the Children's Hospital of Philadelphia, where Sonny would have physical therapy. The team would support Sonny in complying with the program devised under his mother's supervision.

Given the opportunity to be the expert on her son's condition and treatment program, Mrs. Williams blossomed. She quickly observed that the staff of the rehabilitation hospital expected more from Sonny than the family did. Her attention began to shift from what Sonny could *not* do to what he *could* do. For example, while in the inpatient apartment, she expected him to use the toilet, cut his own food, and feed himself, all of which she had been doing for him at home.

Sonny would continue to have special needs related to his physical and cognitive impairments, but the stage was now set for him and his family to enhance his adaptation and development rather than focus on handicaps and limitations.

Generating Intensity

Emotional intensity fuels the therapeutic process along its path toward crisis and transformation. Although certain general principles come into play, it is important to remember that intensity is generated not from the therapist's acting on the family by the use of techniques but through his acting with the family in the context of the relationships of the therapeutic system.

Because interactional patterns in severely symptomatic families are rigid and tenacious, the therapist should be prepared to repeat interventions over and over and in a variety of ways. As Braulio Montalvo says, "The eroding of patterns cannot be brought about by a clever strategy that hits only once" (personal communication). The intervals between sessions and their duration can be also used to generate intensity. It is most useful to end sessions when the therapist and family are satisfied that a particular objective has been accomplished, not because the hour is up. For example, when confronted with situations of great urgency, such as with an adolescent who is violently acting out or starving herself, therapists who are working in conjunction with a team can have marathon family sessions, where team members take turns working with the family throughout the day and night.

The intensity generated in the symptomatic cycle often arises most directly from the symptomatic person, who occupies the most dangerous and powerful position in the cycle. The process of harnessing intensity and channeling it productively often requires that the therapist be willing to sit with or replace the symptomatic person at the hub of the cycle, as in the case of a therapist treating a family with a symptomatic child who is caught in a hostile crossfire between his divorced parents. The therapist knows he is at the hub when he feels the pull of the symptomatic cycle. For example, like the symptomatic person, he may feel like running away or attacking someone in the family, or he may feel starved or abused.

In challenging the family's patterns from the hub, the therapist must not only be prepared to withstand a certain amount of aggression, but he must also be able to use his own aggression in a controlled and constructive manner. The level of uproar and chaos with which these families live is far greater than that with which the average therapist is familiar or comfortable. Therefore, he must develop a tolerance for noise, craziness, conflict, and emotional expression that surpasses the family's threshold, finding ways to amplify his input so that it will register above the roar of chaos in the family, instead of being absorbed and neutralized.

Most interventions to increase intensity hinge on the therapist's proposing a change in the proximity–distance axis of a significant relationship in the system, which may or may not include the therapist. When the relationship selected involves only family members, the therapist has two options: to prescribe a compression of the symptomatic system or to enforce separation.

In a compression of the symptomatic system, family members are requested to perform a task that places them temporarily in extended and intense proximity, such as staying together in one room until the conflict at hand is resolved. By pushing family members together and holding them there, the compression provides them with an opportunity to discover their points of fusion. They can then release each other in a way and at a pace with which they are more comfortable. As will be shown, the consultant to the Monroe's therapist creates a compression when she asks Jennifer's parents to monitor her twenty-four hours a day to prevent her from abusing laxatives.

Alternatively, the therapist may prescribe an enforced separation. Some families need to undergo a therapeutic dismemberment to safely salvage and expand on their remnants of connectedness. In the symptomatic cycle of some families people cast themselves out (or are thrown out) of the family at points of unresolved conflict. This is a common dynamic of families with a presenting symptom of runaway or suicidal behavior, or whenever a symptomatic person has been hospitalized repeatedly without improvement. One way of prescribing disengagement, for example, is for the therapist to request that the parents of a runaway teenage girl locate another family in their community with whom their daughter can reside while treatment with the entire family continues. He thus builds intensity by amplifying the instability of the system and disorienting family members to their expectation that therapists work only to keep families together, regardless of the psychological and physical costs.

When the relationship selected by the therapist for intensification includes himself, there are again two categories of interventions available. One is for the therapist to take an immovable position, insisting that the family reorganize around him and his position. Such an intervention temporarily increases the distance between the therapist and the family and is most effective when the family is experiencing a state of desperation (as when the treatment contract is being developed) or when it is actually in crisis (during the third phase of treatment). The other option is for the therapist to increase proximity between himself and the family by engaging in relentless pursuit of the family. This type of intervention is most effective when the family is in a state of flight and the therapist's goal is to embrace the runaway.

The following vignette illustrates how the process of admission to an inpatient apartment was used to intensify the conflict between a mother and her teenage daughter through the therapist's pursuing the mother, which led to an enforced separation from her daughter. The Morgan family consisted of seventeen-year-old Kathy and her mother. They had been in outpatient therapy for a year in their hometown in a neighboring state, because Kathy was not eating, was hoarding food, and was refusing to attend school. On occasion, Kathy had become physically assaultive toward her mother, leading the mother to back down from her demands that Kathy gain weight and attend classes.

After obtaining this information over the telephone, the therapist scheduled the family's admission for the following week, giving Mrs. Morgan time to arrange for a house sitter and a leave of absence from her job. In the subsequent admission session Kathy refused to speak, so the therapist handed the admission papers to Mrs. Morgan and asked her to obtain Kathy's signature. Mrs. Morgan pleaded with Kathy to sign, and Kathy responded by ripping the papers to shreds and throwing them on the floor. As Mrs. Morgan looked on helplessly, the therapist handed the mother a fresh supply of admission papers, and for forty-five minutes Kathy ripped up one admission form after another. Mrs. Morgan had a dilemma. Although she wanted the approval of the therapist, who had patiently and consistently stood by her, she saw no way of prevailing with her daughter. In addition, the family was six hours away from home, and night was falling.

Having collaborated with the team's psychiatrist, who assessed that Kathy was not at acute risk of becoming dangerous to herself or others, the therapist turned to Mrs. Morgan at the height of the struggle and asked, "Would you like to move in here without her?" Indignant at the therapist's suggestion, Kathy stormed out of the building, and her mother moved her own and Kathy's belongings into the apartment. Mrs. Morgan and the team then developed a plan whereby she would allow Kathy to live in the apartment only if she first admitted herself to the inpatient unit and treated her mother respectfully during daily visits to the apartment. After returning to the hospital later that evening and being informed of her mother's plan, Kathy signed herself into the hospital and finally earned her way into the apartment with her mother three days later.

Using Play and Humor

When inducing crises and responding to emergencies constitute the therapist's normal workday, when he works in an institutional setting with its unending stream of regulations and constraints, and when he is working closely with ravaged families who are struggling to survive, the therapist can become overwhelmed and attempt to find solace in order and predictability. He forgets that the world does not work as he thinks it should and that much of what passes for sanity is absurd. The therapist who takes himself too seriously and has too much reverence for seeking rational solutions to human dilemmas is exquisitely vulnerable to frustration and misery.

Not surprisingly, families who live on the brink of death spend much of their time locked up inside themselves, worrying themselves sick with guilt and thinking monstrous thoughts they cannot seem to escape. The possibility of being childish or playful is remote. For these families, who are held hostage not only by their children's misbehavior but also by the blame that others level at them, playing may be the farthest thing from their minds, yet it is a vital means by which parents and children can connect with each other and with their own creativity and spontaneity (Brendler and Combrinck-Graham 1986, 92–93).

There is no better way to disarm excessive seriousness in the therapeutic process than through the therapist's playfulness. Through his willingness to tease family members when they make a faux pas and to laugh at himself, the therapist creates a context of humanity. It is this context, built on an acceptance and appreciation of human foibles, that fosters the freedom to be daring enough to bring out and enjoy those parts of ourselves that we usually work so hard to guard against, yet without which our lives can become steeped in tedium and arrogance.

A twelve-year-old boy named Lenny had attempted to hang himself. At the point in treatment from which the following dialogue is taken, Lenny was no longer expressing suicidal thoughts and had begun to play with friends again, and his parents were supporting each other more effectively. However, everyone in the family related in a stiff and constricted manner, and the therapist repeatedly found himself becoming bored. Lenny's father, a high-ranking executive in a multinational corporation, conducted himself with the solemn decorum more suitable for a stockholder's meeting, and his wife was preoccupied trying to analyze her son's depression. Sally, Lenny's nine-year-old sister, valiantly struggled to follow the abstract and ponderous discussions. In desperation, the therapist turned to Lenny for help.

THERAPIST: Lenny, can you come up with some ideas to help your dad be less boring? Cause your mom isn't very good at bringing out his creative juices.

LENNY: So?

THERAPIST: Could you give me some ideas about how to help your dad get out of his own head and be less of a stick-in-the-mud?

LENNY: Well, let's say we do somersaults in the mall.

THERAPIST: That's a good idea. But what if your dad's pants ripped? That could get very embarrassing, you know?

LENNY: I would just pretend I don't know him and say, "Who are you?"

THERAPIST: Maybe you could call a taxi and take your dad to an executive meeting on the spot. *(Mother laughs loudly.)* Hopefully, he wouldn't fart with his pants ripped *(more laughter from mother)*. That could get extremely embarrassing. How are you at farting, Lenny? I mean, have you trained yourself to fart yet?

SALLY: He's trained himself to burp. *(Everyone erupts into laughter.)*

THERAPIST: Oh, really? Could I hear?

LENNY: Sure! *(Lenny burps three times, each louder than the one before, then the therapist burps twice, as everyone howls.)*

THERAPIST: Can your dad do that?

LENNY: No, but he can sure fart up a storm. *(Father and son laugh.)*

THERAPIST: That means you need to expand his repertoire, his range of craziness.

LENNY: *(To his father)* Can you burp?

FATHER: Not on the spot, no.

THERAPIST: Can you teach him, Lenny? Try.

LENNY: *(To his father)* You have to bring your tongue down like this. *(He motions and starts burping loudly, and then father starts burping, and then Sally starts burping, and then mother joins in.)*

THERAPIST: Can you do this in class, you know, when it's boring and the teachers drone on and on? *(Father and mother laugh.)* I think your dad needs more practice burping, and also burping and farting alternately, what do you think?

LENNY: I agree. *(To father, laughing)* Let's practice. *(Father and son spend several minutes burping and farting while mother and Sally shake with laughter.)*

THERAPIST: I think you've done very well with your dad—he seems to be improving, so I was thinking that we should show this videotape to his board of directors sometime soon. *(Everyone laughs.)* The only problem I noticed was his farts are kind of loose. Did you notice?

LENNY: *(Laughing)* Yeah. Dad, make your farts tighter from now on, okay?

FATHER: I'll try.

THERAPIST: *(To father)* I think you now ought to teach your wife what you've learned from your son, so she doesn't miss out on the fun, okay? Lenny, would you mind watching your dad for technique, and be his consultant if he needs help?

LENNY: No problem.

FATHER: *(To his wife)* I want to start by showing you how to pick your nose with your toes. *(Everyone laughs.)*

Maintaining Integrity

Integrity is the cornerstone of therapy. Only when the therapist has established himself as someone who can be relied upon, a port in the storm, can the other critical elements flourish. Integrity is neither a technique nor a therapeutic posture. It emanates from the therapist's genuine belief that families are resilient and have the capacity to manage their lives in ways that are more effective and fulfilling. His integrity is communicated most clearly by the limits he sets when he refuses to participate in destructive or futile patterns of interaction, and by the lengths to which he will go to help family members find new ways of resolving conflicts and becoming more human.

When faced with human dilemmas, the therapist should be clear about his ethics and values and feel free to assert them openly and respectfully, expecting family members to treat him and each other with respect and decency. The aim is to be direct without being rude, to capitalize on despair without exploiting the family's hopelessness and depleting its resources, to stimulate hope without making false promises, to increase intensity while maintaining safety, to respect people while challenging their symptomatic behavior, and to take charge of the context while recognizing that the family is always in charge of and responsible for itself.

The therapist must find ways of refusing to participate in the family's destructive patterns, while not abandoning his connections with family members. For example, when a team member found a mother about to beat her son with an extension cord one evening for not brushing his teeth after dinner, he asked the mother for the cord but did not leave her side until he had helped her to get her son successfully tucked into bed. When the therapist takes a stand in order to be true to himself, the family stops for a moment in the midst of its own uproar to listen. When this kind of integrity is not forthcoming from the family, the therapist should insist on it and expect the family to demand the same from him.

The following dialogue occurred between a therapist and the father of a severely ill diabetic girl. The father was running out of steam after spending two full days camped by his daughter's bedside in the intensive care unit in an unrelenting effort to persuade her to stop intentionally overdosing herself with insulin. When she rebuffed all his approaches, he pleaded with the therapist to tell him how to get through to her.

THERAPIST: All it is, is a question of integrity. That's what's needed to save you and her. You know that sometime, somewhere in your life, you had some integrity, and you let it wash out because your daughter got so stubborn, while convincing you she was fragile and weak and sickly. She'll push you hard, and it's going to take a hell of a lot of integrity to help her survive and grow.

FATHER: If you think I've let my integrity wash away, how can you bear to work with me?

THERAPIST: Part of it is that I work with colleagues whom I respect a lot, and we believe in our ability to help you and your family. And part of it is that I believe in you. I believe you have possibilities. I haven't given up on you. I don't want to give up on you, but I have my limits as to how much I will tolerate. Tolerating death is too much.

As families shared the stories of their lives with us and allowed us to participate in those stories, we shared ourselves and our stories with them. One of our favorites is the following tale, told by Rabbi Nachman of Bratzlav, a master of Hasidic mysticism in the late eighteenth century, and repeated by Elie Wiesel in *Souls on Fire* (1972, 170–71). This lovely allegory captures the intermingling of the twin themes of acceptance and disorientation, and each of the six critical elements of therapy.

In a distant land, a prince lost his mind and imagined himself a rooster. He sought refuge under the table and lived there, naked, refusing to partake of the royal delicacies served in golden dishes—all he wanted and accepted was the grain reserved for the roosters. The king was desperate. He sent for the best physicians, the most famous specialists; all admitted their incompetence. So did the magicians. And the monks, the ascetics, the miracle-makers; all their interventions proved fruitless.

One day an unknown sage presented himself at court. "I think that I could heal the prince," he said shyly. "Will you allow me to try?"

The king consented, and to the surprise of all present, the sage removed his clothes, and joining the prince under the table, began to crow like a rooster.

Suspicious, the prince interrogated him: "Who are you and what are you doing here?" —"And you," replied the sage, "who are you and what are you doing here?" —"Can't you see? I am a rooster!" —"Hmm," said the sage, "how very strange to meet you here!" —"Why strange?" —"You mean, you don't see? Really not? You don't see that I'm a rooster just like you?"

The two men became friends and swore never to leave each other.

And then the sage undertook to cure the prince by using himself as example. He started by putting on a shirt. The prince couldn't believe his eyes. —"Are you crazy? Are you forgetting who you are? You really want to be a man?" —"You know," said the sage in a gentle voice, "you mustn't ever believe that a rooster who dresses like a man ceases to be a rooster." The prince had to agree. The next day both dressed in a normal way. The sage sent for some dishes from the palace kitchen. "Wretch! What are you doing?" protested the prince, frightened in the extreme. "Are you going to *eat* like them now?" His friend allayed his fears: "Don't ever think that by eating like man, with man, at his table, a rooster ceases to be what he is; you mustn't ever believe that it is enough for a rooster to behave like a man to become human; you can do anything with man, in his world and even for him, and yet remain the rooster you are."

And the prince was convinced; he resumed his life as a prince.

PART TWO

*THREE FAMILIES IN
TREATMENT*

CHAPTER 4

―――

Madness: Becoming Entangled

It's the frame which makes some things important and some things forgotten. It's all only frames from which the content arises.
—Eve Babitz

IN *A BOOK OF FIVE RINGS,* a guide to strategy for samurai warriors written in the sixteenth century, Musashi calls the process of engagement "soaking in." He counsels, "When you have come to grips and are striving together . . . you 'soak in' and become one. . . . You can win by applying a suitable technique while you are mutually entangled" (Musashi 1974, 78). Although combat and the battlefield are not appropriate metaphors for psychotherapy, the notion of "soaking in," of becoming mutually entangled in an intense struggle, is relevant to the model of crisis induction with families exhibiting life-threatening symptoms.

In this opening phase of therapy, the therapist enters into the family drama by communicating her unconditional acceptance of the family and her conviction that the family has the capacity to change and that she can help it change. The therapist's overall goal in this phase is to assess the nature of the symptomatic cycle so that a properly constructed treatment contract can be developed. This job is accomplished in three sequential stages: (1) obtaining a referral, (2) conducting assessment sessions in which the therapist meets with the family and its professional retinue, and (3) developing a treatment contract to define the framework of therapy and specify the necessary participants and nature of their participation. A therapeutic context is thus established, marking the end of the initial phase of treatment.

The Referral Process

The process of socializing the family into the therapeutic culture begins by obtaining a referral. There are three components to this opening stage: gathering information about the problem from the family and referring professionals, deciding whether to see the case, and determining who needs to attend the assessment sessions.

GATHERING INFORMATION

Important referral information that sheds light on the history and composition of the symptomatic system includes: Who lives in the household with the patient? Who are the professionals currently involved with the symptomatic person and family? What is the nature of their involvement? How long has the problem been present? What efforts have been made to solve it? What obstacles have the family and professionals encountered in implementing their solutions?

When the referring person is another therapist, the receiving therapist should ask the referring person about his relationship to the family, how he views the problem, and what type and level of intervention he is asking for. Does the referring person recognize any ways in which he may be contributing to the maintenance of the therapeutic impasse? Does he wish to continue as the primary therapist (and is therefore requesting a consultation) or does he want to effect a transfer of care? If he is requesting a consultation, will he be present? If the referring therapist sounds ambivalent about continuing treatment with the family, it is necessary to address this issue explicitly at the outset, rather than expecting the consultation or treatment process with the family to resolve his dilemma. If he is requesting help for the symptomatic person only, will he encourage the other members of the family to participate in the process? Failing to obtain sufficiently clear answers to these questions leads to ineffective collaboration between the therapist and the referring person and will likely produce significant problems in the therapy or consultation process (Selvini Palazzoli et al. 1980).

ACCEPTING THE REFERRAL

The decision to accept a referral of a severely symptomatic family has more to do with the therapist than with the diagnosis or the nature of the symptom. The therapist must be equipped with a support system immediately available to her, by having a colleague or supervisor in the room or behind a one-way mirror to whom she can turn for consultation and refuge from the overwhelming demands and stress engendered by these families. It is foolhardy for any therapist to go it alone with families who are so emotionally taxing.

The only sure way to determine whether a treatment contract can be reached with a particular family is by actually working with the family. If administrative constraints preclude an open-ended assessment process—for example, when the court has ordered immediate hospitalization—the family and referring person should be told that the initial stage of treatment will consist of an assessment to determine whether a treatment contract can be developed. If, subsequently, no contract appears workable, this conclusion should be conveyed to the referring person to enlist his support in either motivating the family to comply with the therapist's expectations or identifying an alternative plan for the family. Deciding against referrals based on the explicit or implicit hopelessness of the family or the referring person sells short the potential of the therapist, the referring person, and the family to create a different therapeutic experience.

SETTING UP ASSESSMENT SESSIONS

When the symptomatic person is a child or adolescent, all family members living in the household are expected to attend the assessment sessions, including at least one adult family member who accepts legal responsibility for the child. The participation of the extended family is encouraged, since its involvement in the symptomatic cycle is often significant.

If only a fragment of the family shows up, the therapist can use the session to begin the process of engaging those members who are present, placing on them the responsibility for bringing the rest of the family to the next appointment. If the therapist fails to connect with the family's "scout" who comes to the first session, the assessment process may derail at that point. Although it is possible to start with only one member and work step by step toward bringing in more of the family, the therapist risks developing an inadequate formulation of the symptomatic cycle, since she becomes acquainted with the problem through only one person's eyes. Furthermore, if other family members do join in subsequent sessions, the therapist may be viewed as having established an alliance with the person who had shown up first, complicating her ability to establish relationships with other members.

When a family presents with multiple problems and is entangled with multiple professional systems, it is helpful to ask all the professionals who play a significant role in the family's life to attend the initial session. This integrated approach minimizes the potential for fragmentation and collusion in the system and encourages a collaborative approach to problem solving, as will be seen in the Cabrini case, when Rachel organizes the family, Maria's outpatient therapist, a nurse from her hospital, and Nicholas's protective services worker to come together for the initial assessment session. It is always advisable to invite the referring person to the initial assessment session. It is essential that the referring person attend if he or she plays a controlling role in the life of the family, as does a court-appointed social worker who is responsible for monitoring the parents' contact with their child due to child abuse charges, or a representative of a hospital or residential treatment program from which the symptomatic person has not yet been discharged. In these circumstances, the therapist should not agree to conduct the initial session without the presence of the referring person.

The Assessment Process

The family typically arrives feeling overwhelmed, confused, and helpless. Whether they admit it or not, parents feel like they have failed and blame themselves for causing the symptomatic member's problems. The symptomatic person also feels like a failure, longing to escape the worried looks and accusing fingers of his parents and siblings.

The parents may wonder: Will the therapist blame us for our child's problems, as other therapists have done? Will she understand how frustrated and infuriated our son makes us? Will she side with our child against us? The symptomatic child may ask himself: Will the therapist blame me, like my parents do? Will she understand how my parents drive me crazy? Will she think I'm crazy? Siblings and other family members may wonder: How does this have anything to do with me? Will I get dragged into this mess when I have my own life to worry about?

The therapist must recognize that how she speaks to the family, how she establishes limits and boundaries, how she responds to disorder, and a hundred other things she does or does not say and do, will be perceived by family members as possible answers to their pressing but unvoiced questions. This initial contact, especially the first few moments, sets the stage for treatment. The therapist's manner and style of relating sets the tone and dictates the feel and flavor of the therapy.

The assessment process is not a static process of observing the family from a distance, as often happens in a conventional diagnostic evaluation. Rather, it is a dynamic process of determining the family's responsiveness to therapy, in which the therapist experiences directly the pulls and pushes of the symptomatic cycle. The therapist's internal responses provide an affective understanding of how family members experience one another and how professionals experience the family. These responses can help the therapist to identify with family members' experiences and deepen her understanding of behavior that may seem bizarre if viewed solely from a distance or taken out of context.

The family enters therapy with a story, and through her own involvement the therapist enlarges the story and becomes a character in it. The therapist can obtain an accurate formulation of the symptomatic cycle by carefully tracking the organization of the family and professionals around the symptom, rather than analyzing their isolated behaviors. She can use the answers to her specific questions about who told whom what, when, and why to paint a vivid picture of the strengths and breakdowns of relationships in the system. The timing and style of the questioning is critical to setting the stage for a new experience that challenges the family's tendency to present a rehearsed litany of complaints and plants seeds for a different way of perceiving the problem and relating to one another.

In a family whose teenage daughter was starving herself, the father began the session by giving his view of the problem: "If Trish isn't a full-blown case of anorexia nervosa, then I don't know what she is. She fits the classic definitions. We've read so many articles on the subject, we could discuss it for hours." In the following dialogue, ensuing immediately after the father's comments, the therapist's questions challenge the family's definition of the problem as inherent in Trish, the symptomatic member, while introducing an expanded reality, focusing on how relationships are organized by a disembodied symptom.

THERAPIST: How has the anorexia in the family paralyzed the family? [The therapist is interested in the symptom's effects, not its causes.]
MOTHER: Oh, eating habits—for example, the dinner schedule completely revolves around Trish for the most part.
THERAPIST: In what way—could you be more specific? [The therapist should always obtain as much precision as possible about what actually happens in the family.]

MOTHER: Well, mealtimes are focused to encourage Trish to eat, so if she wants chicken, then everybody has chicken.

THERAPIST: So when a decision needs to be made about—maybe a lot of mundane things, about how you organize the household, how people interact—the first consideration is, what will the anorexia dictate? [She is suggesting that "anorexia" has become part of the family's lifestyle and is not just an eating disorder.]

MOTHER: It's not—she doesn't dictate everything. . . .

THERAPIST: No, I don't mean *her (pointing at Trish),* I mean the *anorexia.* [This disorienting statement invites the mother to consider alternative ways of viewing the symptom.]

MOTHER: Well, I guess that she—I mean the condition—it does influence what we all do where it really shouldn't, because of all the tension. [Mother's shift of pronouns suggests she may be open to alternatives.]

THERAPIST: *(To father)* Who does the tension get played out mostly between? [The therapist focuses on the symptom's effects on relationships.]

FATHER: That's a good question. I'd say all of us, pretty much equally.

THERAPIST: So, actually, you all share the anorexia [implying that the symptom belongs to the system as a whole].

FATHER: I don't quite follow you there.

THERAPIST: Well, does the anorexia have the effect of keeping you and your wife apart, or of pulling you together? [Again, the therapist is suggesting that the symptom is embedded in relationships.]

FATHER: Actually, a while ago we did get separated because of it.

The Treatment Contract

The establishment of a treatment contract punctuates the end of the first phase of treatment. A treatment contract, whether verbal or written, has been specified when the therapist and the family have agreed on the following: (1) a frame for the problem that links the symptom to the system; (2) a delineation of the practical details of treatment (such as who will participate; the frequency, location, and length of sessions; and criteria for ending treatment); and (3) an orientation to the process of therapy.

The frame of the problem needs to describe the relationship between the symptom and the symptomatic cycle. For example, in the Monroe case, Donna, the consultant, links Jennifer's vomiting and laxative abuse, which are her ways of numbing herself to the pain of her parents' relationship, to the lack of connection between her and her parents, and to the impasse between her and her therapist. The contract proposed specifies how roles and behavior will need to change for each member of the system if Jennifer is to become more connected to her family and her therapist, Brian, than to her symptoms.

While the practical details of the contract will vary from one treatment context to another because of differing administrative constraints and demands, the family's relationships with other professionals, such as a probation officer or a school counselor, should be discussed and included. For example, will these people participate in the therapy process, and if so, how frequently and what role will they assume?

The treatment contract should also include criteria for when treatment will end, thus providing a framework in which the family, therapist, and other professionals can work collaboratively toward a common goal without becoming repeatedly distracted by symptomatic behaviors. This is especially important when working in an inpatient or residential facility. Two types of termination criteria should be delineated. The first is specific relational changes within the family and between the family and professionals. For example, "When Mrs. Smith begins to worry about Jimmy's asthma again, she will call her husband to discuss what to do, rather than Dr. Jones." The second is reality decisions that must be made prior to discharge. For example, "The family needs to decide where Tommy will live when he leaves the inpatient unit," or "Mr. and Mrs. Jackson need to decide whether they wish to continue in therapy with Dr. Evans." In inpatient treatment, a tentative discharge date should be specified at the time of admission. Although this can be modified based on feedback generated during the process of inpatient treatment, it serves as a reminder to everyone that the structure and support of the hospital are available for a limited time only.

Too often therapists develop an elaborate reframing of the presenting problem without orienting the family to the process of therapy. The orientation should be communicated clearly at the time of the contract. The gist of the message is that therapy will focus on helping family members change how they participate in relationships, especially those that involve responding to symptomatic behavior. Conflicts and disagreements will have to be expressed directly and resolved without violence, abuse, or disrespect. The therapist will help the family find answers to problems by challenging it to discover untapped competencies and utilize them creatively.

The treatment contract must be developed under the therapist's direction, with input from the family and significant professionals. It is based not so much on what the family wants to change, but on what the therapist believes she can accomplish with the family. Thomas Szasz (1965, 43–44) writes:

This decision will not depend primarily on what the patient *wants* nor on what the therapist believes the patient *needs,* but rather on what the therapist, qua therapist, regards as an appropriate professional activity for himself. . . . A primary duty of the autonomous therapist is to take care of himself: by this I mean that he must protect the integrity of his therapeutic role. If he fails to do this, he cannot "take care" of the patient.

One of the pitfalls during this initial stage is offering a treatment contract to a family before witnessing its willingness and ability to change. With families who have had repeated failures in therapy, it is prudent to hold off offering a contract until the the family has demonstrated behavioral change. The therapist thus becomes an immovable object around which the family must reorganize, holding tenaciously to a position and using the prospect of a contract as leverage to initiate the process of change. This is illustrated in the Cabrini case, where the family had to successfully complete several tasks as a precondition of Maria's admission to the hospital.

Excessive accommodation to the family, especially at the beginning of treatment, when the therapist must establish herself as in charge of the therapeutic context, breeds laziness and disrespect. Most families will respect a demanding therapist and will go to extraordinary lengths to stretch, as long as they trust her and feel truly accepted by her.

The Cabrinis

THE REFERRAL

The inpatient admissions office at the Philadelphia Child Guidance Clinic received a call from Joyce Perkins, a therapist who had been working with eighteen-year-old Maria Cabrini at a local mental health center. Maria was currently hospitalized on an adult psychiatric unit following a suicide attempt two weeks previously, and her condition was deteriorating. Rachel Marshall, the family therapist who directed the inpatient treatment team, told her teammates—a program coordinator, a psychoeducational specialist, a nurse clinician, a psychologist, a child psychiatrist, and several child life counselors—Maria's story, which she had pieced together from the referral information and a subsequent phone conversation with Joyce.

Maria and her three-year-old son, Nicholas, lived with her mother, Angela, her stepfather, Joe, her sixteen-year-old brother, Bruno, and her thirteen-year-old half sister, Anita, who was the only child of the Cabrinis' marriage. Bruno and Maria's father had died in an automobile accident when Maria was six. Nicholas was the product of a brief encounter Maria had had at fifteen with a young man whose whereabouts were unknown.

When Maria was fourteen, her parents felt that her behavioral outbursts had become too difficult for them to manage, and they placed her in a group home for incorrigible teenagers. Since she was sixteen, Maria had been hospitalized on psychiatric units three times following suicide attempts and psychotic behavior, and she was diagnosed as having schizoaffective disorder. More recently, following a neighbor's report to the city's Department of Human Services (DHS) alleging neglect and physical abuse of Nicholas, she had sought help at the mental health center, and Joyce had been assigned as Maria's therapist.

Joyce described Maria as isolated and overwhelmed, frightened of the violent altercations between her brother and stepfather and of the abusive arguments between her mother and stepfather. Maria was also worried about her mother's excessive drinking and Bruno and Anita's truancy from school.

Maria had admitted to Joyce that she hit Nicholas at times to discipline him. His caretaking alternated between Mrs. Cabrini, Maria, and Maria's siblings, and he had not had all of the necessary immunizations and medical care. Joyce tried to persuade Mr. and Mrs. Cabrini to become involved in Maria's treatment, but they refused. Due to DHS's concern for Nicholas's physical and emotional well-being, he had been removed from the home and placed in temporary foster care one month prior to the present referral.

Shortly after Nicholas's placement, Maria's attendance at therapy sessions became erratic. She grew increasingly despondent, began hearing voices, and attempted suicide by overdosing on her psychotropic medication. At that point, her parents had her committed on an emergency basis to a local psychiatric hospital.

Joyce had learned from Nicholas's DHS caseworker, John Williams, that he was planning on extending Nicholas's out-of-home placement, due to the family's disorganization and Maria's "regression." However, Nicholas had begun exhibiting severe tantrums and nightmares in the foster home, and when Mr. and Mrs. Cabrini heard about the situation with their grandson they called Joyce and requested her help in getting Nicholas back. Recognizing the multigenerational nature of the problems in Maria's family, Joyce thought the best course would be a referral to the P.C.G.C's inpatient program.

THE SYMPTOMATIC CYCLE AND THE DEVELOPMENTAL IMPASSE

The therapist should formulate the referral information in a way that sheds light on the symptomatic cycle. In the Cabrinis' story so far, the core dynamic is that Maria's parents repeatedly cut her loose, by turning her over to the professionals, exactly when she became symptomatic. The professionals' efforts to help Maria inadvertently amplified the cutoff by excluding her parents from the healing process. By taking over, the professionals allowed Maria's parents to further abdicate their responsibility.

The stability afforded by this solution was only temporary, because Maria repeatedly decompensated soon after returning home. Now the pattern was repeating itself in relation to Nicholas. When he became too difficult for her to handle, Maria turned his care over to her parents or siblings. His placement was an extension of the same dynamic, in which professionals again took over for the family, creating a deeper rift between Maria and her son. The result of the family's symptomatic entanglement with the mental health system was a blockade of the family life cycle. Nicholas's development was thwarted, Maria could not become an effective parent to him, and her parents could not become effective supports to her and grandparents to Nicholas.

ENGAGING AND ORGANIZING THE PROFESSIONAL NETWORK

When a family experiences repeated or escalating problems despite being involved with several systems of professionals, the therapist must sort out and disentangle the professionals' involvement in the symptomatic cycle to facilitate more straightforward communication and conflict resolution in the entire system. Conflicts arise naturally in such systems because the participants are working to accomplish different goals according to their different roles and responsibilities.

The starting point is to build a respectful collaboration with the referring person and the entire professional network: first, the therapist must validate everyone's perceptions; second, she must capitalize on everyone's concern about the severity of the presenting symptoms; third, she must offer a sense of hope and alternatives. To begin the process, Rachel called Joyce and acknowledged her commitment to Maria and agreed about the urgency of the situation. In addition, she made a commitment on behalf of the team to work with Joyce to engage the family and the other involved professionals.

Rachel made two suggestions about how best to coordinate the treatment effort. The first was that Joyce ask Maria's psychiatrist at the local hospital to make the official referral of Maria to the clinic's inpatient unit, since it was the psychiatrist who was currently in charge of Maria's treatment, not Joyce. Accepting a referral from Joyce would implicitly reinforce the symptomatic cycle, by treating Joyce as if she had responsibility that actually was the psychiatrist's.

The second suggestion was that Joyce ask the DHS worker, John Williams, to refer Nicholas to the preschool program at the Philadelphia Child Guidance Clinic. Nicholas's symptoms were creating a major problem for the foster family, whose services DHS did not want to lose, and the preschool program would provide DHS with a therapeutic resource for Nicholas. In addition, this request could increase the likelihood of Mr. and Mrs. Cabrini's participating in treatment by demonstrating Joyce and Rachel's responsiveness to the Cabrinis' wish to regain their grandson.

Rachel told Joyce that the team was willing to schedule a preadmission assessment session for the following week. Every family member living in the household, a clinical representative from the team currently treating Maria, Nicholas, John Williams, and Joyce would be required to attend.

Through these initial interventions, Rachel asserted herself as in charge of the therapeutic context by taking a clear and nonnegotiable position on how the referral should be made and who needed to participate.

The next week, Rachel was faced with a decision about how to structure the session. The chief advantage in meeting with everyone together in the same room from the beginning is that it reduces the likelihood of miscommunication and blaming, which further erode already troubled relationships. The main disadvantage of this approach, particularly for professionals who have not previously worked together, is that the professionals may be uncomfortable discussing their concerns about the case, including their disagreements with one another, in the presence of the family. Family members may also be reluctant to speak openly.

Rachel chose to meet briefly with the professionals first, separately from the family, to explain the team's general orientation to the assessment process and to understand and review each person's agenda. Then she invited the family to join.

EXPLORING THE SYMPTOMATIC CYCLE WITHIN THE FAMILY

The first few minutes of the initial session are critical. Typically the therapist will begin the session by speaking to the referring person, since her conduit to the symptomatic system is through that person. Beginning in this way also reduces the risk of focusing too quickly on the symptom, a focus that can lead the therapist to inadvertently collude with the family against the symptomatic person and reinforce the symptomatic cycle.

However, in cases where the symptomatic pull is very compelling, such as with the Cabrinis, it is often more prudent to start directly with the symptomatic member to connect with her as an ally in the search to understand how relationships become organized by the symptom. In the following dialogue, Rachel immediately seizes on Maria's plea, "Please don't shut the door," and notes her sense of suffocation. When the family's protectiveness quickly emerges in response, Rachel begins to challenge it.

MARIA: Please don't shut the door!
RACHEL: You don't want me to shut the door?
MR. CABRINI: She doesn't like to feel closed in.
MRS. CABRINI: She gets very nervous and begins to shake all over when she feels closed in.
BRUNO: She's been in the hospital for a few weeks and is always nervous seeing our parents. They don't get along.
RACHEL: I see. *(Looking at Maria)* Do you feel closed in?
MARIA: Yes.
RACHEL: Fine, I'd be glad to leave the door open. That's fine. . . . This is a very helpful family, huh? *(Family members, except Maria, laugh.)*
MR. CABRINI: We try to be helpful.

RACHEL: *(Looking at Maria)* They're very sensitive to you, aren't they? *(Smiles)* Do they often talk for you?

MARIA: Yes.

RACHEL: How old are you, Maria?

MARIA: Eighteen.

RACHEL: Do you really need them to be so helpful, so protective, like talking for you?

MARIA: Not really.

RACHEL: Then why do you let them treat you as if you are so much younger than your age?

MARIA: I don't know. They just do.

RACHEL: Do they treat your brother and sister like they are fragile and unable to talk for themselves, too?

MARIA: Not really.

BRUNO: They worry about her.

RACHEL: They don't worry about you and Anita?

BRUNO: No.

In the first two minutes of the session, the intensity of Maria's panic and the family's rapid mobilization around her helplessness were striking. Maria seemed frozen with fright, her eyes riveted on the floor, her voice barely audible, and her hands and legs trembling. The other family members seemed terrified as well. Perhaps, Rachel thought, in this family it is better to keep quiet when upset, for it may be dangerous to speak.

Like many severely symptomatic families, this family evokes the image of a wheel, with the patient at the hub. The patient is the source of energy, linked to each family member on the periphery while none of the other family members seem connected to each other. The patient seems both paralyzed and powerful at the same time, and is not free to develop in her own way.

To help the symptomatic person free himself or herself, it is necessary for the therapist to take that person's position at the hub of the wheel, using this centrality to connect with each member of the symptomatic system. This connection begins by learning about each person's view of the problem and the nature of his or her participation in the dance around the symptom.

In the course of conversation, Rachel learned that Maria was afraid to leave her bedroom, though she would not explain her reasons for wanting to be secluded. In the following sequence, as Rachel explores how Maria's reclusiveness organizes the family, she intensifies the moment by introducing the theme of death and bringing out Mr. and Mrs. Cabrini's fears of pushing Maria to the point of suicide.

RACHEL: *(Looking at Mr. Cabrini)* How come you're afraid to push her?

MR. CABRINI: I don't want to get her upset. I'm afraid to bother her, I'm afraid if she gets upset. . . . *(He stops talking. The room is dead silent.)*

RACHEL: Are you afraid if you get tougher with her, that you'd kill her?

MR. CABRINI: No. What? No, I'm not afraid of that.

RACHEL: You're not afraid of that?

MR. CABRINI: I don't think so. I'm not sure what I should do. I'm just not sure.

RACHEL: *(Looking at mother)* And you?

MRS. CABRINI: Well, she's been depressed for a long time, and I don't want to set her off. Depression is part of her makeup, but I can't reason with her. She's always liked to stay to herself.

RACHEL: Are you afraid your husband would kill her if he became more demanding of her?

MRS. CABRINI: No, I'm afraid Maria might do away with herself.

RACHEL: No, there is no such thing as suicide. All suicides are really homicides—other people contribute.

MRS. CABRINI: *(Looking puzzled)* Oh, I didn't know that.

Like many parents, Mr. and Mrs. Cabrini become immobilized by the problems of their severely symptomatic child. They view the problems as residing within the child in realms they cannot touch. Emphasizing that death may be the consequence of the parents' continuing the usual pattern of avoidance with a child who presents life-threatening symptoms, and portraying suicide as an interpersonal phenomenon, is a way of disorienting the parents to this view and jogging them out of their paralysis. As Rachel persisted in exploring Mr. Cabrini's fears of pushing Maria too hard, his feelings of impotence came to the fore.

RACHEL: *(To Mr. Cabrini)* How about you? Are you worried that if you pushed her and didn't let her avoid you, would that kill her—are you worried you might kill her that way?

MR. CABRINI: Yeah, I'm concerned about that. Maybe not kill her, but make her worse.

RACHEL: I'm talking about life and death, I'm talking about killing her; you think it might kill her if you pushed her more?

MR. CABRINI: Yeah.

RACHEL: Do you really think she's so fragile, that she couldn't withstand your pushing?

MR. CABRINI: Yeah, that's what I think. So now what am I supposed to do?

The therapist should connect with all members of the family early on in the initial session. Staying too long with any one person risks accentuating family members' sense of alienation. Rachel next turned to Maria's siblings, expanding on the themes of helplessness and protectiveness.

RACHEL: *(To Anita)* You seem very worried about your sister.

ANITA: I am. *(She begins to cry.)*

BRUNO: We're both very worried. I just don't want to see any harm come to her.

RACHEL: Harm? What do you mean?

BRUNO: Well, he *(pointing to his stepfather)* screams and storms around a lot.

ANITA: Bruno and Daddy fight a lot, and Maria gets very upset.

MARIA: *(With her head down, her hair over her eyes)* Please don't scream, please don't.

BRINGING THE SYMPTOM INTO THE SESSION

Suddenly Maria began to hyperventilate and said she was hearing voices. The room grew silent; everyone's eyes were focused on her. Nicholas began to cry, and the DHS worker took him onto his lap.

JOHN WILLIAMS: *(Turning to Rachel)* You see, this is the problem. It's not safe for the boy to be living in their household. It's dangerous.

MARIA: *(Looking at the floor and muttering to herself)* I want my son back.

The entrance of the symptom enables the therapist to do more than simply observe and discuss the symptomatic cycle. Her internal experience of being in proximity to the symptom and to those affected by it offers a compelling way to connect with the family's struggle. The symptom can be a hook for the therapist as well as for the family. Using her own affective experience of the family's struggle allows her to touch the core of the family's paralysis. The power of that touch emanates from the therapist's willingness to share her internal responses with the family. This sharing encourages a more intimate and open therapeutic climate and inspires family members to risk exposing their own vulnerability.

Rachel thus revealed her fantasy of Maria many years hence. She spoke of seeing an old woman who had spent many years in a mental hospital, smoking endless cigarettes and being bathed and fed by her family and nurses, waiting for death's release. Mrs. Cabrini began to cry. When Rachel moved next to her and acknowledged how fearful she seemed, the mother's tears poured forth. She voiced her and her husband's fear of losing Maria to suicide or to a life in and out of institutions, and guiltily acknowledged that they felt ill equipped to help.

CHALLENGING HELPLESSNESS

The Cabrinis, like many families ensconced in the mental health system, felt helpless with respect to Maria and her symptoms and looked to professionals to provide the answers. The challenge for the therapist is to evoke the family's strengths by refusing to accede to its expectations and by repeatedly communicating confidence in its potential to change. Rachel made it clear to Mr. and Mrs. Cabrini that she and her team would work to help the family stay together. "Our belief," Rachel said, "is that before a family submits to any type of cutoff, whether it be divorce, hospitalization, or giving up custody of a child, the family needs to work intensively together, exhausting all other alternatives first. We will need a total commitment from each of you in order to break the cycle of hospitalization and repair the relationships within the family." Mrs. Cabrini nodded and said, "That's good, because it seems like everyone else wants to break us up. Just tell us what you want us to do."

To challenge parental helplessness, the therapist should underscore the need for the parents to go to extraordinary lengths to help their child and family. Questions such as "Is there anything you would not do to help your child?" and "Is there anything so terrible about your relationship that it cannot be changed for the sake of your child?" provoke the family to question the limits of its own flexibility, and will often reinforce its commitment to the symptomatic person and the therapist.

With parents who say "We'll do anything," yet who have not followed through on previous treatment recommendations, it is important to accept their stated willingness to change and to challenge them to demonstrate their competence. The most straightforward way for the therapist to do this in the first phase of treatment is to answer their questions directly, offering concrete suggestions for handling the prob-

lem and requesting that the parents put her advice into practice. Whatever the family then does (or does not do) provides the therapist with
further information about the roadblocks to change—unresolved conflicts associated with the symptom.

Another way to explore parental helplessness is to question the advis-
ability of the family's changing. This approach challenges family members to speak about what they really want to happen, not to mouth
words they think the therapist wants to hear. Although it may be
disorienting and even provocative, such questioning is not intended to
be a paradoxical restraint from change. The process of change in
severely symptomatic families is in fact potentially dangerous and
should be undertaken only with a conscious awareness of its risks.
Dangers are mostly likely to arise when therapists are dishonest with
families, shielding them from the struggles with which they will have
to contend.

Turning to Mr. Cabrini, Rachel said: "I believe you want to change,
but I want to warn you that change is very stressful. Given the history
of violence and depression in the family, I am concerned about the
possibility of you or someone else becoming suicidal or homicidal." Mr.
Cabrini voiced his surprise at Rachel's question and assured her that he
would not act violently. His confident assertion of his ability to control
himself contrasted with the aura of helplessness he had previously
projected.

Rachel then challenged the family's overprotectiveness of Maria by
asking her parents and siblings to move back physically and give her
some room to breathe, in which she could practice calming herself.
Hesitantly they did so, and Rachel began to talk with Maria about ways
in which she could tame her voices and transform them from horrific
demons to friendly imps.

DISRUPTING THE SYMPTOMATIC CYCLE

The DHS caseworker operates under a mandate to protect the safety
of children and strengthen the functioning of families. In many circumstances, these missions seem contradictory. The caseworker may be
caught in coalitions and alliances within a given family and between the
family and other professionals. Thus, the patterns of interaction between DHS and the family can become part of the symptomatic cycle,
particularly when DHS has the power to return or retain custody of a
child. For the Cabrinis, Nicholas's foster care placement represented an
extension of the symptomatic cycle in the family; it was analogous to

Mr. and Mrs. Cabrini's residential and psychiatric placements of Maria. Therefore, an increase in proximity between Nicholas and the family would be an important consequence of disrupting the cycle. Rachel moved to address this issue next in the opening session, setting the stage for the work that would be necessary with Maria and her son later on in the course of treatment.

Rachel asked John Williams, the DHS caseworker, what changes he would need to see in order to return Nicholas to Maria and the family. He said that he needed to be assured that there would be no more instances of violence or neglect, that the family would have to participate in the inpatient program at the clinic, and that at the time of discharge the team would need to provide a statement in court that Maria and Mr. and Mrs. Cabrini were fit to adequately care for Nicholas.

There are several ways of responding to such a request. The therapist and team can agree to the request for evaluation, rendering an opinion about whether the child in question should be returned to the family and reporting their recommendations to DHS and the court. Families and medical or mental health professionals commonly consider the making of judgments about people's competencies to be an aspect of the therapist's role, particularly when mistreatment of children is concerned. From such a perspective, it seems logical to ask a therapist to take this role, and just as logical for the therapist to accept it.

However, accepting DHS's request for an evaluation and recommendation risks jeopardizing the therapist and team's relationship and credibility with the family. For treatment to be effective, family members must view the therapist and team not as a consulting arm of DHS but as an ally of the family. Accepting the consultant role may distract the therapist and team from the job of treating the family, and may even be in overt conflict with it.

Alternatively, the therapist and team can decline the request and tell the caseworker that if he needs an evaluation, he should obtain it from his agency's mental health consultants. Refusing to agree to DHS's request for an evaluation may seem to have the advantage of protecting the therapist and team from possible triangulation. However, this decision diminishes the therapist and team's ability to develop a collaborative working relationship with DHS, a relationship that is necessary if they wish to catalyze a change in the relationship between DHS and the family.

To cultivate collaboration, the therapist can invite the DHS caseworker to observe the family's treatment in the hospital and to meet regularly with the therapist and team. A therapeutic context should be constructed in which the goals, responsibilities, roles, and boundaries of the participants are clearly differentiated and specified in the treatment contract. In this negotiation, the therapist helps the family define its goal (for example, reunification with the child), while the DHS caseworker establishes criteria and a timetable the family must meet to retain or regain custody. The therapist should assist the family in securing a clear statement of expectations from the DHS worker. What the team will or will not do and how the treatment setting can be used to facilitate the caseworker's observations are among the issues that must be addressed. The therapist may also help the caseworker lay out for the family other required aspects of his evaluation, such as home visits or school reports, as well as other services in the community, that can be secured to help the family meet its goals.

With the Cabrinis, the team wanted to align itself as closely as possible with the family, in light of how often professionals had assumed a controlling position with respect to Maria and Nicholas. Rachel explained that the team was committed to working with the family toward the goal of reunification, and she recommended that Nicholas return home with the family unless during the hospitalization Maria or her parents breached their agreement with the treatment contract.

Rachel invited the DHS caseworker to observe the family's progress in the inpatient unit and the preschool program and to confer with the treatment team. The team would provide him with its recommendations regarding the treatment needs of Nicholas, Maria, and the rest of the family. She stressed to him that the team's recommendation of reunification was based on the belief that *all* families have the ability to take adequate care of their members as long as they are sufficiently connected with each other and with their community. It is not the therapist's or the team's job to determine whether the family should be split apart or reunited or whether the family is "fit" to take care of its children; these decisions are the responsibility of the courts and the social welfare system. What the team can do is to identify the ways in which the family's particular therapeutic needs can best be met and to work with the family and DHS to meet them.

John Williams asked how long it would be before Nicholas might return home, as he needed to arrange for continued foster care. Rachel's response was again to invite the caseworker to participate fully in the therapeutic process with the team and the family in order to observe firsthand the rate and nature of the changes that occurred. If his observations led him to feel that the pace of change was too slow, he might need to look for a long-term placement for Nicholas.

Rachel then made it clear to the Cabrinis, in John's presence, that while she and her team would work toward the goal of helping the family convince DHS to allow Nicholas to return home, the family would have to agree that there would be no more incidents of abuse or neglect. If such incidents were to occur, they would be reported immediately to DHS. At that point, the team would work on helping Maria and her family to accept Nicholas's placement and separate from him in as healthy a way as possible.

When there have been allegations of abuse and neglect, there must be open discussion of these issues in the family's presence. While seeking assurances that safety will be maintained, the therapist cannot wear blinders and deny or minimize the potential for abuse. Nor should she naively or prematurely accept the family's reassurances and recommend the removal of external controls. Supporting DHS's role as the societal monitor of Nicholas's safety was not contradictory to the team's position of supporting the family's reunification efforts. It is often necessary to maintain such external controls throughout the course of treatment.

To reinforce the differentiation of roles and responsibilities between the team and DHS, Rachel made another request of the caseworker. She asked him to prepare a list of specific guidelines delineating the behaviors the family would be expected to demonstrate in the course of treatment in order for Nicholas to return to the family. John said he was not in a position to offer any guidelines at that moment, but he agreed to discuss the idea with his supervisor and call Rachel back. A subsequent session would be held to review the guidelines with the team and the family.

THE TREATMENT CONTRACT

Joyce Perkins had previously agreed to continue individual therapy with Maria after discharge if the team recommended it. She said the caseload at her center was heavy, so that she would be able to attend at most two sessions during Maria's hospitalization at the clinic, but she would be available by phone. The nurse, Francis Turner, who accompanied Maria, stated that the attending psychiatrist was willing to transfer Maria to the clinic's inpatient unit, as her condition was not improving in their unit. Mr. and Mrs. Cabrini spoke up in favor of an immediate transfer to the clinic, and Maria said that although she didn't like being in the hospital, she did not feel ready to go back home with her family.

Transferring a patient directly from one hospital to another can repeat a pattern of preempting the parents' responsibility and keeping them on the periphery of treatment, thus perpetuating the symptomatic cycle. Therefore, any contract for hospitalization proposed by the team should incorporate conditions that force changes in the family's interaction with professionals. Admitting the symptomatic person should be contingent on the family's making the specified changes.

Taking this position is disorienting to family members, who expect changes to be a consequence of hospitalization, not a prerequisite for it. However, without some degree of disentanglement from the larger system of family plus professionals prior to hospitalization, the family is less likely to learn to take responsibility for itself in the long run.

After conferring with the team regarding possible ingredients of the contract, Rachel returned to the interview room and made the following statement: "The team is very concerned about Maria and Nicholas, as are all of you. Since the two of them have been separated, each has developed severe symptoms; we feel that they are so important to each other that they may not survive if they continue to be separated. However, Nicholas is too young to care for himself, and we do not see Maria as able to care for Nicholas by herself yet.

"We think you, Maria, first need to learn to care for yourself, but to do that you will need a great deal of support from your family. We believe you will then be better able to care for your son. We would very much like to help your family, and we believe we can help. There are several conditions, however, which must be met before we can agree to admit you to the hospital."

First, Maria would need to be discharged to the care of her parents from the hospital in which she was currently a patient. Accepting Maria as a hospital transfer would only perpetuate the symptomatic arrangement in which her parents were allowed to avoid assuming responsibility for her.

Second, since the other hospital was reluctant to discharge Maria to her home in her current condition, Mr. and Mrs. Cabrini would need to assist Maria in acting more competently in that hospital. Rachel suggested that the parents convince the hospital staff to allow them to spend more time with her on the ward, so that they could encourage her to participate more actively in group and milieu activities. They could help her negotiate with the hospital staff to obtain passes to the community and to home, where she would need to comply with her parents' expectations. All this would enhance the Cabrinis' ability to convince the hospital staff that they could keep Maria safe at home.

Third, Maria would be admitted to the inpatient unit at the clinic after she had been discharged from the local hospital and was acting responsibly for three days at home. Admission should be predicated on the family's competence and success rather than incompetence and failure.

The remaining components of the treatment contract dealt with issues to be addressed after Maria's admission.

Fourth, during the hospitalization, the entire family would participate in daily family therapy sessions, as well as in other activities of the inpatient unit during the day and evening. The overall goals of treatment would be for Maria to speak up and communicate her needs directly rather than through symptoms, for the siblings to support one another and help Maria to find her own voice, for Mr. and Mrs. Cabrini to assist Maria in acting more responsibly as a young adult and as a parent, and for the entire family to resolve conflicts more constructively.

Fifth, if there were any further incidents of physical violence in the home or the hospital between any family members, Maria would either be discharged to her home or transferred to another psychiatric hospital if she was acutely at risk of harming herself or anyone else. The team took a strong position on this matter to emphasize again its categorical opposition to violence and its refusal to participate in treatment with any family in which there were ongoing acts of abuse.

Sixth, Maria's treatment would commence without medication since various psychotropic drugs had been used in the past without benefit. Because her parents tended to rely on the "magic bullets" of experts, the use of medication would be discussed only after Mr. and Mrs. Cabrini had demonstrated a willingness to lean on each other for support, rather than on chemical substances, and to consistently expect responsible behavior from Maria regardless of her symptoms.

Seventh, Maria would either need to have a job to go to following discharge, or else attend a partial hospitalization program.

Rachel spent some time reviewing the expectations with everyone and secured an agreement from each family member and from John Williams, Francis Turner, and Joyce Perkins.

Rachel held two subsequent sessions with Maria, her parents and siblings, the outpatient therapist, and the nurse. Her objective was to help the family accomplish the first three conditions of the treatment contract. Mr. and Mrs. Cabrini reported that they had become more involved in Maria's treatment and that in response Maria had begun to demonstrate more initiative herself. After her discharge from the other hospital, and after meeting with the clinic's preschool staff to begin the intake process for Nicholas, the parents called Rachel to set up the final assessment session.

In the session, they reported that John Williams had joined them in the meeting with the preschool staff. He had presented a set of guidelines the family needed to meet in order for Nicholas to return home. Examples were: "Family is to set up and keep regular medical appointments for Nicholas in collaboration with foster parents, and provide documentation of this to DHS" and "Maria is to maintain a consistent schedule of contacts with Nicholas, demonstrating an ability to set limits in an age-appropriate manner."

Rachel and the team used the treatment contract to begin to disrupt the entanglements of the symptomatic cycle prior to Maria's admission to the hospital. Such an intervention disorients the family to its expectation that professionals will take responsibility for its symptomatic member and instead challenges the family to take responsibility for itself.

The Harmons

CONSIDERATIONS OF HOSPITALIZATION

The referral to the inpatient service at the Philadelphia Child Guidance Clinic came from Frank Hirsch, a therapist in private practice. The symptomatic person, thirteen-year-old Josh Harmon, was described as out of control at home and at school and had recently made a suicide attempt.

Josh lived with his seventeen-year-old sister, Suzanne, and his parents, Robert and Barbara. His parents were in their forties and had been married for twenty-four years. Mr. Harmon was the manager of a restaurant, and Mrs. Harmon worked part time in an insurance company.

Outpatient therapists generally request hospitalization when they feel that their own resources and those of the family are exhausted. The therapist and family may be working toward common goals but find they need the additional resources provided by an inpatient unit to break through a therapeutic impasse. An inpatient unit provides possibilities for containment, compression, separation, a sharpening of focus, and an increase in intensity, which may be more difficult to sustain on an outpatient basis.

The inpatient unit can serve as an arena for a referring therapist and family to work together intensively for a concentrated period of time, with the support and collaboration of the inpatient therapist and team.

Sometimes changes occur in the symptomatic system as a result of the outpatient therapist's decision to refer for inpatient hospitalization, and hospitalization no longer seems necessary. But while the referral process can initiate a change in the symptomatic cycle, it can also be part of that cycle, as occurred in the Cabrini case. The inpatient therapist must carefully assess and understand the symptomatic cycle, then respond in a way that does not incorporate her into the problem.

At times, the referring therapist will describe himself as stuck or overwhelmed; he may feel that he is on a merry-go-round, a treadmill, or a roller coaster. Anxious about the symptom, he may be overly focused on the behavior of the symptomatic member and may express hopelessness about the family in general. In such situations, hospitalization may be best viewed and defined as a consultation to the referring therapist, with the goal of catalyzing a more effective therapeutic process for him and the family.

There are also times when a referral for hospitalization is implicitly a request for "divorce" between the referring therapist and the family. When the therapist or family experiences their work together as not helpful, the negotiation of a separation may be in order. In such cases, part of the inpatient therapist's job is to help the referring therapist extricate himself in a respectful and explicit manner, freeing the family to seek what it needs elsewhere.

THE OUTPATIENT THERAPIST'S PERSPECTIVE

After receiving the intake information sheet from the admissions worker who had handled the initial telephone call, Paul Rogers, the inpatient therapist, called Frank Hirsch to discuss the referral. Here is what Frank reported:

"Josh was diagnosed as perceptually impaired and has been in special education classes throughout school. He has been a behavioral problem since the first grade, and now he is in junior high school, doing poorly academically, and always in trouble. He is immature, provocative, and intrusive. The teachers are fed up with Josh, and the school is planning to put him on homebound instruction.

"I like Josh. He is basically a good kid, but very insecure, with low self-esteem. Over the past four months, he has been meeting weekly with a drug and alcohol counselor at school. Three weeks ago, since things were going downhill, the counselor referred Josh and his family to me for family therapy.

"The older sister is now a senior in high school. She had some problems in school with drinking and drugs a couple of years ago. The family saw two therapists then, but the father didn't like either one of them and the family dropped out of treatment both times. The parents say that Suzanne straightened out on her own.

"I have seen the Harmons for four sessions. They are quite cooperative, but things are getting worse. Josh and his sister are very close to the mother, and the father is much less involved in the parenting. I have tried to involve the father more, but he gets so angry and punitive toward Josh that the boy acts out more.

"One week ago, Josh took an overdose of Tylenol at school following an angry exchange with father. In our session this week Josh got very angry, his father was full of rage, and mother criticized father for being 'too harsh.' She tried to coax and cajole Josh into talking about the problem, but he only became more resistant and withdrawn.

"After the session, I got a call from mother saying that she and Josh had gotten into a fistfight and everyone in the household was upset and scared. Frankly, I'm worried myself. I am calling to discuss the possibility of hospitalizing Josh before someone gets hurt."

Inpatient admission is only one of a number of alternatives to be considered in responding to a referral for hospitalization, and it is not necessarily the best option. The first step is to assess the symptomatic cycle and to determine whether or not available outpatient resources have been exhausted. The inpatient therapist should start by assessing the referring person's relationship with the family. After listening to Frank Hirsch's description of Josh's problems, Paul began the assessment process.

PAUL: How can I be helpful to you, Dr. Hirsch?
FRANK HIRSCH: The bottom line is keeping Josh from hurting himself or someone else. I could see him twice a week, but I'm not sure that would hold him. He's a pretty impulsive kid.
PAUL: Sounds like you don't trust that the parents can keep him safe.
FRANK HIRSCH: I do think they care about Josh and probably would watch him all the time if I told them to do that, but then I would worry they would start fighting amongst themselves. I'm not sure I want to take that risk. I think it would be easier to get to the bottom of this and figure out what they are all so angry about if Josh was in a safe place.
PAUL: Do you see any other uses for hospitalization?
FRANK HIRSCH: Yes. I don't fully understand what Josh's behavioral problems in school are all about. He probably could use a good psy-

chological and educational workup. I'm not sure why he has such trouble with peers, but he gets into fights all the time. I considered a psychiatric evaluation, but I didn't want to see Josh on medication. Actually, I think the father might benefit from an antidepressant.

When an outpatient therapist refers a patient for inpatient treatment and leaves himself out of the referral, as Frank Hirsch did, the inpatient therapist should ask him directly about his relationship with the family and his expectations regarding his involvement in treatment, both during the hospitalization and after discharge.

PAUL: What role do you see yourself playing in the hospitalization and the evaluation process you're describing? If Josh is admitted, will you continue with the family after discharge?

FRANK HIRSCH: To be frank with you, I really like these people, but I think they are a multiproblem family and should be treated in an agency where there are more services available. It's not like I'm at a mental health center and work with a team. I'm seeing them on my own and it feels a bit too much for me. After Josh is discharged, could he be followed in your outpatient department?

DISENTANGLING THE REFERRING PERSON FROM THE FAMILY

An inpatient referral made by an outpatient therapist who is ambivalent about his ability to help can be experienced by the family as an abandonment. It is essential that the receiving therapist have the referring therapist specify under what conditions he is willing to continue treatment with the family. This clarity allows the family to choose whether, given those conditions, it wants to continue working with him. The inpatient therapist can also use the referring person's conditions to generate intensity during the hospitalization if the family wishes to continue with the referring person after discharge.

There is nothing wrong with a therapist's defining what families she will or will not treat. Limit setting is part of all mutually respectful relationships. For the therapeutic relationship to have integrity, the therapist should specify these limits explicitly at the outset, so that if a parting of the ways occurs prior to a mutually negotiated decision to end treatment, it can happen without the family's feeling betrayed.

Paul's conversation with Frank Hirsch clearly indicated the referring therapist's interest in using a hospitalization to separate from the family. In concluding their conversation, Paul asked Frank to state his position to the Harmons before Paul saw the family for the first time. The statement would be something like this:

"I am referring you to Paul Rogers at the Philadelphia Child Guidance Clinic. I have suggested that he consider hospitalizing Josh for his own safety and that of the family. Mr. Rogers will schedule an appointment to meet with you for an inpatient assessment. He may or may not recommend hospitalization, but in either case, I think you will be better served at his clinic, where they have more of the resources your family needs. You may choose to work with him and his team and to follow their recommendations or not, but either way, I think it would be best for me to bow out at this point."

Frank expressed relief about this disposition, feeling that it gave him a way to leave the family that was respectful and saved face for everyone concerned. Even so, the family's anxiety would undoubtedly heighten as it anticipated the initial session with Paul, its fifth therapist.

FOCUS ON THE FATHER

Therapists connect with families in different ways based on their unique personal styles and idiosyncrasies. Rachel entered the Cabrinis' world by seizing on a trivial event, Maria's request to keep the door shut, and used it to begin challenging the family's symptomatic patterns. In contrast, Paul took a more deliberate approach. He began his first session with the Harmons by asking family members to describe their experience of the problem and their attempts at solutions.

Mr. Harmon began in a sheepish tone, stating that the family was close. He described Josh as a behavior problem and said he "couldn't get a handle on him." Although Suzanne was concerned about her brother, she was embarrassed by his "weird behavior" at school. Mrs. Harmon was worried about Josh's Tylenol ingestion, but she was most alarmed by the fistfight she had had with him. She felt that her behavior was as much a part of the problem as Josh's.

Mrs. Harmon and Suzanne did most of the talking, while Josh stared at the floor and remained silent. After being repeatedly interrupted by his wife and daughter, Mr. Harmon faded into the background, and no one in the family attempted to include him.

One way to increase instability in a system is to enter through the family member who seems most disengaged. By persistently engaging this person, the therapist exerts a pull on the rest of the system to move closer to herself and the peripheral member. In this case, Paul elected to start with Mr. Harmon, especially since Frank Hirsch had emphasized his role in the family and the family acted as if his participation was irrelevant.

A mother who is accessible and a father who is physically and emotionally distant are part of a dynamic that is frequently seen early in therapy. As Goldner points out, too often therapy becomes organized by the sexual politics within the family and within the field of family therapy that identifies "women as good patients . . . because their socialization sensitizes them to the feelings of others and promotes the notion that caretaking is their responsibility, indeed, perhaps their raison d'être" (1985, 41).

Therapeutic myopia results from the belief that the *only* way to engage a distant father is by first engaging the mother and then requesting that she engage the father. The therapist must also be willing to engage the father directly. To connect with a family only through the mother, placing the responsibility for change solely on her shoulders, is to reinforce what Goldner calls "the structures of thought and the structuring of power that keep women (and therefore their families) trapped in cycles of toxic devotion and recrimination" (1985, 45). To avoid this trap and to challenge the family's pattern, Paul continued the session by requesting additional information from Mr. Harmon.

Going against the family's grain is stressful—like swimming upstream. Directing questions to someone whose participation is seemingly not valued requires that the therapist be prepared to continually block interruptions and distractions that emanate from other family members. As Paul explored Mr. Harmon's experience of his relationship with Josh, Mr. Harmon began to express his sadness. Throughout the conversation, Paul maintained a disorienting refusal to see Mr. Harmon as unhelpful or irresponsible.

MR. HARMON: Josh doesn't use good judgment. He doesn't think things out before he does or says something.

PAUL: So it's like he's tripping over his own feet and putting his own foot in his mouth and a few other things.

MR. HARMON: Yeah. He just doesn't think before he acts or speaks.

PAUL: And when you find that happening what goes through your mind, and what are you trying to do?

MR. HARMON: I try to correct him all the time.

PAUL: So anytime you're with him, you're on his back.

MR. HARMON: A lot. All the time. I'm always at his throat.

PAUL: How does that leave you feeling?

MR. HARMON: Terrible. I'm his father. I don't know what to do.

PAUL: So it ends up with you feeling hopeless and sad.

MR. HARMON: Uh-huh.

PAUL: And almost like you don't know your own boy.

MR. HARMON: I'm always apologizing to him. Always thinking I'm hurting him. It's tough.

PAUL: I get the sense that your son and daughter are important to you.

MR. HARMON: Very. The most.

PAUL: So then to have this kind of thing between you and one of them must drive you nuts.

MR. HARMON: It does. Even when I argue with Suzanne, I can't handle it.

PAUL: How come?

MR. HARMON: I don't like fighting with my kids. I don't like fighting with anybody, really, but with my kids, it bothers me a lot. I apologize, even though I'm right.

Paul was struck by Mr. Harmon's softness and touched by his sadness about feeling like a failure as a father. The prospect of cultivating a connection with him seemed promising. Mr. Harmon's fluctuation between emotional absence and fiery rage suggested a pattern frequently seen in families with severely symptomatic members. Often the parents themselves, especially the more isolated parent, have experienced disconnected relationships in their own families of origin, such as the death of a parent, divorce, or abuse, from which they have not yet healed. Carrying the weight of that trauma impedes the parents' ability to reach out to their children and be intimate with each other.

As Paul communicated to Mr. Harmon his sincere interest in hearing what he had to say, Mr. Harmon allowed Paul into his private world. Searching for a way to change the lens through which the family viewed Mr. Harmon, Paul introduced his own empathic response into the dialogue. He began by making an attribution that was disorientingly at odds with the family's usual way of seeing Mr. Harmon.

PAUL: How did you get to be so gentle?

MR. HARMON: From my father.

PAUL: How do you mean?

MR. HARMON: He was a very gentle guy. He never hit us. Never yelled at us. He was a good guy.

PAUL: How many of you were there?

MR. HARMON: Me and my sister.

PAUL: Are you the oldest or youngest?

MR. HARMON: I'm the oldest. My sister has a mental problem.

PAUL: What kind of mental problem?

MR. HARMON: Paranoid schizophrenia.

PAUL: Where is she now?

MR. HARMON: She's home with my mother. She has beat mom up a few times. She was down in Texas doing drugs.

MRS. HARMON: She refuses to take her medication or be hospitalized. There's nothing to do, except keep her home and out of her mother's way.

PAUL: That must be a weight on you.

MR. HARMON: It is.

PAUL: Are you afraid of being too hard with Josh, and driving him crazy?

MR. HARMON: Yeah. I'm afraid he might go crazy, like my sister, or run away. But I'm afraid also of being too soft. I'm just not sure how to be.

PAUL: I see. You're afraid to follow your gut?

MR. HARMON: Yeah.

PAUL: And what about your dad?

MR. HARMON: He's dead.

PAUL: When did he die?

MR. HARMON: Eight years ago?

MRS. HARMON: Six years ago.

PAUL: How did he die?

MR. HARMON: Cancer.

PAUL: He must have been fairly young.

MR. HARMON: Sixty-one. It was very tough on my mother. She couldn't handle it.

PAUL: What happened to her?

MR. HARMON: That's when she went downhill. From that day on.

After losing his father, Mr. Harmon became embroiled with his mother, his sister, and the mental health system in ways that left him feeling helpless and inadequate. For many years, he had watched the destructive interactions of his mother and sister, feeling powerless to help. Finally, about three years before this session, he decided to stop speaking to his mother and sister. Since then, his wife had taken over the job of communicating with his family in an effort to help him with his pain, but to no avail. In spite of refusing contact, he could not stop thinking about them. Much of his time and energy were absorbed by this futile and painful preoccupation; he seemed to be living in a perpetual state of mourning.

Paul surmised that Mr. Harmon's despair about the torn relationships of his family of origin was the source of his rages. It seemed that his anger at Josh, when Josh acted irresponsibly or incompetently, was fueled by his associations with his sister. Professionals had failed to help Josh much as they had failed to help his sister, and the symptomatic cycle had extended into the next generation.

BRINGING JOSH INTO THE PICTURE

In an initial session where younger children or adolescents are present, therapists often err by focusing too much attention on the adults. Failing to encourage the children's participation will deprive the therapy not only of valuable content but also of the spontaneity and playfulness that children add to a family. Although the parents' personal concerns and their relationship with each other are important aspects of the symptomatic cycle, it is a mistake at this early point in the therapeutic process to focus too much attention on these areas. It is not true in severely symptomatic families that the child's behavior will spontaneously improve if the parental relationship changes. Disruptions in parent–child relationships require direct attention.

Accordingly, Paul next moved to connect with Josh. He was uncomfortable with Josh's silence in the beginning of the session and wanted to hear about the problems from his perspective. Josh stated that he could not control what he did. He described himself as frequently not knowing the right thing to do, and he generally felt lonely and inept. He said that he quickly became frustrated with his father and that "no matter how hard I try to patch things up, something always gets in the way." Developmentally, he seemed about ten or eleven years old, ineffective at modulating his impulses and his relationships.

Both Mr. Harmon and Josh were dissatisfied with their relationship. They tried to get closer and ended up farther apart. To construct a framework within which the father and son could repair and rebuild their relationship, Paul introduced an idea that he hoped would link them together. "I find the two of you very similar," he said. "You are both isolated in the family and from friends, and you really don't know each other well. I think life would be much more satisfying for both of you if you got to know each other better."

Josh and his father readily agreed, and Paul elaborated, suggesting that when Mr. Harmon's father died, a part of him had died, too. In an important sense, Mr. Harmon and Josh had each lost their fathers. By sharing more of himself with his dad, Paul continued, Josh would be helping his father discover his own qualities as a father. Although this process might lead Mr. Harmon to experience a heightened sense of loss vis-à-vis the missed opportunities with his own father, working through those feelings would allow Mr. Harmon to give more freely of himself to Josh. It might also allow Josh to grow up without being burdened and held back by his father's grief. As Paul spoke, Mr. Harmon was nodding with interest, and Josh occasionally looked up with a slight smile at Paul and his father.

THE MOTHER'S POINT OF VIEW

As the therapist increases instability in the family by engineering changes in the proximity–distance axis of relationships in the symptomatic cycle, she must monitor the responses of all members of the system. Although Paul was encouraged by Mr. Harmon's and Josh's acceptance of his proposed framework for their relationship, he needed to connect with Mrs. Harmon to hear her response to the proposed increase in proximity between father and son, and to understand her view of their relationship.

MRS. HARMON: I don't know why they push each other away. I think maybe my husband's a little too hard on Josh. See, I'm a lot easier with him. Robert's beginning to accept that Suzanne's growing up, but he wants to keep Josh his little boy. And I think Josh may be rebelling against that, even though he needs his father's direction now.

Having heard Mrs. Harmon's perspective, Paul challenged her to enlarge her vision by including herself in the cycle.

PAUL: If you feel that Josh needs his dad to be more involved with him, how come you have let Robert off the hook?
MRS. HARMON: I knew Robert was hurting from his own family, and wanted to protect him. I didn't want to rock the boat.
PAUL: You think maybe you sold him short by being so protective, you know, sent him and the kids a message that you didn't find him competent to deal with your son?
MRS. HARMON: I can see that now, but I didn't see it before.

Mrs. Harmon's responsiveness to Paul's directness and her willingness to accept responsibility for her participation were encouraging. It seemed to Paul that her going easy on Josh and feeling bad for him were related to her going easy on and feeling bad for her husband.

CHARACTERIZING THE SYMPTOMATIC CYCLE

Once a therapist has plunged into the symptomatic system and begun to map its entanglements, it is helpful to step away to formulate the symptomatic cycle from what has been described or demonstrated so far. Physically leaving the therapy room is useful for this.

Here is how Paul sketched out the Harmons' cycle during a break: When Josh has difficulty in school, Mr. Harmon hears echoes of his experience with his sister and becomes frightened and furious with his son. Mrs. Harmon, respecting her husband's pain and wanting to avoid conflict with him, compensates for his anger by being soft and going easy on Josh. Feeling that she couldn't turn to her husband, Mrs. Harmon conferred with professionals about her son, further distancing her husband from herself and Josh. Mr. Harmon felt cut off, but dealt with it as if his wife was intentionally colluding with professionals to deprive him of his parental role. The distance between the parents grew; Josh's underlying needs were not addressed; he expressed his difficulties in increasingly dramatic ways; and the cycle repeated itself.

When Josh was in grade school, Mr. Harmon was absorbed by his grief and his efforts to try to help his mother and sister. Mrs. Harmon tried not to intrude on his world with the children's problems, and Mr. Harmon left their rearing to her, remaining distant from all of them. Paul surmised that with Josh's entry into adolescence and junior high school, the operation of the cycle left the family stuck in a developmental impasse.

In junior high school, Josh was faced with more advanced academic subjects, a larger number of teachers, more complex peer relationships, and the psychological and physiological onslaught of puberty. Josh had never liked school, and now he felt even more out of place. He was accustomed to relying on his mother to handle school problems for him, but now his mother's presence at school became more of an embarrassment than a help. Lacking the physical or social skills to draw positive attention to himself, he had developed a style of provoking attention with obnoxious and aggressive behavior. The only way he found to connect with peers was through using drugs.

Josh's sense of isolation was amplified by his father's emotional distance. Mrs. Harmon felt frustrated in her single-handed attempts to help Josh, but she did not know how to enlist her husband's help. The previous stress of dealing with Suzanne's problems had drained much of the parents' energy, and there was little in reserve. Emergency calls from the school roused Mr. Harmon from his apathy, but he backed off as soon as things calmed down. Josh was growing older, but he was not maturing. His development was at an impasse.

These were the elements of the symptomatic cycle in which the family was caught, a cycle that had taken Josh from a young boy with learning difficulties to an adolescent with a psychiatric emergency.

With each repetition of the cycle, new professionals were called in, new diagnoses were added (perceptual impairment, conduct disorder, and now depression), and the parents became increasingly mystified and uncertain and less trusting of themselves, each other, and the professionals, reinforcing everyone's sense that the situation was out of control.

CHALLENGING PARENTAL HELPLESSNESS

After a therapist has developed a connection with family members and a map of the symptomatic cycle, she must decide who is most pivotal to the initiation of the process of change. Paul saw Mr. Harmon and his relationship with Josh as the key. He did not feel Mr. Harmon was any more competent than Mrs. Harmon, but he saw Josh's symptoms as most severely entangled in his distant and strained relationship with his father. If Mr. Harmon were to participate more actively in Josh's life and become more emotionally available to him, then Josh could feel more accepted and confident.

Paul also saw his efforts to reach out to Mr. Harmon as implicitly supportive of Mrs. Harmon, who had already expressed her wish to help her husband deal with his longstanding conflicts with his mother and sister so that he could become more of a husband and father. Her recent loss of self-control with Josh had frightened her enormously. Although she had been stymied for years in finding a constructive, proactive way of involving her husband with Josh, she had not given up. She felt Josh needed his father's direction, and she still seemed eager for her husband's participation.

Upon his return to the session, Paul told Mrs. Harmon he agreed that her husband's increased involvement in the family was essential. Mrs. Harmon was relieved that Paul would share with her the weight of her husband's pain and help him develop a stronger voice.

When family members are adept at avoiding the resolution of conflicts by withdrawing into their own separate spheres, the therapist needs to close off their escape routes. For example, she can spell out the consequences for a child of the parents' remaining disconnected. "Josh needs your help, Robert, your involvement in his life, if he is to break out of his isolation," Paul said firmly. "If you stay cut off from him, he will drift farther away. You can make the difference, but he needs you to change. You'll need to get to know your son well enough to help him stay out of trouble. You can no longer respond just to emergencies, running in to put out fires and then backing off."

Families like the Harmons can be articulate and insightful about their situation as they sit in the therapist's office, talking calmly about the violent episodes at home. The therapist must go beyond descriptions and interpretations of what happens outside the session, however, if she wants to generate enough intensity to help the family break old patterns and discover new ones. The therapist must actively bring the family's passion into the room.

Although Mr. Harmon nodded his agreement with everything Paul was saying, he looked exceedingly uncomfortable when Paul insisted that he challenge Josh right then and there on how he would deal with future conflicts without resorting to self-destructive behavior. Within minutes, the symptomatic pattern had emerged: Josh was staring at the floor, pouting, and Mrs. Harmon began to explain Josh's feelings to Mr. Harmon, who was rapidly getting angry.

As Paul blocked Mrs. Harmon's intrusion, she backed off and actively encouraged Mr. Harmon to persist with their son until Josh began to express how he felt. Bolstered by the encouragement of Mrs. Harmon and Paul, the father and Josh began to talk, and Mr. Harmon secured a commitment from Josh that they would talk whenever Josh felt sad or angry. With Paul's continued encouragement, the parents worked out a plan to assist each other in supervising Josh.

Paul was comfortable with their plan because the parents' verbal and behavioral accommodation to his suggestions during the session led him to trust them to stay connected to each other and to Josh. If the therapist does not trust the parents' ability to monitor a youngster who is at risk of hurting himself, she should ask the family to seek out trustworthy adults in the extended family or community who are willing to monitor the youngster on a twenty-four-hour basis. If none can be uncovered, hospitalization should be considered.

Paul next challenged the pattern of the parents' interactions with the school, because (as is typically the case with a symptomatic child who has special educational needs) this appeared to be an important part of the symptomatic cycle. He said that if Josh were not going to be hospitalized, he should return to classes immediately. The parents, therefore, would have to convince the school to rethink its plan for homebound instruction. When Mrs. Harmon asked Paul if he would speak to the school counselor, he agreed to do so only after the parents had negotiated Josh's reentry into the school.

Paul's position expressed his belief in the parents' ability to intervene successfully with the school in their son's behalf. It set the stage for them to approach the school administrators with a plan of their own, instead of turning to the school in helplessness, asking for advice. Challenging them to work more effectively with the school would in turn help them collaborate more effectively at home. Also, since a child's symptoms generally reflect dislocations in his relationships with his family and community, an increase in his parents' constructive participation in his relationships at school will enhance the child's sense of security and self-esteem and decrease the probability of symptomatic behavior.

An alternative to insisting that the parents collaborate directly with the school to negotiate their child's return is for the therapist to initiate or facilitate the return. Although this option is often more palatable to the parents and to the school, it is better for the therapist to be more challenging of the parents in the beginning, placing the responsibility for change squarely on their shoulders. The therapist can always modify her position based on the degree to which family members are initially willing to stretch themselves.

Paul persisted in challenging the parents because he felt that they would respond positively to his pushing. He said he would be willing to commit himself to a contract for treatment as soon as the parents succeeded in working together to ensure Josh's physical safety and return to school. This commitment was predicated on the parents' demonstration of a change in how they dealt with one another and the school. The treatment contract would thus be a sign of Paul's appreciation for their competent and responsible action in taking steps toward breaking the cycle of abdication and helplessness.

THE TREATMENT CONTRACT

The family returned for the next session more confident and relaxed. Josh participated more freely, and the parents actually talked with some zest about their strategy in approaching the school and their success in having Josh reinstated. In response, Paul offered the family a treatment contract. He would see the entire family twice a week during the next two months. Sessions would last between one and two hours. Paul outlined the details of the treatment contract: (1) Mr. Harmon would get to know his son, would learn his strengths and difficulties, and would develop ways of supporting Josh's maturation and self-control; (2) Mr. and Mrs. Harmon would collaborate in decisions about their children; (3) Mrs. Harmon would support her husband with their son and not intrude to protect the two of them from each other; (4) Mr. and Mrs. Harmon would work with the school to help both Josh and Suzanne experience success in that arena; (5) Josh and Suzanne would be expected to present their needs and wishes directly and respectfully throughout treatment; and (6) Paul would expect Mr. and Mrs. Harmon to let him know of any concerns they had about the treatment process. Additional goals and modifications could be added as Paul or the family deemed necessary. Paul emphasized that an important barometer of progress would be changes in Josh's social relationships, including those with his family, and in his behavior at school.

The Monroes

THE REFERRAL

Brian Ross was the outpatient therapist for a young woman with a complicated history of depression, self-mutilation, anorexia, bulimia, and suicidal behavior. Therapy was at an impasse, so he called a colleague, Donna Jacobson, whom he had met several times at local professional meetings. Although they didn't know each other well, they had discussed several cases before and had a familiarity with each other's way of thinking and style of approach. "Hello, Donna," Brian began. "I'm having trouble with a young woman and family whom I've been working with for over a year, and I was hoping you could give me some help. Are you available for a consultation?" Donna said she was glad to hear from him and would be interested in discussing the case. They agreed to meet later that day in Donna's office.

When a therapist feels that a case is not going well, the request for a consultation generally takes one of two forms. Most often, the therapist says, "This person has a severe case of such-and-such a condition. He is not responding to treatment. Can you suggest something that might work?" The language of the therapist locates the problem in the patient (or family) and suggests that a therapist is a technician whose

task is to fix the problem. The consultant may conclude that the therapist has misdiagnosed the problem; that the diagnosis is correct and the
therapist needs a different technique; or that the problem is just too hard
to solve. If consultant and therapist agree to work together, their goals
are identical: to solve a problem belonging to someone else.

Less commonly, the therapist states, as Brian did, "I'm having trouble
and would like your assistance." Here, the therapist's language suggests
that he experiences himself and his relationship with the patient (or
family) as a part of the problem. Often therapists working with severely
symptomatic families do not recognize their role in the system, perhaps
because the enormity of the family's problems obscures their awareness
of difficulties in the therapeutic relationship.

When a referring therapist recognizes that she is contributing to the
problem and that she will need to become disentangled if she is to help
the family become disentangled, the consultant has reason to be opti-
mistic. The therapist and consultant agree implicitly on a crucial assumption, namely that any therapeutic impasse indicates a breakdown
of relationships in the treatment system. With this shared framework,
the consultant's initial work can focus on identifying what is blocking
the relationships from developing further.

In both types of consultation request, the consultant's first task is to
assess the symptomatic cycle, much as a therapist does at the outset of
treatment with a family. This assessment requires a delineation of the
boundaries of the symptomatic system—who is inside and who is outside. Although with the first type of request the therapist defines herself
as outside and with the second, as inside, the consultant is best advised
to believe that the therapist is always inside the system. When symptomatology persists or worsens, the therapist should examine all relationships in the treatment system, starting with those that include her
as a participant. A consultant can be helpful in this process, but only
if she sees the therapist as inside the system in which the symptom is
located. An exception occurs when the therapist has met so briefly or
infrequently with the family that no therapeutic relationship has
formed.

MEETING WITH THE THERAPIST

When Donna and Brian met later that afternoon to discuss the case,
Donna began by requesting a brief overview of the whole course of
treatment, including what Brian wanted to see happen in the consulta-

tion. Seeing the problem through Brian's eyes would constitute the first step in assessing the symptomatic cycle, since he was a member of the symptomatic system. The following was Brian's account.

"Jennifer is twenty-two, and was referred to me for treatment following a six-month hospitalization for severe depression and self-mutilation. Although those symptoms abated within a few months, while she was in the hospital she became anorectic and bulimic, and remained so at discharge.

"I worked with Jennifer and her parents, Carl and Nancy Monroe, but after a few months, I felt like there wasn't much that could be done, so I ended treatment with them. Later on, Jennifer requested individual therapy, and I have seen her regularly for a number of months. At first it went well, but recently things have been going downhill, and her symptoms have escalated a lot.

"In the middle of Jennifer's sophomore year of college, the chain of clothing stores Carl managed was bought out by a large corporation, and he quit after a conflict with the new boss. Faced with serious financial problems, Nancy found a job in a department store and Carl took a series of menial jobs and began drinking heavily. The marital conflicts that had existed for years became worse. Jennifer dropped out of college, returned home, cut her wrists on several occasions, and wound up in a psychiatric hospital. Six months later she was discharged and referred to me for treatment of the eating disorder she had developed while hospitalized. By that time Jennifer had lost thirty-five pounds. She weighed eighty-five pounds and was five feet, four inches, tall. Her parents were supporting her financially while she was starving herself and popping laxatives like candy."

Brian went on to say that he was not able to develop any traction with the parents to "get Jennifer to gain weight," in spite of having the parents set up a behavioral paradigm with clear incentives and consequences contingent on weight gain. He described being particularly stumped by Carl, who presented himself as warm and nurturant, but wasn't willing to push or challenge his daughter in any way. Nancy would watch critically and say to Brian, "I know you're trying to get Carl to change, but I think it's a lost cause. I really wonder why I stay with him."

Brian found that though Nancy seemed more aware of Jennifer's need for firm expectations and limits, her way of trying to meet that need came across as highly controlling. To support Nancy's parental expectations, Brian tried to engage Carl as a collaborative co-parent. After four months of therapy, frustrated with the parents' ineffective collaboration and supervision of their daughter, Brian ended treatment and gave the parents names of several other therapists whom he had contacted and who were willing to see the family in therapy. However, the Monroes didn't call any of the other therapists. When Jennifer called Brian a few months later to request individual therapy, he acquiesced. He liked Jennifer, knew she was in serious trouble, and felt he might be able to get somewhere with her without the distracting presence of her parents and their many conflicts.

MAPPING THE SYMPTOMATIC CYCLE

Using the information presented by the therapist, the consultant constructs a map to serve as a framework for the consultation. The map identifies the symptomatic cycle at two levels: the level of the family system itself, and the level of the system of family plus therapist. The development of the symptomatic cycle in the Monroe case can be understood in the following way: the Monroes' marriage was at an impasse, in which the parents' struggles with Jennifer's symptoms blocked the way for either a clean separation or a reconciliation in their relationship with each other. Jennifer's development as a young adult, including successfully leaving home and maintaining new relationships with peers, had been brought to a standstill by her symptoms and by her involvement in her parents' conflict.

After Brian had established an initial treatment contract with the Monroes, aspects of the symptomatic cycle reemerged. Repeatedly, someone in the system gave up on someone else without first having pushed conflicts to a clear resolution. Nancy remained focused on her ineffective efforts to control Jennifer, while Carl sat back and watched his wife fail. Instead of pursuing Carl with greater intensity or confronting Nancy's ambivalence by pushing her to pursue Carl, Brian ended treatment.

In the beginning Brian had worked very hard to support Nancy. Yet, Brian had identified with aspects of Nancy that did not further their therapeutic goals: her desire to be in charge of Jennifer's behavior; her sense of helplessness in influencing Jennifer to change; her distrust of her ability to convince Carl to be a different kind of husband and father. He also identified with her ambivalence about separation because he ended treatment with the family but later agreed to see Jennifer individually. These points of connection left Brian as immobilized and helpless as Nancy. Faced with a runaway in the family, Brian had wound up fleeing, thus becoming incorporated into a key dynamic of the symptomatic cycle.

Brian's focus on getting Jennifer to gain weight indicated that he may have lost sight of one of the purposes of a treatment contract, namely, to establish a framework in which the therapist can gain further information about the pattern of relationship breakdown in the system. Donna wondered why Brian had become so focused on symptom control. Why did he quit when the parents seemed unable to work together, rather than interpreting this as feedback from the family to use in revising the contract? Given Brian's lack of success in engaging Carl directly, Donna also wondered why Brian had not worked through Nancy to engage him, thereby creating a context in which Nancy could face and resolve her ambivalence about staying in her marriage.

Donna shared with Brian her sense that he had joined a runaway in the family out of his anxiety for Jennifer. She asked him to say more about his experience. Brian explained the pressure he felt to please the referring physician and to live up to his reputation as an expert on eating disorders. His distrust of Nancy's ability to engage Carl and his frustration with trying to accomplish that himself led to his decision to quit. He added that he felt Jennifer was "wasting away for want of a sustaining and nourishing relationship with either parent"; he did not see how she could grow without being more solidly connected to at least one of them.

INDIVIDUAL THERAPY IN THE SYMPTOMATIC CYCLE

Donna then asked Brian to discuss his experience of individual therapy in order to understand his current role in the symptomatic cycle. "Initially," Brian said, "therapy with Jennifer went well. Our main focus was on exploring and understanding Jennifer's feelings of emptiness and her social isolation. Although progress was slow, I felt we were developing a trusting relationship, and Jennifer began to emerge somewhat from her shell, participating in some group activities with young adults in the community. I had little contact with Carl or Nancy, although they said that they supported our working together. Within a month after we started individual therapy, Nancy left Carl after a blowup over his drinking and moved in with her mother.

"During all this time," Brian continued, "we didn't really talk too much about Jennifer's symptoms. I could see she had gained weight, and she told me she was staying around ninety-eight pounds. I had been in contact with her family physician and he felt she was not in any acute medical danger, although she was still quite thin. However, Jennifer continued to binge, vomit, and overuse laxatives.

"Finally, after seeing her frail body week after week for eight months, I began to push Jennifer to gain weight, and in spite of Jennifer's insistence that I was pushing her too hard, I stood my ground. Her binging and vomiting began to escalate, and she intensified her use of laxatives to the point where she had to be repeatedly admitted to a local hospital for medical treatment of dehydration and severe electrolyte imbalances. She quit her part-time job and became increasingly isolated. What made everything worse was that I felt I had to focus on the symptoms even more now, because their intensification interfered with our dealing with any of the therapeutic issues we had been working on previously.

"I feel like I'm caught in a vicious cycle. I've thought about referring Jennifer for inpatient psychiatric treatment, and I'm willing to do that, but she came to me when she was discharged from a six-month hospitalization, and I'm not sure how that would help Jennifer now. I know she doesn't want to be rehospitalized, and I'm afraid she would experience it as my giving up on her. I gave up once before, with her family—I hate the idea of doing it again."

Many therapists would have referred Jennifer to a psychiatric inpatient program well before the point at which Brian consulted Donna. In light of the severity of her symptoms, few would argue with such a decision; there are a variety of medical, legal, and social rationales for inpatient referral. From a psychotherapeutic point of view, however, no one "needs" to be hospitalized psychiatrically, no matter how severe the symptoms.

This is not to say that hospitalization is always unnecessary or antitherapeutic. The point is that the indication for hospitalization is not solely the level of symptomatology or the need to provide physical safety. Rather, hospitalization is indicated when the patient's interpersonal relationship systems have repeatedly demonstrated ineffectiveness in sustaining and nourishing functionality and development, despite the symptoms. The goal of short-term psychiatric hospitalization should be the same as the goal of crisis induction in general: to catalyze a change in the context of the symptoms. Viewed in this manner, inpatient treatment can be a powerful therapeutic intervention.

From a practical standpoint, however, most psychiatric hospitalizations are fraught with pitfalls. The patient's outside relationship systems tend to assume that responsibility for solving problems lies with the professionals who have taken temporary custody of the patient, and most hospital staff members are only too willing to accept this responsibility. Members of the patient's outside systems also tend to see the hospitalization as concrete proof of their inability to help. In addition, a hospital, like any large system, inevitably develops goals and agendas of its own. These goals are typically oriented toward the stabilization of the patient, and they may be directly in conflict with the goals of a family or a referring therapist.

Since the Monroes' family physician deemed Jennifer medically stable and able to leave the hospital, Donna decided to continue the consultation on an outpatient basis. She asked Brian to arrange for a meeting with him and the family the day before Jennifer's discharge from the medical unit. She also asked Brian to have Jennifer's physician give her a call.

Donna's meeting with Brian, the first step in the consultation, was long. Donna had carefully tracked Brian's experience with the Monroes, revealing the symptomatic entanglements, while commenting about her reactions and hypotheses about Brian's work with the family. Donna was cultivating a relationship with Brian based on directness, respect, and owning responsibility, knowing that such a relationship would be the anchor Brian could count on to support him in changing his relationships with the family.

MEETING WITH THE THERAPIST AND FAMILY

Although Donna had not expected Jennifer to look fit, she was taken aback at the sight of her. Jennifer was excruciatingly thin. Her complexion was sallow, her eyes sunken in their sockets, her hair disheveled. Nancy Monroe was a tall, well-dressed woman in her late forties, and Carl was a stylish man with graying hair and a mustache.

The consultant should rely on her map of the symptomatic cycle to keep herself oriented throughout the consultation. In this case, the starting point was Donna's belief that the impasse in Brian's therapeutic relationship with Jennifer was connected to the impasse in the parents' relationship. She chose to start the interview with Brian because her entry into the system was through him.

DONNA: *(To the family)* Brian and I talked the other day, and he gave me a lot of background information. What I wanted to do with all of us together was to ask him to summarize what his experience has been. So *(turning to Brian),* where are you stuck?

The consultant can help the therapist begin to disentangle herself from the symptomatic system by asking her to share her thoughts about how she may be reinforcing the symptomatic cycle. This discussion has a powerful impact on family members when it occurs during a session; the therapist's response may include how she feels about the family and the areas in which she is particularly vulnerable to being hooked by the family's symptomatic patterns. If this had been Donna's first encounter with Brian and their relationship were more formal, she might have simply asked, "How do you see the problem?" Donna's question, "Where are you stuck?" was more direct and challenging. It reflected her assumption that Brian was a member of the symptomatic system, as well as her confidence in his relationship with her. Not only can such a question elucidate how the therapist is inducted into the symptomatic cycle, it can also stimulate an openness on the part of the family. The consultant and therapist's ease in speaking directly with each other establishes a climate for talking about difficult problems in an honest and straightforward way.

BRIAN: Okay, you want to know how I'm stuck. Well, as I was raking my leaves yesterday, I was mentally rehearsing what I would say to you about the problem. All of a sudden it occurred to me that I was sounding to myself exactly like I have heard countless parents of anorectic daughters talk! Everything that I was hearing myself say about what my goals for treatment were, what I hoped would come from your consultation, it all sounded like I was talking not as a therapist but as a parent! I think I'm stuck in the wrong role.

When I agreed to work with Jennifer by herself, I never realized that on some level I was trying to replace her parents, whom I had dismissed as unworkable. It wasn't until I tried to take care of her symptoms, and she went through all these hospitalizations and everything else, that I realized that I was really stuck and needed help. I guess what I really want, Donna, so that I can be helpful to Jennifer, is for you to help me change my role, without my having to bail out of the system, or be kicked out of it, as a consequence. Does that make sense?

DONNA: Sure, it makes a lot of sense. Sounds like you're stuck with trying to take over her parents' job, that it's become your responsibility to keep her alive, while they are watching anxiously from the sidelines. I'm not surprised that arrangement isn't working out too well. So how come you haven't quit?

BRIAN: Why haven't I quit? Because I was afraid of what would happen to Jennifer if I quit. It was a classic damned-if-you-do, damned-if-you-don't situation. We weren't getting anywhere trying to work with her symptoms; actually, it's been getting worse. And yet I was worried that if I quit, that would be the end of her.

NANCY: *(Unable to contain herself)* That's exactly how I've always felt about all these problems! I don't want to deal with them, and why should I have to? Jennifer's twenty-two now, she's old enough to take care of herself, but she won't. Even though her father isn't working the long hours he used to, he can't seem to get himself involved with her and her problems, despite the therapy we went through last year. Since he lost his job, I've been earning my own income, and I'm thinking about maybe trying to start a career. I'm a single woman now for all practical purposes—and that's all right, except I can't do a thing for myself because of Jennifer. When she began seeing Dr. Ross, I thought everything would be okay, but . . . *(She begins to cry, as Jennifer stares at the floor and Carl looks out the window.)*

Brian's opening comments set the stage for change. Clearly his role needed to be different if he was to be helpful. But change in his role would require corresponding and complementary changes in the family. Nancy's outburst poignantly summarized her dilemma: How could she leave an unsatisfactory marriage and take care of herself when Jennifer was sinking and neither her father nor her therapist could rescue her? Donna would need to explore Nancy's dilemma further, looking for an opening to challenge Nancy's perception of the problem and open her view to alternatives.

DONNA: *(To Nancy)* What do you think the problem is right now?

NANCY: Right now, I'm afraid Jennifer is going to die, and that's why I'm so glad that you're involved, Dr. Jacobson. I've felt that she needs to see Dr. Ross more often, and maybe other doctors as well. It was especially bad when Dr. Ross was out of town two weeks ago, and Jennifer overdosed again. She called me from home—I was working—and I told her to call an ambulance and go to the hospital. Then . . .

DONNA: *(Breaking in)* Did you leave work and meet her at the hospital?

NANCY: No, not then I didn't.

DONNA: You relied on the doctors?

NANCY: Yes.

DONNA: Can I ask you something? For how long have you been relying on the doctors? Are you still waiting for *them* to cure your daughter?

Nancy: Well, she needs help; she needs a treatment program with different types of therapy.

Donna: Why do you think that will help?

Nancy: Because it doesn't work when she's by herself. It just hasn't worked. She gets too depressed, and she needs to be talking to someone and there's no one around during the day because she stays in her room, and I'm at work. If her father could just *be* with her more. They used to be close when she was little, but he's so impossible now, I can't talk with him at all, I don't think anyone can reach him. *(Nancy sighs deeply and looks to Brian for corroboration. Brian looks to Donna.)*

Nancy's statements reflected her own disconnection from Jennifer, a void that she somehow hoped could be filled by the right doctor with the right treatment program. Donna next asked Carl about his understanding of the problem. He said he thought Jennifer had a communication problem, that she kept her feelings to herself, especially the angry ones, and that she didn't know how to ask people for help in a direct way.

Donna: What do you mean by that?

Carl: Jennifer's not demanding. If she wants something, rather than demand, she'll take one swing at it and if it doesn't work out, she won't stay with it.

Donna: Like what?

Carl: Well, I suppose, like demanding more time from me.

Carl's comments implied that he might be open to a different kind of relationship with his daughter. Donna then turned her attention to Jennifer. By exploring Jennifer's perception of her mother and father's portrayal of her as helpless and fragile, Donna elicited Jennifer's profound sense of despair.

Donna: I guess the main reason that everyone is here today is because they're all so worried about you, Jennifer. People seem afraid to push you for fear of what might happen. Do you think you're really so fragile?

Jennifer: Yeah, I guess I do.

Donna: But what would happen if people were firm with you, if they confronted you?

Jennifer: It seems crazy, but I feel like it would kill me.

Donna: Kill you? How could it do that?

JENNIFER: By making me face things I don't want to face, by removing my options so that I have to deal with my feelings, so that I couldn't run away from them. Like making it impossible for me to throw up or making it impossible for me to take laxatives—somehow creating a situation where I couldn't use the only outlets I have.

DONNA: And how would that kill you?

JENNIFER: I don't know—it doesn't make sense, but there would just be too much loneliness and pain. I mean physically it doesn't seem possible but I really think that I would die. I don't know how. I guess what I mean by dying is that I can't see beyond that point. I can't imagine there being a life after that.

DONNA: Is it kind of like being on a roller coaster? And when you get to the top, and you start to go down, and you don't know whether you're going to make it, or what might happen?

JENNIFER: I guess so—it's like being on a cliff. Everything is black, and maybe it's only a little fall and maybe it's endless, and I just don't know and I'm not going to step off if I can help it.

Like many severely symptomatic people, Jennifer had paradoxically turned her symptoms into her lifelines. They were the parts of herself that felt the most real. Giving them up, therefore, was tantamount to dying.

THE CONSULTATION CONTRACT

In articulating a frame for the consultation, it is important to use the family's language, since the most effective metaphors are not the ones devised by the therapist but those offered by the family. Donna returned to Jennifer's image of being on the edge of a cliff, at risk of freefalling into a black void, and used it as a means of intensifying the moment and exploring possibilities for change.

DONNA: Tell me, Jennifer, what if your mother were at the top of the cliff with you and she didn't let you drop? Do you think that it would still kill you? See, what I understand you to be saying is if she pushed you to the brink—wiping out your options that you've been using—and then backed off, you would fall, and die. But what if she didn't back off?

JENNIFER: *(Astonished)* But I can't imagine that. I can't conceive of anyone not backing off. *(Shaking her head)* I can't conceive that anyone could stay . . .

DONNA: So what you're saying is that you're not sure how she'd handle it, whether you could trust her not to back off.

JENNIFER: What I know is that I'm not sure I could trust her.

DONNA: Whether you could trust her *not* to disengage, *not* to let go of you—

JENNIFER: Yeah, I'm afraid that she would drop me.

DONNA: How about your dad?

JENNIFER: I'm even more afraid that he would . . . he doesn't like, um, you know—

DONNA: Living on the edge?

JENNIFER: Right.

The symptomatic cycle had been transported to the edge of Jennifer's cliff, where she stood alone and terrified. For a transformation to occur, someone would need to join her there, being prepared to hang on tight and take a leap with her into the unknown. Jennifer could not imagine either of her parents exhibiting that degree of courage and commitment to her. But she was their daughter, not Brian's or Donna's. So Donna would need to take a strong position about the core component in the consultation contract.

DONNA: You know, Jennifer, you haven't been making it on your own, and Brian and the doctors haven't been able to cure you. Maybe what you need—is it possible that what you really need, and what you've needed for a while, is for your parents to be more intimately connected to you—to push you and be there for you and demand more of you, and not to let you drop? So that you don't end up living in a medical or a psychiatric hospital for the indefinite future, or worse, that you end up dead? And that maybe this is what it's going to take, and I don't know how yet, exactly, but that what you need is for your parents to do this, and there isn't any substitute?

JENNIFER: I think that *is* what I really need. I mean, it always seems to come back to them. I get to a point in my relationships with other people and I don't—I get stuck and I guess it's because I've never really gotten past that point with my parents. And they're too important just to say, well, I can't do it with them so I'll do it with somebody else. . . . I can't seem to do that.

Jennifer's last statement was an eloquent portrayal of her developmental (and therapeutic) impasse: she became stuck in her relationships with others at a point isomorphic to where she was stuck in her relationships with her father and mother.

Now that Donna had a clear sense of the symptomatic cycle and developmental impasse, she returned to Brian. She stated that the primary goal of the consultation, as she saw it, was to help Brian renegotiate his relationship with the family. He would have to remove himself from the untenable position of being the caretaker of Jennifer's physical and emotional needs if he were to return to his role as her therapist. That meant that her parents would have to step in to do the job of parenting Jennifer.

It seemed that the Monroes were heading toward divorce. However, their efforts to amputate themselves from each other while their daughter was still entangled with them was having the predictable consequence of cutting through Jennifer. To free Jennifer from the messy triangular arrangement in which she was caught, helping her to individuate from her parents, it would be necessary to help her parents separate in a healthier way from each other. To accomplish this, Donna felt it would be necessary first to acknowledge the bind in which Nancy was caught, and then to help Nancy free herself.

Donna began by noting the years Nancy had spent as a mother and wife, economically dependent on her husband and unprepared to make it on her own financially, pressured by society to make her marriage work, and overwhelmed by her daughter's life-threatening behavior. Donna recognized Nancy's desire to leave the marriage and her right to establish a life of her own, while highlighting that for her to feel secure about separating, she would need to see Carl more solidly connected with Jennifer. To really know when this had happened, Nancy, not Brian, would have to be the one to reengage Carl.

Brian's relationship with Nancy would thus have to change. Previously, they had joined with each other in their feelings of helplessness about Carl's imperviousness and in their attempts to take charge of Jennifer's behavior. The consultation contract proposed that Donna would help Brian to struggle more effectively with Nancy. This struggle would be focused not on Jennifer's symptoms but on developing enough intensity in their relationship to support Brian in his pushing Nancy to engage Carl.

The very act of presenting a treatment contract that mandated relational shifts was followed by an enactment of the symptomatic cycle. Donna seized this event as an opportunity to raise the level of intensity by exposing and challenging the abandonment dynamic of the cycle. As Donna presented the contract, Jennifer became increasingly agitated and upset. She protested that it was entirely too much to expect of her parents. In the following dialogue, as Jennifer reclaims the responsibility for her problem, her father jumps in to collude with her.

JENNIFER: I know I said that I feel like nobody could stay with me, that they'd drop me, but I guess I haven't taken a lot of risks myself. I guess I make it very hard for anybody to be there, because I'm so afraid . . . I'm so afraid that nobody will be there for me that I don't even try to give it a chance. Because I'm so sure that I'm going to fail, that I'm going to get hurt, or let down. That I'm going to fall apart, or die, or . . .

CARL: Well, honey, what would it take for you not to do that?

JENNIFER: I don't know, Dad *(appearing frustrated),* that's exactly what I don't . . . I don't know what it will take!

CARL: But unless you know, unless you can tell me specifically what you need, then there's no way I can help. So what do you need?

Carl's offer to help is conditional: "I will help you *if* you specifically tell me what you need." This statement captures the interpersonal abdication that is a characteristic part of the cycle in which severely symptomatic people are trapped. Statements like this leave the symptomatic person alone and terrified on the edge of a cliff. The way out is for the parent to join the child where she is and collaborate with her in her struggle to grow. The therapist can facilitate this process by pushing the parent to move toward the child and hold her in a nurturing embrace and by not allowing the parent to place the responsibility for change on the child alone.

DONNA: *(interrupting)* Why are you asking her that?

CARL: I'm trying to figure out—this is the whole problem—I'm trying to figure out what we're talking about here, what I need to do to help.

DONNA: Would it matter if it required you to be with her around the clock?

CARL: Around the clock?

DONNA: Yes. It's your daughter's life we're talking about here. She's not making it on her own, and she's not making it with you disengaged. She may need you to be with her twenty-four hours a day.

CARL: I guess if that would do the job, if it would solve it . . .

DONNA: Without knowing whether or not it would solve it. She's your daughter. It's clear that she can't make it on her own, and doctors and hospitals can't cure her. *(Nancy and Jennifer watch this interaction with increasing interest.)*

CARL: *(Pauses, shifts in his chair, looks at Nancy, then at Donna)* It seems to me that this is all being shoved on the parents; the parents are going to have to do the job and you all *(gestures at Donna and Brian)* will help, but all responsibility is on the parents.

Now I think to myself, well, the parents have tried and done a pretty damn bad job of trying to get things done, to get Jennifer to a point of independence, and I keep coming back to the same thing which is, How can I help? and I haven't gotten that answer yet. I'm like a ditchdigger, and I'm not getting any younger. I do have a lot of strength and desire but I still don't know which direction to dig, how deep, how far, or anything . . . I'm totally at a loss, and trying to get an answer from you is like trying to get blood from a stone.

Donna felt herself becoming angry with Carl's insistence that unless someone told him what to do, he couldn't be helpful. The issue here goes beyond content. When it is a matter of life and death, the therapist has to push people to find new ways of being together and experiencing a greater degree of relatedness without having to know every detail in advance. Donna experienced Carl's comments as a betrayal of Jennifer; they explained in part how Brian had become stuck in a parental role. Carl's asking the professionals for advice and asking his daughter to tell him what he would need to do to help would be reasonable if this session had been the first one he had ever been in, or if Jennifer's problems had been of recent onset. But in this context his request made as much sense as asking a crying three-month-old infant to tell him whether she needed to be fed, changed, or held. As the dialogue continued, Donna's outrage at Carl's abandonment of Jennifer fueled the intensity of her interaction with him.

DONNA: I want to ask you something.

CARL: *(Shaking his head in exasperation)* I never get an answer, just another question.

DONNA: That's right. Are you here to sacrifice your daughter to a graveyard?

CARL: Obviously not. We're here to help her.

DONNA: Are you sure? Is she helping herself?

CARL: Well, just by her being here she's trying to—

DONNA: She's been hospitalized how many times in the last few months? How many overdoses? Take a good look at her *(gesturing at Jennifer)*—does she look like she's helping herself?

CARL: But ultimately she has to be the one—nobody can do it for her—it's basically up to her.

DONNA: *(voice begins to rise)* Either I'm not expressing myself clearly, or you're deaf.

CARL: I hear you, but I don't understand. My understanding is that if a person wants to live, they ultimately have to—their mind has to say . . . If Jennifer wants to live, then ultimately she has to make that choice, and all we can do is help her. Isn't that right?

DONNA: *(Moves closer to Carl)* No.

CARL: Then what is right?

DONNA: *(Slowly and loudly, emphasizing each word)* Look at me, Carl. Your daughter is dying. As surely as she is sitting in the chair next to you, she is dying. She's not helping herself and the doctors haven't helped her. You talk as if you're blind, totally blind, or psychotic.

CARL: *(Getting uncomfortable with Donna's affect)* Okay, okay.

DONNA: *(Continuing as before)* It's *not* okay, it's *absolutely not okay*. *(Everyone in the room is motionless, watching Carl; he seems oblivious to everyone but Donna.)* I'm not getting through to you, Carl, and I didn't get through to you earlier. Jennifer is dying and she needs help and she needs your help and she needs your wife's help and the doctors aren't going to cure her. *Do you understand that?*

CARL: *(Shaken)* Yes, I understand that. *(Without breaking his gaze, Carl reaches out and takes Jennifer's hand.)*

DONNA: We're talking about life and death right now—nothing else! She's not my responsibility. She's not Brian's. She's *your* responsibility *(pointing at Carl)* and *your* responsibility *(pointing at Nancy)*. She is too weak to take care of herself, to do what she needs to do to stay alive, and that's your job. Brian and I will help the two of you. But it's your job, and no one else's. Am I getting through?

CARL: I think I got the message that time. Did you get it, Nancy? *(He turns to his wife.)*

NANCY: Loud and clear. Let's get moving on it.

In dealing with impasses that are associated with life-threatening symptoms, the therapist may need to fight aggressively to disrupt a tenacious pattern in a parent's relationship with a child. Here, Donna disciplined her anger as she hammered at Carl's blandness and blindness. She was not challenging him for the sake of being dramatic, nor was she exaggerating the consequences of his abdication. The therapist must go beyond simply mobilizing her affect; she must channel it constructively. The intensity of the therapist's affective confrontation and the willingness of family members to accept it are both predicated on the mutual sense of trust in their relationship. Here, it was the family's trust in Brian, and Donna's relationship with him, that allowed her to push as hard as she did.

As a result, Donna experienced a shift in Carl's responsiveness to her. At least for the moment, he had stopped denying and defending. He had become open to her depiction of the frightening reality of the situation. Donna's earlier hypothesis about his availability for a different kind of relationship with Jennifer had been confirmed by his move toward a more nurturing physical contact with her. It appeared that Nancy sensed this also, because when Carl turned to her she sounded prepared to work with him. Brian and Donna had established a sufficiently clear therapeutic context, with some stirrings of shifts in interactional patterns, to end the session at that point. To solidify the frame, Donna reiterated the components of the contract, and with Brian's agreement, recommended that they all meet again in three days.

In the interval between sessions, Donna continued, Nancy and Jennifer should live in the house with Carl, and Nancy and Carl should work out a schedule of monitoring Jennifer around the clock, preventing overdoses, vomiting, or any other life-threatening behavior.

Donna's objective was to construct a context in which the relationship conflicts in the system could be activated and then negotiated in a different way. Donna was not trying to control Jennifer's symptoms; she wanted to encourage the parents to collaborate in a way that would provide Jennifer with the sense of security and protection she needed.

CHAPTER 5

Chaos: Embracing the Runaway

The manifestation of chaos is the evidence that the system is responding. It is open.
—Virginia Satir, "The Tools of the Therapist"

The Onset of Chaos

CHAOS, the second phase of treatment, marks the point at which the family's symptomatic pattern recurs after the family has agreed to the treatment contract. The therapist may feel anxious or angry with the appearance of symptomatic behavior and may respond by distancing from the family. Therapists in flight can readily be identified by their use of words such as *resistance, unworkable,* and *burnout* and by their inclination to resort to administrative (that is, managerial and controlling) stances vis-à-vis the family.

Runaways may be figurative or literal, depending on whether family members abandon each other (and the therapist) emotionally or physically. The therapist can recognize a runaway by the behavior of the symptomatic person, as will be demonstrated in the Cabrini case when Maria begins to hear voices and in the Monroes when Jennifer takes an overdose. The runaway is also signaled by the behavior of others in the system that is characteristic of interactions in the symptomatic cycle, as illustrated in the Harmon case when Mr. and Mrs. Harmon do not speak to each other for three days following a conflict about how to handle a problem with Suzanne. Whether the runaway takes the form of overt episodes of dangerous behavior; escalations of interpersonal conflict; angry, explosive outbursts; or impotent withdrawals, the therapist can be certain of one thing: he is being offered an invitation to embark on a roller-coaster ride with the family. The therapist's primary task is to accept this invitation in a manner that fortifies his connection with the family.

But why does a runaway emerge at this particular point in the therapeutic process? Although the family's pattern of flight recurs throughout the course of crisis induction, it is particularly characteristic of the second phase. Family members' past experiences with each other and professionals have reinforced the belief that closeness and acceptance in relationships are conditional, so it is only normal that they should respond to the therapist's unconditional acceptance during the first phase of treatment with skepticism, suspicion, and trepidation. They return to symptomatic patterns, relating to one another through ultimatum and capitulation.

The runaway is thus an enactment of the symptomatic cycle. Scientists are discovering that many dynamic systems displaying apparently chaotic and unpredictable behavior are in fact operating according to specifiable principles (Gleick 1987; Stewart 1989). A number of researchers are now engaged in investigating applications of chaos theory to behavioral sciences, including psychotherapy (see Woodcock and Davis 1978; Langs 1989). It is not surprising, therefore, to find that the events of the runaway at the onset of the second phase of treatment are anything but random. Their appearance and even their details can be predicted by the therapist in advance. A strategic therapist might see such a prediction as a paradoxical attempt to reduce the likelihood of the runaway. In crisis induction, however, runaways are a natural part of the process, and predicting them affords the therapist an opportunity to further his relationship with the family. It is honest to tell the family that the process of change will not be smooth or devoid of pain and that recurrences of symptoms in the symptomatic person or in other family members are an inevitable part of the struggle of growth. This warning can help to lessen the sting of symptomatic behavior when it occurs.

Virginia Satir (1988) describes the entry of a new person into a significant involvement with a family as analogous to an organ transplant. Using this analogy, one can foresee the possibility of two undesirable responses. One is for the family to extrude the new person—the therapist—from the system, that is, to reject the transplant outright. With severely symptomatic families this happens frequently, aborting the therapeutic process even before the end of the first phase, without establishing a treatment contract. "You're not listening to us," the family spokesperson tells the therapist. "You're saying the same things the last doctor said, and it isn't helpful. All you people do is criticize and blame us. This is our last visit; we won't be coming again."

A second response in the system is for the therapist and family to become joined—but for the transplanted organ, that is, the therapist, to begin to exhibit the same pathological processes as the host. The therapist may begin to fear, contemplate, or enact the same kinds of abandonment, betrayal, and coercive ultimatums that existed in the symptomatic system before the therapist became a member. Family members will then begin to distrust the therapist. Conflicts will flare, an impasse will develop, and the symptomatic cycle continues.

Embracing the Runaway

One of the risks posed by the runaway is for the therapist to be caught unaware and experience an impulse to flee. Therapists tend to flee along one of two paths. They may insist rigidly on compliance with the contract, believing that the words of the contract have more weight than the factors that reinforce the continuation of the symptomatic cycle. Such a focus can lead the therapist to attempt to control the family, thus abandoning his posture of unconditional acceptance. Or he may accommodate to the symptomatic behavior, abandoning the treatment contract altogether. In either case, the therapist distances himself from the family and diminishes his credibility.

The therapist *embraces the runaway* by not allowing himself to be distanced. Regardless of the efforts of family members to shake him off, the therapist's embrace takes the form of relentless pursuit. For example, when Maria starts to hallucinate and becomes highly agitated, Rachel pursues and accompanies her into her private world of taunting demons. For runaways that take the form of immobility, where the family is paralyzed by depression and feelings of helplessness, the embrace may take the form of finding active and creative ways of being with the family while waiting for movement. Remaining *with* the family, the therapist persistently offers authentic, nonmanipulative contact. This principle is illustrated in the story of Winnie-the-Pooh, when Pooh overate on a visit to Rabbit and ended up stuck, half in and half out of Rabbit's entrance hole. Christopher Robin's assessment of the situation was that the only course of action was to wait the week or so that it would take for his friend to become thin again, a decision received by Pooh with much anxiety and unhappiness. Pooh achieved a measure of solace, though, as Christopher Robin passed the time by reading to him "a Sustaining Book, such as would help and comfort a Wedged Bear in Great Tightness" (Milne 1926, 30).

Just as Christopher Robin goes to Pooh where Pooh is, so does the therapist need to go to the family where it is. When the runaway occurs, it is more meaningful for the therapist to maintain a connection by accompanying family members to their own hideaways than for him to insist that they remain on, or return to, territory that is more familiar and comfortable for him. However the therapist chooses to embrace the runaway, a successful intervention is only superficially a matter of technique. It is the therapist's demonstration of his commitment to maintaining connectedness with the family that counts.

The therapist's pursuit and his refusal to be derailed by symptomatic behavior is at once disorienting and engaging to the family. As he convinces the family of his determination to stay connected and to participate in its experience with the symptom, the family invests trust in him. This process of pursuit leads to a deepening of the therapeutic relationship and the formation of a true therapeutic system.

But how will the therapist know when his attempted embrace is succeeding? The therapist pays careful attention to the family's feed-back. One marker is his intuitive feel that the family trusts and accepts him, demonstrated, for example, in its desire to hear the therapist's perspective before deciding on a course of action. For example, we will see that Brian feels that he has embraced the runaway with Nancy Monroe when, after he invites her to talk about her dissatisfactions with him and his therapy with her daughter, she shares her feeling of being understood by him for the first time. Another marker of success is when communication with the therapist begins to occur directly instead of through symptoms, such as when Maria Cabrini stops speaking through her voices and tells Rachel about her fear of death.

Further evidence of success in embracing the runaway is seen when the family is able to contain symptomatic behaviors without escalating into a full-fledged symptomatic cycle. This will be exemplified when Nancy Monroe responds to Jennifer's refusal to eat and threats of sui-cide by sitting with her and reading to her from her favorite childhood storybook and when Mr. Harmon accepts his wife's anger at his refusal to accompany her to the police station without withdrawing or verbally attacking her.

To signify the deepening of the therapeutic relationship as a result of the therapist's pursuit, we say that the therapeutic context, marked by the establishment of the treatment contract, is now superseded by a therapeutic system, in which at least one relationship between a family member and the therapist embodies expectations of mutual account- ability. To demonstrate accountability to this new relationship, the therapist may need to modify the treatment contract based on feedback obtained during the process of embracing the runaway, as Donna and Brian will do with the Monroes.

The milestone marking the end of this second phase is the experience of at least one family member forming a relationship with the therapist characterized by integrity, persistence, and conflict resolution, rather than betrayal, abandonment, and conflict avoidance. This experience is disorienting—it is not like the experience of self that accompanies par- ticipation in the symptomatic cycle. It is the therapist's unconditional acceptance, his willingness to negotiate and compromise in order to stay connected, that offers a way out of the cycle. As the family strives to maintain this new relationship, shifts will be engendered in the relation- ships of the symptomatic cycle as conflicts within the family are precipi- tated and intensified in the next phase of treatment.

The Cabrinis

THE RUNAWAY

A runaway can strike at any point following the family's acceptance of the treatment contract. In the Cabrini family it began at home follow- ing Maria's discharge from the local hospital and erupted in the two- hour admission session, which the entire family and Joyce Perkins, Maria's outpatient therapist, attended, as planned.

Maria had become more depressed and withdrawn at home, and her parents were retreating from their agreement to be involved during this hospitalization, casting the responsibility to care for their daughter to the team.

MR. CABRINI: I don't think we know enough to handle her. I think she'd be better off in the hands of professionals.

MRS. CABRINI: We don't have the energy to deal with her or keep up with the therapy. We'd just like to keep Nicholas while Maria gets everything straightened out here in the hospital and works with Joyce afterwards.

The speed with which a family can surrender to its anxiety in the face of the patient's return to symptomatic behavior highlights the importance of the therapist's anticipating the runaway and preparing for the reemergence of the symptomatic cycle. Otherwise, he may become angry with family members for abdicating responsibility and reneging on the agreements made, rigidly insist on the family's complying with the contract, or threaten to end treatment, running the risk of exacerbating the family's feelings of abandonment. Anticipating the runaway frees the therapist to embrace it.

INITIATING THE EMBRACE

On the heels of her parents' expression of helplessness, Maria turned to her private connection with God. As seen in the following dialogue, she spoke in an idiom the family did not understand or feel comfortable with. Her parents' response was to sit silently and shake their heads in frustration, retreating into their own worlds. Here, Rachel joins Maria in her world and then encourages Mrs. Cabrini to reach out to her daughter and become an ally in her struggle.

MARIA: I asked the Lord, and he says you're too young, and it just goes and comes back.
RACHEL: What do you mean, it goes and comes back?
MARIA: It's, it's evil, it's not in the right form, it's devilish. Um, you ask to be God, and . . . that's a devilish thing to do.
RACHEL: *(To mother)* Do you know what the "it" is? Can you find out from Maria?
MRS. CABRINI: You told me that you told the devil you could beat him, you could take him on, right?
MARIA: Yes.
MRS. CABRINI: Is that what you mean when you say "it"?
MARIA: Yes.
MRS. CABRINI: The devil?
MARIA: Yes.
MRS. CABRINI: And you're fighting it?
MARIA: Yes.
RACHEL: *(To mother)* And what is she fighting?
MRS. CABRINI: The devil. She is saying it controls her.
MARIA: Yes.

The appearance of the symptomatic cycle in the session presents the therapist with an opportunity to influence the parents to alter their pattern of either disengaging from or engulfing the symptomatic member. To accomplish this, the therapist needs to demonstrate that he can accept the symptomatic person with her symptoms, tolerate the intensity of her suffering, and remain connected to her. In this way, he can offer the parents a sense of hope.

Rachel's response to Maria's statements as meaningful communication contrasted with the parents' response of distancing and disregarding Maria when she did not seem to make sense. Rachel continued with this approach, suggesting that Maria was communicating about the family.

RACHEL: *(To mother)* Do you know where the devil is?

MRS. CABRINI: In her thoughts, I guess.

RACHEL: Well, I'm not sure. Maybe she thinks the devil is someone in the family. Find out who the devil is that is making her feel so weak and small.

MARIA: *(Adamantly)* There is no devil in the family!

MRS. CABRINI: Are you sure? Say it, no matter who it is, say it.

MARIA: Oh, okay, I asked for help and the help said it needs more help, and the feeling inside says, you will overcome when I feel too much suffering inside.

Tracking Maria's relationship with the devil, Mrs. Cabrini revealed her belief that Maria's problem lay inside her head. It is understandable that with this view of the problem the family is likely to increase its distance from Maria and turn her over to professionals. To expand the family's field of vision to include alternative ways of interaction, Rachel depicted the devil within Maria in interpersonal and concrete terms, using the language and metaphor Maria introduced. The challenge for the therapist is to understand the symptomatic member's communication and relate it to her interpersonal context without blaming the family, respecting the fine line between responsibility and blame.

RACHEL: So, you're suffering very much now?

MARIA: Yes, yes.

RACHEL: *(To mother)* See, anybody who suffers as much as she does thinks she has very strong shoulders.

MRS. CABRINI: Uh-huh.

RACHEL: Strong enough to take a lot on her shoulders, and to be willing to pay the price of suffering.

MRS. CABRINI: *(Nodding)* Yes.

RACHEL: I don't know what the load is, but she is clearly carrying too heavy a load on her shoulders, to make her suffer like this. *(Rachel, having sensed Maria's responsiveness to her throughout the session, slowly turns toward her and lightly places her hand on her shoulders.)*

MARIA: *(Looking at Rachel)* That's right.

RACHEL: *(Responding to Maria's acceptance of her touch, she stands up, slowly moves behind Maria, and gently begins massaging her shoulders.)* Can you feel this load right here? *(Pressing more firmly on her shoulders.)*

MARIA: Uh-huh *(deep sigh)*.

RACHEL: *(Looking to mother and father)* So, for how long has your daughter been acting like Christ, suffering and holding up the weight in the family?

MRS. CABRINI: It's been many years she's been this way.

RACHEL: *(Continuing to massage Maria's shoulders and feeling her muscles relax)* Let's find out from Maria what she has been worrying about. I'd like to hear Maria tell you in her words, and as she begins to talk straight, her shoulders may feel heavier and heavier, and that's fine. So find out from her.

Embracing the runaway began with Rachel's acceptance of Maria's position as a suffering martyr. By conveying comfort with the intensity of feelings that Maria's strange behavior evoked, Rachel hoped to loosen the parents' paralysis. Rachel also offered the family a more workable definition of the problem by relabeling the devil as a symbol for the load that Maria was carrying in an effort to help the family, while in desperate need of help herself.

Rachel reached out to Maria not only through words but through physical touch. This contact deepened Maria's trust in Rachel, potentially strengthening the parents' willingness to listen and reach out to their daughter.

STAYING IN PROXIMITY: INTENSIFYING THE EMBRACE

A therapist may feel he should back off and stop pushing when family members communicate intense emotional pain. However, it is precisely then that the therapist needs to remain close. Treating family members as fragile and moving away emotionally or physically is liable to accentuate their sense of isolation.

To catalyze a release of unspoken feelings, it may be necessary to amplify instability by adding intensity to an already painful experience. As Rachel continued to guide Maria to focus on her worries about her family, Maria began to speak about her feelings of loss over the deaths of her maternal grandmother and a younger sibling who had died some years earlier at the age of eight. In the following dialogue, Rachel helps Maria unleash her rage by introducing an even more frightening notion, the death of her mother. Rachel's goal here is not to calm or control Maria but to stay connected with her and keep her family involved no matter how intense and extreme the expression of Maria's terror becomes.

MARIA: The feeling just came that everyone is dying! You just don't know what to do! And you tell them, one by one, that you need help, but they just think what *they* want to think, that you don't need help.

RACHEL: Your family didn't hear your cry for help.

MARIA: Right. You know, you don't want to feel it either.

RACHEL: You mean, to feel sad and scared your mother will die?

MARIA: *(Looks at Rachel with shock)* Yes!

RACHEL: Then who would take care of the family?

MARIA: Right!

RACHEL: But they haven't heard you.

MARIA: No!

RACHEL: They really haven't heard you.

MARIA: No! *(Becoming louder)*

RACHEL: And they *still* haven't heard you.

MARIA: Right! *(Increasingly agitated)*

RACHEL: And you have things to tell them.

MARIA: *(Looking out into space, she begins to shout at the top of her lungs and shakes her head furiously.)* Leave me alone! Leave me alone!

RACHEL: Uh-huh.

MARIA: *(Shaking her head and shouting)* Go! Get out!

RACHEL: That's fine.

MARIA: *(Still shaking)* Get off me! Get off me! Don't touch me! Don't touch me! Go!

Maria's eruption felt like an earthquake. Her parents appeared stunned, and Maria's eyes looked glazed as she stared blankly ahead. Her outcry of "Leave me alone, get off me, don't touch me," can be understood on several levels. Perhaps she was responding to voices that terrorized her from within. Perhaps Rachel's physical touch triggered a flashback to some trauma from her childhood. Perhaps she was telling Rachel to stop the pressuring contact that was haunting and encircling her.

Distancing from Maria at that moment would once again have left her deserted and responsible for overcoming her suffering by herself. Instead, Rachel stood close by, accepting and validating Maria's degree of stress.

RACHEL: Maria, do you think that if your family could hear you, things would get better?
MARIA: *(Looking intently at Rachel)* Yes!
RACHEL: Okay. I think you're probably right. Can I ask you something?
MARIA: Yes.
RACHEL: Have you ever heard your family talk about the people who have died, and about their fears and anxieties about death?
MARIA: No.
RACHEL: Isn't that crazy?
MARIA: Yes, and it must go. .
RACHEL: Yeah, I think so. Wouldn't it be better if the rest of your family would talk with each other and with you openly and honestly about their own hidden monsters, so you don't have to continue to go crazy and sacrifice yourself?
MARIA: *(Sighs with relief)* Yes!

Pursuing a connection with Maria and linking her intense suffering with the losses in her family eased Maria's pain. Maria could afford to rest comfortably for a moment once she felt understood and accepted. Rachel proceeded to describe Maria's suffering as an act of loyalty to her family, an attribution that freed Maria to tell her parents how much she feared and resented their shutting down on her.

Seeing that the symptomatic person's pain can be contained within a trusting relationship allows the family to accept expressions of that pain more comfortably. Witnessing the results of the therapist's tenacity in staying with the symptomatic person strengthens the connection between the parents and the therapist, while making the therapist's subsequent challenges to the parents' pattern of distancing more palatable to them.

EMBRACING A RUNAWAY ON THE TEAM

Working with severely symptomatic families renders the treatment team susceptible to replicating the ambivalence and conflicts within the family. While contending with the runaway in the family, the team may find itself experiencing a runaway of its own. The therapist must be alert to this possibility, realizing that the same persistent pursuit and embrace of the runaway that is called for with a family is needed in working with the team.

Behind the one-way mirror the team was engrossed in observing the Cabrinis' session. As the intensity built, team members began to experience the tension radiating from the therapy room. When Rachel began to deal with Maria's intense suffering by massaging her shoulders, controversy arose. "She's pushing too hard; she's going to push Maria over the edge," one person said. "Why is she touching her? She's getting too close," remarked another. "Have some faith in Rachel," said a third team member. "She is giving Maria a chance to experience someone getting very close, even touching her, without violating her."

When Rachel entered the observation room to talk with the team, she heard words of encouragement. However, several members of the team looked anxious. The psychiatrist looked particularly concerned and said, "I think you're doing a nice job of staying in there with the family and your use of metaphor is great. I'm very worried about Maria's mental status, though. I think I'd better meet with her alone and reassess her need for medication."

To Rachel, the psychiatrist's comment signaled a runaway. In formulating the treatment contract, the team, including the psychiatrist, had agreed that the use of medication would be predicated on a convincing demonstration of the parents' commitment to help Maria responsibly manage her behavior. Prescribing medication, like using any other therapeutic tool, would need to be discussed among team members and between the family and the team. It seemed to Rachel that taking Maria off by herself to be evaluated for medication, rather than counting on the family and the rest of the team for support, was a reflection of the psychiatrist's anxiety. To deal with this runaway, Rachel told the family that there was a disagreement on the team that needed to be ironed out before the session could proceed, and the team went to another room to hash out its differences.

Rachel stated that she thought the use of medication as a stabilizing agent at this juncture ran the risk of maintaining Maria as the locus of pathology, perpetuating the pattern of the professionals taking over responsibility for Maria and keeping the parents at a distance. She recognized that medication might very well have a role in Maria's treatment. However, the way in which it was being proposed was a problem for her. Rachel asked the psychiatrist why he was considering medication for Maria, and he spoke of his fear that she would become so out of control that she might hurt herself in some way or attack someone else. He pointed out that the plan to maintain close contact between Maria and her family could be problematic in that "her parents are subtly provocative of her, and when she reacts, they drop her like a hot potato." Another team member voiced a similar fear.

Just as Maria's lack of trust in her family led her to communicate in symptomatic ways, the psychiatrist's anxiety about whether he could count on the team and family to supervise her—whether he could count on relationships to contain Maria's symptoms—led him to suggest imposing control via medication. Rachel acknowledged the validity of the psychiatrist's concern for Maria's safety and asked the team to consider ways of addressing this concern that were more consistent with the treatment contract.

A team member suggested that if Maria appeared to be in danger of harming herself or someone else, the parents should be requested to stay with and supervise her on a twenty-four-hour basis. A team member would then be assigned to monitor the parents' monitoring of Maria. The team's program coordinator checked with the milieu director to ensure that accommodations for the parents could be arranged on the unit. The psychiatrist said that he was comfortable in theory with this plan, but he expressed considerable skepticism about the parents' ability to follow through. Because the psychiatrist's doubts had led to the development of this plan, Rachel felt that the team's runaway could be further embraced by inviting him to join the session with her, so that he could challenge the parents himself about their commitment.

Bringing a conflict between team members into the room with the family serves multiple purposes. It models effective conflict resolution while communicating respect for family members by including them in the discussion. The team's conflict often mirrors the family's ambivalence, wherein a sense of duty and desire to respond to the patient's needs conflict with a sense of helplessness and desire to turn her over to someone else. Listening to this conflict discussed in the open by the professionals can free parents to intentionally commit themselves to one course of action or the other, rather than being pulled back and forth by their own ambivalent feelings. Using a conflict between two team members as a way of challenging parents can also be diagnostic. Mr. and Mrs. Cabrini's response to the psychiatrist's challenge would provide feedback concerning the strength of their connection with Rachel.

The psychiatrist and Rachel reentered the therapy room. The psychiatrist stated that in order to honor the treatment contract, and not to resort to an immediate use of medication, he would need a full-time commitment from Mr. and Mrs. Cabrini to monitor Maria if she were

at risk of hurting herself or others. With Rachel's support, and with
some reluctance, the parents eventually accepted the responsibility to
monitor their daughter, and the psychiatrist accepted their commitment. Embracing the runaways both in the family and on the team
would allow Maria to be admitted without her parents' abdicating their
responsibility. They agreed to supervise her, rather than expecting the
hospital, team, or medication to function as agents of control.

EMBRACING THE PARENTS' RUNAWAY

In severely symptomatic families it is necessary to challenge the patterns of the symptomatic cycle from several directions simultaneously.
By staying with Maria during her symptomatic eruption, Rachel had
forged a connection with her. By securing the parents' agreement to stay
close to Maria in the hospital, the team had established a way to work
with them in the present, day by day. Now Rachel wanted to establish
a deeper relationship with Mr. and Mrs. Cabrini by understanding the
roots of the runaway in their past.

Many parents have experienced a betrayal in their relationship with
each other and harbor enormous resentment. A debt has accrued, repa-
rations remain unpaid, and the wall between them grows. Rachel suggested that Maria would be better able to tame her monsters if her
parents were more forgiving of each other and could reveal more about
the monsters that haunted them from their families of origin. In this
way, they would become more human to their children. She began with
Mr. Cabrini, asking about his relationship with his parents as he was
growing up.

He said his mother had left the family when he was a young child.
He had had no contact with her for years thereafter until his father's
funeral ten years ago, and he had not seen or spoken with her since. As
an adolescent he lived in and out of foster homes, running away from
them in search of his father. He was quick to say he did not miss his
mother at all, in fact he had never liked her, but he missed his father
terribly and agreed with Rachel's interpretation that his wildness was
linked to his rupture with his father.

Bruno seemed startled to hear this information and said he had never
known anything before about his stepfather's background. Anita and
Maria, however, began to speak about their anger toward Mr. Cabrini
for his violent, unpredictable explosions. Mrs. Cabrini said she had been
occasionally hit and frequently verbally abused by him to the point that

she was now emotionally numb. Rachel asked her why she had toler-
ated the abuse, why she had not left with her children. She replied that
she had left several times on her own, but always came back. She had
very strong feelings about family loyalties.

To continue the process, Rachel asked Mrs. Cabrini about her childhood. Mrs. Cabrini reflected for a moment and sighed, as if surrendering
to an internal struggle that had long been keeping her hostage. She
hesitantly began to share her story, describing a very rough time with
her parents, including physical abuse from her mother while her father
was out drinking and frequent episodes in which her mother would
disappear from home for days at a time. The recurrent trauma had
gutted Mrs. Cabrini's insides and robbed her of her spirit. As with all
victims of abuse, a part of her had died with each assault, leaving her
more and more empty, frozen with her pain, mistrustful of relationships. She learned at a young age that depending on others, especially
parents, was dangerous, and that the only safeguard was to remain
detached. Isolation had been her means of survival, but it had been
crippling her relationships with her husband and children.

Rachel used the rapport she was developing with Mrs. Cabrini to
challenge her stoical manner of keeping her pain secret. "I don't understand why you don't trust your children. You pretend you don't have
pain, but all the while the pain has been leaking out, and all of them,
especially Maria, have been absorbing it. By hiding your pain from
them, you give them the message that they're too weak to handle seeing
you hurt, like they'd collapse if you expressed your feelings more directly. I think you're selling them short." Rachel teased her about how
foolish it is to be a stoic, pretending to be tough while cheating her
children of the experience of sharing her suffering. Mother laughed, and
Maria looked over and smiled.

So far, the family had been seen together in each session. To promote
the further development of differentiation and boundaries, the therapist
also has to orchestrate separations. The team recommended separate
sessions for the siblings during the first few days of Maria's hospitalization. This would allow Rachel to establish a stronger alliance with the
sibling subsystem.

EMBRACING THE RUNAWAY: MEETING WITH THE SIBLINGS

In the early phases of crisis induction, especially in an inpatient or
residential facility, it is necessary for the treatment team to go out of

its way to create a supportive network of adults who can engage the symptomatic person and her siblings. When, later on in therapy, they are prepared to become more independent of their parents, they will have allies to turn to.

The Cabrinis' team felt that the children were joined in their anxiety about their parents but were otherwise disconnected from one another. Though Mr. and Mrs. Cabrini had agreed to monitor Maria, the team was skeptical about the likelihood of the parents' compliance and wanted to enlist the siblings' assistance in pressuring their parents. To expand the siblings' view of the team as resources to them, Rachel invited several team members to sit in on the meeting.

In the session, all three siblings voiced the view that the primary problem was Mr. Cabrini. Rachel learned that Bruno and Anita stayed home from school because they felt a responsibility to protect Maria and their mother from his violent temper. In exploring how the siblings dealt with violence in the family, Rachel discovered that each of them acted independently of the others, and consequently suffered alone. As they continued to talk, Bruno and Anita expressed feelings of hopelessness and depression. Each admitted to having had thoughts of suicide.

In light of Bruno and Anita's level of despair and their distrust of their parents' ability to give them the necessary balance of support and structure in their lives, Rachel suggested admitting Bruno and Anita to the inpatient unit so that they could get more intensive training from the team in becoming an effective support system for each other.

Admitting siblings of the patient to the hospital, provided that they exhibit symptoms of sufficient severity to justify hospitalization, is a powerful intervention, particularly if the parents do not trust each other and the children do not trust the parents to provide protection. All three siblings were enthusiastic about the idea, but were anxious about their mother's safety without their presence as a buffer between her and Mr. Cabrini.

To lessen their fear of leaving their mother unprotected, Rachel suggested they tell Mr. Cabrini that they would call the police and press charges against him the next time he became violent toward anyone in the family. They could take this initiative to help their stepfather take responsibility for controlling his anger, something he had already promised Rachel he would do. The siblings discussed this suggestion with Rachel at great length, reviewing the pros and cons, and finally agreed with the logic of taking such a stand. They spent the day and evening talking more about it with the team, planning how to present the plan to their parents. In her session with the siblings, Rachel challenges them to assume more responsibility for supporting each other.

RACHEL: *(To Bruno)* I think you and Anita need to change the way you're helping your parents.

BRUNO: Uh-huh.

RACHEL: Because if you continue to give up on them, they will continue to act as if they're giving up on Maria. Do you know what is likely to happen then?

ANITA: Nothing will change.

RACHEL: I think there will be another death in the family. I think your parents need to change, and you all need to help each other in a different way to help your parents change, so we don't have a funeral.

BRUNO AND ANITA: Yeah.

Opening up access to outside control is critical in working with families in which there is physical violence and abuse. External supports can anchor a reorganization in the family that might otherwise collapse under the weight of the symptomatic cycle. Efforts to exclude these agents can result in the therapist inadvertently colluding with the family to keep the violence a secret. Empowering the Cabrini siblings to seek police protection and to expect their mother to do the same was thus essential.

In the next day's session, with the entire family and team present, Rachel presented the idea of admitting Anita and Bruno to the hospital and solicited the parents' assent. Then Bruno spoke to Mr. Cabrini in a calm but firm voice: "Anita and Maria and I are afraid of your temper, and if we move into the hospital, we're worried that Mom won't be safe. We've decided that if you become violent again, we will call the police and press charges."

Bruno's strong assertion that he and his siblings would not tolerate any further violence on Mr. Cabrini's part represented a major challenge to the symptomatic cycle. It resulted from Rachel's and the team's orchestration of the siblings, rallying them to push for the restoration of order and control in the family.

Let us review the steps involved in embracing the runaways. First, Rachel connected with Maria in her state of agitation and isolation. Through her relationship with Maria, she invited Mrs. Cabrini to listen to and understand her daughter's symptomatic pleas for connectedness.

Rachel used her embrace of the runaway on the team to challenge the parents to assume more responsibility in caring for their children, especially for Maria. Then Rachel pursued each parent, seeking an understanding of their suffering that was rooted in their past experiences with their families of origin. Finally, still not trusting the parents' resolve to stop fleeing from each other and their children, Rachel and the team pursued the siblings to enlist their support in assuming more responsibility for taking care of each other.

Two significant relational shifts emerged from embracing these runaways. First, Rachel's accompaniment of Maria into her impassioned outburst and back led Maria to trust that Rachel really wanted to understand her suffering, not just control or cure it. It also increased her siblings' and parents' confidence in their capacity to reach her. Second, the siblings had begun to create their own holding environment by convincing their parents of their desire to move into the hospital and by taking a clear and nonnegotiable position about Mr. Cabrini's violent behavior. A significant change seemed to have occurred in Bruno. As a result of strengthening his ties with his sisters and the team, he was less tempestuous and more effective in asserting himself with his parents.

The Harmons

THE RUNAWAY

In inpatient treatment, runaways are typically manifested in blatant behaviors from the symptomatic cycle, such as Maria's fight with the devil or her parents' early announcement of their intention to relinquish care of her to the hospital staff. In outpatient therapy, however, runaways may be more subtle. They may be signaled only by subdued or angry looks or tones of voice, reflecting the family's sense of frustration and helplessness.

As soon as the Harmon family entered Paul's office for their third session, one week after the initial session, Paul wondered about a runaway, for the formerly friendly and talkative family was now sullen and tense. Each person stared angrily at the floor, as if daring someone to say the first word. Then Barbara broke the silence and told Paul what had happened since the last session. "We haven't been together for three days," she said, and related the following series of events.

The day after the session, she had received a phone call from the local police informing her that Suzanne had been arrested for shoplifting. Barbara was advised to come to the police station to bail her daughter out, whereupon she grabbed her coat and asked her husband to come with her. He refused, shouting that Suzanne could "stew in her own juices and cool her heels in jail for a while," and that if his wife wanted to "mollycoddle the delinquent" she could, but he wasn't going to participate. Barbara did not want to go without him, and she argued with him for forty-five minutes. Finally she gave up and went alone, bringing Suzanne home after persuading a policeman to give her a stern lecture. Suzanne and her father avoided each other, Josh kept to himself, and Robert and Barbara didn't speak to each other. A meeting had been arranged at Josh's school during that time: Barbara attended, Robert did not. "Like I said," Barbara concluded, "we haven't been together for three days."

Suzanne's acting out had precipitated a replay of the symptomatic cycle, in which her parents abandoned one another in stressful situations and began looking outside the family for help. In this instance, father retreated behind a wall of angry silence and mother turned in desperation to a policeman to provide a stern rebuke to her daughter. The parents' split, marked by their going outside their relationship for help following an agreement with the therapist that they would go to each other, was not unexpected. Why should the parents be successful at working collaboratively at this point, simply because they had agreed to a treatment contract?

Although Mr. Harmon's behavior could be explained as an attempt to undermine treatment, such a disparaging description is usually a projection of the therapist's frustration; it obscures his vision and hinders his effectiveness. It is more accurate to recognize that the family is simply not used to assuming responsibility for relationships, and has had little practice maintaining a sense of mutual accountability, initiating collaboration, negotiating conflicts, or finding ways to accommodate each other. The therapist's challenge is to respond to the symptomatic pattern without becoming organized by it.

Paul considered various ways he could respond to Barbara's statement. He could express alarm about Suzanne and offer his thoughts about how to deal with her behavior. However, he realized that in light of the symptomatic cycle, this intervention could be seen as abandoning the parents (as they had done to one another) by taking over their job of dealing with Suzanne. It might also be a reaction to his own concern that he had erred in not working more with Suzanne in the first two sessions. Yielding to his impulse to deal with the symptomatic behavior would keep him in the position of the expert and the parents in positions of helplessness.

A less obvious but more useful way of viewing Barbara's statement— "We haven't been together for three days"—is that she saw the pressing problem to be in the relationship between her and her husband, and not that with Suzanne. Viewed from this perspective, her statement would indicate that her perception of the situation was informed by the treatment contract—that she was maintaining some accountability in spirit to the agreement to work together with her husband, even though they had failed in practice.

EMBRACING THE RUNAWAY

The runaway included two elements: Suzanne's behavior and the parents' quitting on each other before an adequate airing and resolution of conflict occurred. This definition of the runaway had implications for the current session. Paul would need to forge a connection with at least one of the parents to outweigh that person's inclination to bail out of the next conflict that occurred. A pitfall at this juncture is for the therapist to push too quickly for conflict resolution in an attempt to establish order, leading to a pseudoagreement that is reached out of fear of the emotions associated with the conflict. Here, Paul pursues the runaway by exploring and accepting each parent's view of the problem, elongating the presentation of both sides of the issue in the process:

PAUL: You guys haven't been together since Tuesday?
BARBARA: Not really.
PAUL: Great! Why don't you sit next to your husband and we can talk about that. If you guys haven't been together since Tuesday, I would say in my view that's fine, because now we have an opportunity to talk about it. So tell me in more detail how it went.

When he felt both parents trusted that he had heard them, he said that they had wound up polarized because they had misinterpreted each other. "Barbara, I think Robert misinterpreted your request for help," Paul said. "He didn't understand that your request for him to come to the police station was for *your* sake, that *you* needed him to be there for you, not for Suzanne." "That's exactly right," Barbara responded, pleased that Paul had understood her request correctly. Paul continued, "I think *you* took his refusal to go as his unwillingness to carry his weight as a parent and support you, but *I* think he didn't go because he was furious at Suzanne and he thought you'd continue to go easy on her." Robert nodded emphatically in agreement. "I just think," Paul concluded, "that you don't know each other well enough yet."

Paul then increased the intensity by encouraging Barbara, who was accustomed to turning to professionals for solace, to pursue her husband right then and there, making demands of him in a way that he could hear. As she began to do that, Paul shifted some of his support to Robert's side of the conflict.

PAUL: *(To Barbara)* You define when you need support; he doesn't define that. But you've got to help him to hear you, or else you won't get what you need.

BARBARA: When I did tell him what I needed he said, "No you don't."

PAUL: So then you tell him that's disrespectful. And you don't like him fighting with you that way.

BARBARA: Right. I don't.

PAUL: Keep going. Tell him right now.

BARBARA: I don't like you fighting with me that way. If I need you, you have to be there whether *you* think I need you or not. Just like I'm there for you when you need me. You say, "Barbara, leave me alone for a while." And I do. And when you want to talk, I talk. But I needed you to come with me that evening. I was scared.

ROBERT: I didn't know that.

BARBARA: I said you have to come with me. I said that over and over, you have to come with me. I didn't say you had to go for Suzanne's sake.

PAUL: Barbara, you just have to say, "It's for *me.*"

ROBERT: Okay, I see it now.

Having experienced a more direct approach on Barbara's part, and some flexibility from her husband, Paul turned to Robert and supported him by challenging Barbara's indirectness.

PAUL: *(To Robert)* She was asking for herself, not for Suzanne. But I don't think that she explained it clearly enough to you.

BARBARA: Probably not.

ROBERT: *(To Barbara)* You didn't say it at all.

PAUL: How are you supposed to support her if she doesn't tell you what she needs? Are you a mind reader? If she doesn't make it clear, how can you know what she wants you to do to support her?

ROBERT: *(To his wife)* You need to tell me what you want.

BARBARA: How can I tell you when you blow up, walk out, or come home and sit and watch television for two hours?

ROBERT: Well, I was upset at the time.

PAUL: She says she needs you and then goes and deals with the school all alone. She goes to the meetings, makes decisions, and acts like Josh's sole parent. Where does that leave you?

ROBERT: I wanted to go, but I was so angry at Suzanne. And then I thought, this is all happening because Josh takes up so much of our time, and I was angry at him too. I remember how my parents were always taking my sister to doctors. They had no time to pay attention to my schooling. The money for my college education went to my sister's treatment, and a lot of good *that* did. I was just angry at everyone, especially Suzanne. I have needs, too.

BARBARA: *(Tentatively)* It's okay to be angry at her for what she did, but I think what happened is that you took it out on me.

Paul heard the echoes of Robert's unresolved anger and unfinished issues from his past, but he thought that venturing too deeply into that world at the moment might provoke another runaway, one into a past full of blame and guilt, detouring the discussion at hand. Paul felt it would be better to postpone delving into the past until he felt that Robert had a stronger connection with his wife in the present.

Thus, instead of pursuing Robert into his world of defeat and despair, Paul decided to focus the couple on how they could help each other solve the concrete problems facing them at that moment. He uses his affect to push the parents to return to a discussion about handling their childrens' behavior so that he can assess the extent of their rapprochement with each other and with him.

PAUL: What happens is that the gulf between the two of you *(gesturing at Barbara and Robert)* allows your kids room to screw up, and when they screw up they make the gulf even bigger. What is Suzanne doing stealing? I mean, really! And what is Josh doing taking pills and getting himself beat up? Unless you two can stick together, all the heat stays between the two of you, and none of it comes over here *(gestures at Suzanne and Josh)*. One day Josh is going to hassle somebody who's got a knife in his pocket—

ROBERT: Absolutely.

PAUL: —and it'll be in his guts. So carry it on. Figure out what you're going to do.

BARBARA: *(To her husband)* Okay, what do you want to do with Suzanne?

ROBERT: Well, like I said before. I think you're too lenient with her.

BARBARA: We're not talking about that. We're talking about what you want to do with her. I don't care what you think right now about whether I'm too lenient or not. What do you think is the right punishment for her?

ROBERT: *(Angrily)* Well, I think she should be grounded. I really do. And whenever we're out of the house, she's got to be in the house. That's one thing.

BARBARA: All right, I can go along with you on that.

The parents' discussion continued in this direction, with Paul helping to keep the conversation focused on immediate concerns. Allowing Robert to express his anger seemed to help Barbara realize that the children needed to be held more accountable for their actions. The parents decided on a punishment for Suzanne as well as to make her pay the fine and damages. With pencil and paper, Robert helped Suzanne work out a payment plan that she could manage. Robert agreed to attend another meeting at school for Josh, but insisted that Josh also be present and expected to participate more actively on his own behalf. He and his wife helped Josh identify and rehearse specific things he would say in the school meeting.

By the end of the session, the parents looked more confident, and Paul felt that he had successfully embraced the runaway, holding family members accountable for finding a new way through the resurgence of the symptomatic cycle. Paul had encouraged Barbara to insist that her husband deal more directly with her so that she could obtain support for herself as a person in her own right and as a wife, not simply as an advocate for her children in her role as mother. Barbara was experiencing a developing sense of differentiation, as reflected in her comment to her husband, "It's okay to be angry at her [Suzanne], but . . . you took it out on me." Making this distinction allowed Barbara to talk with her husband about their childrens' difficulties in a more direct, less encumbered manner.

Paul's taking a position at the hub of the wheel from which to pursue each parent created a therapeutic alliance that he used to help them find a more effective problem-solving process. Both parents, in fact, found themselves operating in substantially different ways in the process of asking for and receiving support from each other and Paul.

The Monroes

THE RUNAWAY

Three days after the initial consultation session with the Monroes, Brian phoned Donna and said nervously: "Things have broken loose with the Monroes, Donna. About midnight last night I got a call from Dr. Frank Carmody, the Monroes' family physician. He was with Nancy and Jennifer in the emergency room—Jennifer had taken a bunch of sleeping pills. They pumped her stomach in the emergency room and she seemed to be in stable condition, but he wanted to admit her to the hospital overnight as a precaution.

"I asked Frank where Carl was, and he said apparently Carl and Nancy had had a fight so he had stayed at home. Before Nancy left the hospital, Frank thought he ought to call me and let me know what had happened. He said that he was feeling very frustrated with the whole situation. Remembering the task we had assigned, I urged Frank not to let Nancy leave, and asked him if he could arrange for her to spend the night in Jennifer's hospital room. I also told him Carl should come in and stay as well, and that I would call him, but Frank said he'd take care of it himself."

The therapist's anticipation of the runaway prepares him to embrace it, but it does not protect him from the emotional distress involved in facing the violence and pain the family inflicts on itself.

Although she was accustomed to working with severely symptomatic families, Donna was upset about Carl and Nancy's abdication of their agreement to monitor Jennifer; this was their part of the runaway. When a therapist feels angry, dejected, or puzzled at a given moment in therapy, it can be helpful for him to step back and review the map of the symptomatic cycle as a way of gaining perspective and reviving his sanity, which can flag at times in working with such complex and overwhelming problems. Reflecting on the cycle, Donna realized that another aspect of the runaway had to do with Brian's behavior. Brian had told Frank Carmody that *he* would contact Carl and ask him to come to the hospital, despite the fact that an explicit part of the contract was for *Nancy* to be responsible for engaging Carl. Brian was still a participant in the cycle, taking over Nancy's job for her. This confirmed for Donna the importance of persisting with and strengthening her efforts to help Brian and Nancy struggle more directly with each other.

EMBRACING THE RUNAWAY: THE CONSULTANT SPEAKS WITH THE FAMILY

As scheduled, Brian and Donna met with the Monroes later that day in Donna's office. The first step in Donna's embracing the runaway was to track carefully what had happened. The first two days after the initial session had been uneventful. The parents had worked out a plan in which they alternated supervising Jennifer's activities. They confiscated her laxatives, took her cash so she couldn't purchase more, and were both present at mealtimes. Jennifer voiced no protest about being continuously chaperoned, and even ate moderately well.

The day before the breakdown that constituted the runaway, it had been Carl's turn to supervise Jennifer during the day. Nancy had called from work to say that she might be home late from the store; since Jennifer answered the phone, Nancy asked Jennifer to tell her father. Rather than saying, "You discuss it with Dad yourself," Jennifer accepted the job of go-between. And rather than calling Nancy back, Carl complained to Jennifer that he had tickets for a ballgame that evening and that her mother was doing this on purpose. Listening to Carl, Jennifer became increasingly upset, started crying, and said she was going to her room. There, she took a handful of her mother's sleeping pills. When Nancy arrived home, she discovered Jennifer sleeping on the floor in the bathroom while Carl was at work on his second martini in the kitchen. After finding out from Jennifer about the pills, Nancy rushed Jennifer off to the emergency room, screaming at Carl but not insisting that he accompany them.

The outcome of such runaways is further divisiveness within the family, where everyone blames someone else for what happened to justify their sense of helplessness. In actuality, family members have no idea that any other response is possible because they are still operating under the assumptions of the symptomatic system.

An advantage of viewing problems in terms of interpersonal systems and symptomatic cycles is that more points of potential intervention are created. However, this can also be a disadvantage, because the therapist must then choose among competing alternatives, none of which may seem to be any better than the others, at least in theory. And simply moving from one to another in sequence seldom generates enough focus and intensity to facilitate change in severely symptomatic families.

The way out lies in understanding that although systemic therapy can be conceptualized according to various mechanistic theoretical models, the actual work is in creating, modifying, and transforming living relationships, relationships in which the therapist is an active participant. Decisions about who to connect with whom and how to do it have more to do with who the people are and what their relationships are like than with technique.

A temptation for Donna would be to go after Carl for his lapse in supervision, similar to what she had done in the session three days previously. In doing so, however, she would be expanding the cycle to include herself. Part of the original cycle as Brian had described it was precisely that dynamic: when the parents weren't working together, the professional tried to engage Carl while Nancy watched. Even if Donna were more successful in activating Carl than Brian had been, the attempt would be missing the point. Although Donna had initially been willing to pursue Carl directly as a way of challenging the myth of Carl's unreachability, her real objective was for Carl to be more available to Nancy and ultimately to Jennifer.

The relationship that Donna trusted the most, the one that offered her the most therapeutic leverage, was the one between her and Brian. Brian had been open from the outset about seeing himself as stuck, and it was explicit in the contract that a goal was for Donna to help him renegotiate his role with the family. Although she couldn't be sure where it would lead, accepting and exploring Brian's contribution to the runaway was the most suitable point of departure.

EMBRACING THE RUNAWAY: THE CONSULTANT SPEAKS WITH THE THERAPIST

To look for an opening to challenge Brian's way of thinking about his role, Donna decided to ask him to say more about how he saw the situation. Her assumption was that successfully embracing *his* runaway would facilitate his embracing the family's runaway with her help.

DONNA: Brian, it seems like the more involved people get with the family, the more things escalate. How do you see it?

BRIAN: Right, that's how I see it. It's like a flashback to how it felt when I first started working with them. Now you're involved, too, and Jennifer OD's on sleeping pills. I'm really afraid she may kill herself or die of physical deterioration.

NANCY: I'm afraid of that, too. You can see how much help my husband is. I think he was half drunk by the time Dr. Carmody convinced him to come to the hospital last night. Can't you try again to get him to see what he's doing?

JENNIFER: *(Shouts angrily at her parents)* I can't stand it—I hate both of you! Next time, I really will kill myself—then you'll be sorry! *(Carl looks at her despairingly, then bolts out of his chair and clutches her in a big hug.)*

NANCY: Don't start in with your fake affection, Carl. You're not fooling anyone. *(Carl looks at her in disgust and sighs heavily. He abruptly lets go of Jennifer and returns to his chair, while Jennifer cries softly.)*

In response to Donna's inquiry, Brian expressed his sense of being caught in a powerful bind, where his efforts to help paradoxically seemed to be hastening Jennifer's demise. At that point, almost as if on cue, the family's symptomatic cycle entered the session: Nancy echoed Brian's helplessness, directed her impotent rage at Carl, and requested help from the expert, whereupon Jennifer threatened suicide. Jennifer's symptomatic outburst engaged her father, but when Nancy challenged him, alluding to his failures as a husband, he pulled away, leaving Jennifer alone at the edge of the cliff with her pain.

Donna returned to Brian's participation in the runaway. She asked him why he had not spoken to Nancy after his conversation with the family doctor so that (in keeping with the contract) he could request that *she* solicit Carl's involvement. Initially Brian was not sure, but as he and Donna talked, he recognized that he had simply assumed that Nancy would refuse to deal with Carl, despite the agreement. "You know, Donna," Brian mused, "I wonder why I'm doing Nancy's thinking for her." Brian acknowledged that not only had he been thinking for Nancy, he may have been taking over for her in other ways. He began to experience his identification with Nancy as considerably more than the intellectualized construct it had been previously. He began to consider that perhaps his own feelings of frustration, anger, helplessness, and despair, which he felt so acutely in relation to Jennifer and Carl, might also be feelings that he was carrying for Nancy.

Donna's pursuit of Brian's participation in the runaway—that is, his accommodation to Nancy's disengagement from Carl—awakened Brian to the necessity of confronting Nancy's behavior. Brian's process of embracing the runaway with Nancy would mirror Donna's process with him.

EMBRACING THE RUNAWAY WITH THE FAMILY

Donna's job at this point was to be alert to any signs that Brian was reinforcing Nancy's feelings of powerlessness as he challenged her to reengage Carl in the task of parenting Jennifer. For example, as the following dialogue unfolds, Brian begins to collude with Nancy's attempt to restore their previous impotent coalition against Carl. Donna intervenes to challenge Brian, who, in turn, challenges Nancy again.

BRIAN: *(To Nancy)* Why didn't you insist on Carl's coming with you to the hospital last night?

NANCY: Are you kidding? The whole thing was his fault to begin with. You know how he is—you've seen the same irresponsibility; even *you* said you couldn't work with him!

BRIAN: That's true—I know how infuriated you get when you try to deal with Carl, and he is awfully difficult to get through to.

DONNA: Of course, but that's no reason to quit on him. In fact, Brian, to the extent that Carl didn't come through last night, it seems to me that it's even more essential for Nancy to involve him in a different, more constructive way, so that this doesn't happen again. Don't you agree?

BRIAN: You know, you're right, Donna. Thanks. *(Turns back to Nancy)* So let's get back to last night. I understand how you felt, but we're talking about how to change things, not about understanding or accepting them the way they are now. Is this a two-parent family or a single-parent family?

NANCY: A single-parent family, always has been. Carl's never around.

BRIAN: *(In an accepting and understanding tone)* Why do you keep him out?

NANCY: I don't keep him out—he keeps himself out. He has a lot of things he has to do, and no matter what I need, he's not available for consultation.

BRIAN: We're talking now specifically about Jennifer.

NANCY: Sometimes I think he makes matters worse. If I really push him, he blows up at me, and says do I want to sit on her and force her to eat?

BRIAN: You haven't done such a good job working by yourself—look at her.

NANCY: That's true, I haven't.

BRIAN: You're going to lose her, you know, if you continue to operate the way you've been operating.

NANCY: Yeah, that's true, too.

BRIAN: Well, do you want his help, or don't you?

NANCY: Maybe, as long as I knew that he'd really be there, and not evaporate at the first sign of tension.

CARL: All I've ever wanted is for you just to ask me directly for what you want, instead of going through Jennifer. So many of these crises come up because you and I just don't communicate.

NANCY: I never felt that I could depend on you because as soon as you stepped in, you'd make matters worse.

CARL: Well, I could sense the disaster ahead and you'd get so angry and upset, and I figured there's no point in standing there and watching things deteriorate further.

NANCY: Right, so then you leave.

CARL: You got it.

NANCY: *(To Brian)* So you see, I end up abandoned and alone.

BRIAN: But the problem I'm talking about here, Nancy, the problem with that situation, is that you let him go.

With Donna steering him back on track when he deviated, Brian began to follow a more consistent course. He continued to challenge Nancy, becoming less accepting of her disengagement from Carl without withdrawing his acceptance of her. In fact, he encouraged more intimacy by staying with her despite her protestations of incompetence to get through to her husband. Brian's refrain was that regardless of the correctness of Nancy's position or her intentions, her efforts to help were not working; in fact, Jennifer was rapidly getting worse. The therapist's purposeful use of the patient's symptomatic behavior is a powerful way to challenge relationships in the system. Not only can this help motivate family members to change, it can also take away some of the power of the symptoms.

As the session continued, Brian intensified his pursuit of Nancy. Although their struggle over this issue lasted longer than on any previous occasion, no resolution seemed imminent. Brian and Donna took a break to discuss the situation, and Donna suggested that perhaps it would be best to put a hold on the discussion where they were and reconvene the next day to work more on the issue. But Brian seemed uncomfortable with that idea. "I feel like I'm close to understanding what Nancy's problem with this is," he said, "and I think knowing that would be very helpful to her and the family. She and I have hung in there with each other this far, and I don't want to quit now. Anyway, something about the process doesn't feel right. I think I'm missing something somewhere."

As Brian and Donna talked about what might be missing, Brian recalled his earlier insight. He wondered whether some of those feelings that he had been "carrying" for Nancy needed to be relocated within *her.* "And maybe," Brian pondered, "something similar is going on with regard to Nancy and Carl. She keeps talking about how Carl can't help her, as though *she* wants his help but *he* isn't giving it, as though the obstacle is in him. I agree with you that I need to keep pushing her to find a way to enlist Carl's support with Jennifer. But maybe my pushing in this way simply reinforces some mechanism that leads Nancy to view the problem as being inside Carl, and she keeps feeling helpless and defeated."

Brian said that perhaps Nancy did not accept the premise that she needed her husband's help. Trying to convince her that she *did* need Carl, he continued, was trying to graft on a belief that did not fit with her experience, so the graft would not take. Brian wanted to develop a deeper understanding of Nancy's experience. Donna agreed to continue the session until Brian felt more comfortable in his connection with Nancy because she wanted to support Brian and Nancy's relationship, which she felt would lead to Brian's having more therapeutic traction with the entire family.

When the session resumed, Brian shared with Nancy his hunch that she did not yet believe that she had done everything she could on her own to help Jennifer. Given that, Brian went on, he could understand why she resisted his efforts to turn her toward Carl.

NANCY: *(After a long pause)* Well, I don't know where to go from here. I'm just not sure.
BRIAN: What is it you're not sure of?
NANCY: *(Hesitantly)* Whether I could save her on my own.
BRIAN: Right, you don't know. That's what I thought, that you're not totally convinced you can't do it without Carl. If you *were* convinced, you'd know it. Since you *don't* know, you're not sure.
NANCY: You know, Brian, you're right. I'm *not* sure about it.
BRIAN: So maybe, Nancy, despite what Donna and I have been saying, maybe you don't need Carl's help after all.

Brian and Nancy continued this discussion for a good while. Although Carl and Jennifer listened attentively, Nancy seemed oblivious to the presence of anyone but Brian and herself. Brian asked Nancy how she had felt about his earlier work with Jennifer and the family. Nancy appeared surprised by the question, but Brian said that it was important to him to know how she felt. Nancy spoke haltingly at first, then with increasing fluency about how she had hoped that Brian would make things right for Jennifer, as well as somehow find a way to improve her marriage to Carl. A new dimension to Nancy emerged—she told Brian that she had felt hurt and angry when he had discontinued treatment with the family: "It was very confusing to me, because first I was pulled into treatment, and then I was kicked out."

While Nancy spoke, Brian listened quietly. When she finished talking, he apologized for having underestimated her determination to participate in the family's struggle, revealing a new part of himself to her. As he did so, he became aware that he had never talked with Nancy about her experiences in any role other than as a mother and wife. He asked her what it was like for her at work, and learned how she had discovered that she felt valued and appreciated in her job in a very different way from how she was perceived in her family or in therapy sessions.

As they continued to talk, Nancy's doubts, fears, anguish, and guilt poured forth. Brian's sincere and straightforward acceptance of her turmoil, devoid of any effort to fix or mute it, provided Nancy a secure place in which she could own her pain. It was the first time, she said, that she remembered being able to express her conflicting feelings without someone trying to take them away, or without her trying to hide them in someone else. She described a feeling of being more of a whole person.

Brian told Donna that he felt that the understanding between himself and Nancy was greater than ever before in their work together. Donna felt that she and Brian had successfully weathered this encounter with the symptomatic cycle. By challenging and embracing Brian's role in the runaway, she had helped him to substantially renegotiate his relationship with Nancy, and in doing so to expand the potential of his therapeutic role. She proposed ending the session and meeting again the next day. Donna wondered aloud how Nancy and Carl would decide to monitor Jennifer between now and then in a way that would be respectful of the work that had been done in the session. She left the task unspecified, so that Carl, Jennifer, and in particular Nancy, could determine for themselves how to use the experience in ways that were meaningful for them.

CHAPTER 6

_____

Violence: Struggling for Survival

There are always risks in freedom. The only risk in bondage is that of breaking free.

—Gita Bellin

The essence of crisis is struggle.

—Donald Langsley and David Kaplan,
The Treatment of Families in Crisis

AFTER the therapist has embraced the runaway, a relative lull in the therapeutic process often sets in. Although no enduring change in family relationships has taken place, a sense of mutual accountability exists between the family and therapist. At this juncture, the therapist intensifies her push to challenge the family's severe and longstanding unresolved conflicts and destructive entanglements in which life-threatening symptoms have been embedded. *Violence* refers to the process of relentlessly eroding these patterns and to the intensity of the ensuing struggles among family members and between the family and the therapist.

As conflicts emerge, the newly consolidated state of mutual accountability and integrity in the therapeutic system serves a catalytic function, allowing the conflicts to be safely contained, despite intense affect. The therapist's goal in this phase of treatment is to help family members struggle with the elicited conflicts until they reach a new resolution by using the relationships of mutual accountability established in the second phase of treatment. This outcome leads to a transformation in at

least one significant relationship of the symptomatic cycle and a dissolution of the developmental logjam.

Violence in Relationships and the Symptomatic Cycle

The breeding ground for violence is an interpersonal context in which
family members experience only conditional acceptance. That is, they
feel respected and valued only as long as they conform to others' expectations. A family member learns quickly that to be accepted, he must
deny or hide those parts of himself that are unacceptable to others.
These little "suicides" have their counterparts in the little "murders"
that occur as family members disqualify and reject each other, attempting to destroy the parts of others that remind them of the hidden parts
of themselves. People communicate in indirect and mystifying ways to
camouflage these murderous behaviors. Nevertheless, the underlying
hostility leaks out, increasing the isolation and scapegoating in the
family.

As the acts of violence mount up, family members feel increasingly
helpless and powerless. In their efforts to exert control they are prone
to express more overtly the accumulated violence. The ensuing eruption
can be physical or emotional, directed toward others or themselves,
explosive or implosive, short-lived or smoldering, episodic or persistent.
The trigger for the explosion is an abrupt change in the proximity–
distance axis of an intimate relationship, an act that threatens or sym-
bolizes loss of the relationship through abandonment or engulfment.
The actual outburst is provoked by an act, or a sequence of actions,
which is controlling, coercive, or intrusive and which is perceived as a
betrayal by the person who becomes violent.

Family members who have been dealt with in such a violent and
unilateral way feel justified in acting similarly. Violent behaviors thus
become entrenched in the interactions of the symptomatic cycle, both
as stimulus and as response. The unresolved conflicts of the cycle gradually become more and more dangerous to broach. Over time these
conflicts begin to feel irreconcilable as they become inextricably intertwined with the violence. The prospect of change becomes increasingly
frightening, for the family fears that the hidden and seemingly unacceptable parts of its members will emerge. Thus any change, whether
environmental or internal (that is, part of the normal developmental
process), threatens the survival of relationships.

Inducing Change

Having developed an initial understanding of the symptomatic cycle in the first phase of treatment and a stronger grasp of it through embracing its outbreak during the second phase, the therapist is now prepared to engage the struggle. Any event can ignite the process. At times the crisis can be precipitated from a statement or action made by a family member or from a random environmental event. At other times the therapist needs to precipitate it by deliberately altering the distance between herself and at least one member of the family. For example, in the case of the Cabrinis, Rachel will propose an increase in distance between herself and Maria by suggesting that Maria be discharged from the hospital. In the Harmon case, Paul will encourage proximity by challenging Mr. Harmon to adopt a warmer, more understanding relationship with Josh.

The therapist, working from a relationship of trust, encourages family members to challenge her and each other. The question of which relationships to challenge, which conflicts to engage, is the primary one for the therapist in this phase of treatment. The content of the challenge will vary from family to family, although the challenge should be connected to the symptoms, either directly ("Your daughter will die of starvation if your husband continues to pay more attention to his job than to you and her") or through metaphor ("By continuing your affair with your job, you are starving your wife and family"). Relentlessness is the key. The therapist must be comfortable with the intensity; otherwise she may inadvertently respond to her own discomfort by detouring conflict and perpetuating the cycle. She must push for a continuation of the struggle over the precipitated conflict until something new emerges. This may take the form of helping one family member give up the struggle through accepting a new and different reality and grieving the loss of a former belief system. Or the therapist may insist that family members struggle with each other beyond previous thresholds until they arrive at a mutual redefinition of their relationship, resulting in a dissolution of the conflicts rather than, as the family fears, a dissolution of the relationship.

At the outset of treatment it is essential to create a context that ensures physical safety. The therapist must do whatever it takes to prevent physical aggression from breaking out, even if it means stopping a session or insisting that certain family members leave. The therapist who does not attend to and take care of her own needs first cannot be of much value to the family, for such self-denial is part and parcel of the dynamics of the symptomatic cycle. If the therapist feels that danger is imminent, it is prudent to say so. Expressing her own anxiety is likely to elicit the subterranean fears of others in the system, allowing those fears to be dealt with openly and straightforwardly.

By the third phase of treatment, safety has a broader, yet more subtle, connotation than physical protection. A safe context is one built on trusting relationships. Although members of the family may not yet trust each other, they must trust the therapist in order to submit to the stress of change in a way that fosters growth. The same holds when larger systems, such as social agencies, hospitals, and the courts, are involved. If these systems do not also trust the therapist and concur with the goals outlined in the treatment contract, they may withhold their support, leaving the therapist at sea with the family.

Therefore, the safety that is felt at this time means that family members are now willing to take a leap into the unknown with the therapist, viewing their relationship with her as a safety net. This relationship allows the participants in conflict to remain in proximity, preventing escape and simultaneously providing a safe space in which the family's unleashed passions can be channeled productively.

Safety also emanates from the therapist's willingness to accept a variety of outcomes as satisfactory resolutions of the conflicts precipitated in the family during this third phase. If the therapist becomes invested in the details of the resolution, violence may result from the therapist's intention to control the outcome. For example, if Donna believes that Nancy and Carl Monroe should remain married in order to take better care of Jennifer, she may try to force a configuration that is not suited to the needs and desires of the family. The therapist's willingness to accept the family's choice of outcome is not a passive accommodation, but a reflection of her willingness to continue the exploration of new patterns with the family, as treatment enters the fourth phase.

The Cabrinis

AFTER THE EMBRACE: THE LULL

During the two weeks following Maria's admission, the team used the interpersonal and physical contexts of the inpatient milieu and the day treatment program to chip away at the symptomatic cycle. Having solidified her relationship with the family by embracing the runaway, the therapist could now move to use such external resources to assist the family in its reorganizational efforts.

Mr. and Mrs. Cabrini came regularly for therapy sessions, for scheduled activities with their children, and for informal visits day and evening. Maria remained quiet and self-absorbed, but she appeared less frightened. Rachel met daily with the family, and every other day team members met with the siblings as a group. In family therapy sessions a primary focus was for the parents to establish behavioral expectations and activities for Maria that would help her practice in the inpatient unit the skills she would need to function more effectively in the community after discharge. Sessions with the siblings were organized around discussions about family and peer problems and how they could be more supportive of one another. They remained worried about outbreaks of violence.

To increase the siblings' sense of security, the team participated with them in play fights with batacas, bats made out of canvas-covered foam. These fights, which were organized and monitored by the team, allowed people to play out their violent fantasies without literally becoming violent. As Whitaker and Bumberry write: "It's a way of acting dangerous . . . but not being dangerous. It's the people who don't have a chance to play out their violence who become violent" (1988, 188).

Twice a week Mr. and Mrs. Cabrini participated in parent-run group meetings that helped parents of inpatients develop a sense of community regardless of differences in socioeconomic or cultural background. The group organized projects with each others' children based on their own areas of expertise. A parent skilled in mechanics, for example, might teach a child from another family how to build a bookshelf or work on an automobile engine. Having these additional interpersonal resources to draw upon for sustenance and support increases both parents' and childrens' sense of connectedness and diminishes the risk of violence.

All in all, the family and team were settling into a comfortable routine. But that comfort began to concern Rachel. Although the team was building various contexts to encourage differentiation and reorganization in the family, Rachel felt the therapeutic relationship was losing the creative tension that arises from a shared sense of anxiety.

LAYING THE GROUNDWORK FOR CRISIS INDUCTION

A comment made in the next day's team meeting sparked Rachel and the team to increase the system's instability so that new patterns of resolving conflict could unfold. As the team was discussing the lull the Cabrinis had settled into, Tony, one of the child life counselors, remarked: "Joe is awfully private and distant, and Angela still acts like she's in a fog. I'll bet Joe's been molesting Maria, and everybody's keeping it a secret."

Once it was actually voiced, no one on the team was shocked to hear Tony's speculation. Team members talked about how they could best support the family and each other if this speculation proved to be true. Giving up control of such secrets leaves a person vulnerable to the anxiety engendered by being disloyal to her family and can lead to further retreat into isolation, anger, blame, and guilt.

The question facing Rachel and the team was how to act on their hunch—that the family was sitting on a secret that was maintaining Maria's (and perhaps Nicholas's) symptomatic behavior—to induce a crisis. When a therapist senses that family secrets are crippling development and breeding symptoms, she must find a way to deal with them. Her goal should not be simply to find out what the secret is, but more important, to bring the conflicts with which the secret is entangled into the open so that the family can resolve them differently. To do this, the therapist must be prepared to counter the fragmentation in the family that can easily result from the disclosure of the secret. Some groundwork would need to be done by the team so that whatever reaction the family might have could be safely contained.

The team trusted the siblings to be the most effective support system for Maria. Rachel and the team worked out a plan whereby Tony and Joan, the team's psychoeducational specialist, would meet with Maria, Anita, and Bruno to plan for the next family session, while Rachel would observe from behind the one-way mirror, prepared to consult if necessary. In that meeting, the discussion focused quickly on Mr. Cabrini's violence. Here, Tony challenges the siblings' inclination to be indirect with their parents and run from conflict:

TONY: You guys won't get anywhere walking on eggshells around your parents, or hiding from them. There's got to be some other way.

JOAN: *(To Bruno)* So you'll fight? *(To Anita)* You'll be quiet? *(To Maria)* And you'll split? That's no way to settle anything. Don't you trust us to help your parents stay in control?

BRUNO: Nobody's ever done that before. No matter what happens, no matter where we are, Dad first gets mad, then he yells, especially at Mom. She can't defend herself and just shrinks away. It's awful to see.

JOAN: I think we need Rachel in here. We need to find out if she can handle your parents. Because if she can't, maybe you should just keep things the way they are.

Joan left the room to get Rachel, who said: "This is excellent. If they feel free to challenge us and can come to trust us, then they will be closer to trusting their own ability to make difficult things happen." Joan reentered the room with Rachel. Rachel assured the siblings that she would support their confronting their parents and keep the situation under control; however, she also needed help from them.

RACHEL: I'm not going to quit on you. But I need something from you guys. I need you to stick together, support one another, so I can work with your parents. I need you to decide with Tony and Joan who's going to speak up, and how you're going to support each other, no matter what happens. If you abandon each other, then we're all lost.

All three siblings nodded in agreement, although Maria said she was afraid. Bruno agreed not to lose control and Anita agreed to talk even if she was scared.

PRECIPITATING THE CRISIS

Feeling confident that the siblings' protective network had been mobilized, the team was ready to precipitate a crisis. Rachel proposed the following strategy. In the family session that afternoon Rachel would raise the possibility that Maria be discharged from the hospital within a day or two. This proposal of an abrupt change in the proximity–distance axis of the family's relationship with the team would test the family's apparent stability, crystallizing hidden conflicts that might still lurk beneath the surface.

At the family session later that day, Rachel began by asking how things were going.

Mrs. Cabrini: Well, everything's going well at home. Joe and I are talking more. I've not been drinking as much, and the kids are doing better here, even Maria.

Rachel: We agree things are going smoothly. In fact, we were thinking that perhaps since things are going so well, Maria ought to be discharged tomorrow or the next day. She could continue in outpatient therapy at the mental health center.

Maria: *(Looking anxiously at Rachel)* No, no *no!* I can't go home yet. I'm not ready. No, no, it's too soon. *(Silence in the room)*

Mrs. Cabrini: *(Impatiently)* Come on, Maria, what's the matter now? *(Maria is silent.)* What is it, what's the matter with coming home? *(Maria remains silent. Bruno and Anita get restless.)*

Mr. Cabrini: We've been through this before. She just gets quiet. Nothing happens. *(Shouting) I'm sick of it!* She always shuts up and ruins everything.

Rachel: Joe, hold on. *(Speaking quietly but firmly to Mrs. Cabrini)* I think there must be some reason, some problem at home, that leaves her scared and feeling unsafe. I don't know if she'll say what it is. Will you listen to her and handle whatever it is? No matter how bad, no matter how upsetting?

Mrs. Cabrini: *(Haltingly)* If I have to, I will. Maybe she should just come home; maybe some things are better left unsaid.

Rachel: That won't work anymore. She needs you, needs a mother to listen to her, to understand, to talk with her. Silence won't solve anything; you've been that route before.

Mr. Cabrini: *(Upset and angry)* Lay off—can't you see that Maria just needs some space to get herself together?

Rachel: *(Quietly confronting Mr. Cabrini)* Joe, hold on a second. You need to have more faith in your wife. Inside her there's resilience and strength. If anyone can hear what Maria has to say, it's her. *(Turning to Mrs. Cabrini)* Isn't it, Angela?

Mrs. Cabrini: Yes.

Rachel: *(Softly and warmly)* Angela, she needs to know that you want to hear. Maybe she still doesn't realize all that *you've* been through in your life.

Mrs. Cabrini: *(Nodding)* Maybe not. Maybe no one does.

Rachel: Why don't you tell her? Tell her straight out; don't sugarcoat it.

CRISIS: THE SECRET IS DISCLOSED

Mrs. Cabrini spoke again of her childhood, of the physical abuse at the hands of her mother, the constant belittling and criticism. She said she never let on how deeply it upset her. For years she cried only when she was alone. There was no mistaking Mrs. Cabrini's pain and sense of isolation, no overlooking how her own pain during Maria's childhood had blinded her to Maria's needs.

Responding to her sense that there was even more to be said, Rachel asked Mrs. Cabrini what the worst part of it had been. There was a long silence, and then with her face to the floor, in a shaky, muffled voice, Mrs. Cabrini said she had been sexually abused as a child.

There was a stunned silence. Rachel asked how long it had gone on, and Mrs. Cabrini said, "For years, on and off. I never told anyone. I couldn't tell, my parents would have killed me." Maria began shaking. Mr. Cabrini's eyes were glued to his shoes. Rachel asked Mrs. Cabrini who had done it. Mrs. Cabrini hesitated a few seconds, then murmured that it had been her brother, Billy. The words were no sooner out of her mouth than Bruno erupted, "What the hell is he doing still living in our house?"

Before Rachel could even ask who this person was, and why no one had ever mentioned him before, Maria abruptly blurted out, "That's why I can't go home. He did it to me, too!" She began sobbing loudly, hiding her face in her hands. The emotional tidal wave that surged through the room in the wake of Maria's disclosure was as strong as if someone had dropped dead. As with death, no amount of anticipation of the event could take away the raw shock of it.

It was not surprising that the Cabrinis had hidden from the team the fact of the uncle's presence in the house. A veil of secrecy is characteristic of severely symptomatic families. A major threat to the family's connection to the team was necessary to precipitate the disclosure of what was really going on at home. As the session continued, the room was engulfed in uproar.

BRUNO: *(To Maria)* Why didn't you tell me?
MARIA: *(Barely audible and crying)* It wouldn't have made any difference.
BRUNO: What do you mean? How can you say that?
MARIA: They knew all the time.
BRUNO: Who knew?
MARIA: Mommy and Daddy.
MR. CABRINI: Don't say that, we didn't know.

RACHEL: Joe, stop it. Let her finish talking.

MARIA: They're the ones who are sick, not me. They see and hear only what they want to, not what's really happening.

BRUNO: You knew they knew?

MARIA: Yes.

BRUNO: Did anyone else know?

MARIA: No, I never told anyone.

ANITA: How do you know Mom and Dad knew?

MARIA: Because I knew she walked in on him in my room and then went back out. Not just once, several times. She just played dumb, like she didn't see it.

BRUNO: I'll kill that son of a bitch.

MR. CABRINI: You'd better calm down and shut up. *(He gets up and begins to move toward Bruno.)*

MARIA: Oh, no! *(She jumps up and runs out of the room.)*

CHANGE: THE SIBLINGS EMBRACE MARIA'S RUNAWAY

Maria's flight in the heat of conflict reflected the family's pattern of isolation and fragmentation: the heart of the symptomatic cycle. To capitalize on the increasing strength of the sibling group, Rachel asked Bruno and Anita to pursue and comfort their sister and return to the session with her when they felt prepared to face their parents again. Rachel also asked Joan, who was in the session as a support to the siblings, to accompany them to provide additional support, while she stayed with the parents to understand why they allowed Uncle Billy to stay in the house.

RACHEL: *(To Mrs. Cabrini)* I know you're very upset, but I need to understand why you've allowed your brother to stay in the house.

MR. CABRINI: You can't believe everything Maria says.

RACHEL: Hang on a second, Joe. Let's listen to Angela.

MRS. CABRINI: He did it to me, but that was long ago. I didn't want to face it with her all over again. I knew he had touched her once, but I told him to stop, and I thought he had. This whole thing is a nightmare.

RACHEL: Say more, Angela.

MRS. CABRINI: My brother, Billy, he's slow, you know. He doesn't understand things. I promised my mother I'd take care of him. She never knew what he did to me. I couldn't tell her. It would've broken her heart. We always go easy on Billy—we have to. Oh, God *(sobbing)*, we can't kick him out—he's got nowhere to go; he can't survive on his own.

RACHEL: *(To Mr. Cabrini)* Your wife needs your support now. *(Mr. Cabrini moves toward her and tentatively takes her hand.)*

Meanwhile, the siblings returned. Maria was distraught, but she walked in with Anita, Bruno, and Joan and sat down between her brother and sister. Mr. Cabrini was trying to comfort his wife, and the room was quiet. Rachel took a moment to think.

Maria's having kept her sexual abuse secret had obviated the need for her mother to deal with a number of longstanding conflicts, such as her ambivalence about having to take care of the brother who had molested her and having to choose between her daughter's needs and her brother's. Mrs. Cabrini's intense need to be a loyal sister to her brother allowed her to neglect Maria. She was even able to persuade her husband to have Uncle Billy—who without Mr. Cabrini's knowledge had molested his wife and daughter—live in their home. Yet the toxic effects of the secret had permeated the family, leaking out and igniting explosions of various other sorts, probably including Maria's outbursts and the fights between Mr. Cabrini and Bruno. Although the team had provoked the disclosure of the secret, the next step would be considerably more important. That step was to help the family reorganize in whatever way was necessary to protect Maria from the threat of continued violation, while attempting to prevent the total breakdown of the family in the process.

Rachel's thoughts raced with all the issues that would soon need to be dealt with. Now Maria would need to talk more about the abuse, when it occurred, what had actually happened, when it stopped if it had stopped, how to stop it if it had not, and how to avoid future abuse. The team would need to find out whether Anita, Bruno, or Nicholas (and for that matter, any other children in the community) had been abused. Mrs. Cabrini would have to deal with her sense of guilt concerning her brother and her daughter. Mr. and Mrs. Cabrini would have to begin to make their home secure to demonstrate to their children their commitment to change. They would also need to involve the authorities to be sure that Billy would not abuse anyone else.

Rachel did not want to debate with anyone what had "really" happened with Uncle Billy. The immediate task was to use the revelation to assist the parents in taking care of Maria in ways they had not done previously. To capitalize on the instability of the moment, she focused on the concrete steps the family would need to take to keep Maria and the other children safe. Here, Rachel challenges the parents to remove Uncle Billy from the house.

RACHEL: *(To Mrs. Cabrini)* I know you're loyal to your brother and I understand you feel obligated to care for him, but things have gone too far. For Maria's sake, you need to have him leave the house, and get some help for him.

BRUNO: I agree. He's got to leave. We need him out of the house, *now.* Look at what he's done. *(Anita nods in assent.)*

RACHEL: Right. *(To parents)* I agree with your kids. He needs to leave. And you need to take care of that. There's been too much accommodation and protection, too many secrets. Maria also needs to consider pressing charges. She may not be up to it now, but we should talk more about it.

MR. CABRINI: *(Raising his voice and turning to Rachel)* Wait a minute, it's up to her *(pointing to his wife).* She'll do what she wants. It's her brother. Why don't you stay out of it? It's not your business.

RACHEL: Hang on a moment, Joe. It *is* my business, because you want me to help you with Maria. I don't want to see her trying suicide again, and she's at risk as long as Billy is still around.

MR. CABRINI: You can't tell my wife what to do. I don't think you understand. Why don't you just leave her alone? *(Turns to his wife)* Come on, let's get out of here; this is ridiculous!

MRS. CABRINI: Wait a minute, Joe, calm down; we can't just leave now and run. *(Turning to Rachel)* I don't know what to do. I know Maria needs me, but I'm afraid of what will happen if my husband gets too upset.

MR. CABRINI: I've had it with this bullshit! *(He stands up and looks at his wife.)* I'm leaving. Are you coming with me? *(Mrs. Cabrini looks at the floor, and Mr. Cabrini storms out of the room. No one moves. All eyes turn to Rachel.)*

CHANGE: BRUNO EMBRACES MR. CABRINI'S RUNAWAY

When a family is in a state of disorientation and disequilibrium, suspended between the old and the new, as the Cabrinis were, it is most open to change. This is the most opportune moment for the therapist to induce change in the relationships between herself and the family and among family members. Rachel's map alerted her to the danger of stepping in and taking over for the family at moments of intense stress, as other professionals had done before. Instead, she felt the challenge to the parents' pattern of abandonment should come from within the family. Trusting the relationship she and the team had developed with Bruno, Rachel will look to him to pursue Mr. Cabrini and interrupt the symptomatic cycle. Notice how Mrs. Cabrini reverts back to the cycle in her anxiety over Rachel's suggestion, attempting to avoid conflict by first pulling in Rachel, then Maria.

MRS. CABRINI: *(Turning to Rachel)* I don't know what to do when he gets crazy like that. He won't listen to me.

RACHEL: What do you want to do?

MRS. CABRINI: I don't know. Maybe he'll listen to you. Can you get him?

RACHEL: I think it would be better if someone in the family would go after him and talk with him. When there is conflict in the family, people give up on each other and the professionals rush in and take over. I don't want to do what everyone else has done—that doesn't help. I would suggest that Bruno talk with him.

MRS. CABRINI: Bruno? Are you crazy? Bruno always provokes Joe, and Joe explodes, and they end up fighting.

RACHEL: Well, I think that Bruno has grown up a lot. He understands his father better and is able to control his temper.

MRS. CABRINI: *(Looking at Maria, who begins shaking)* What do you think?

MARIA: I'm scared. I'm afraid they'll get into a fight, like they always do.

RACHEL: *(Looking at Bruno)* Can you talk with him and listen to him without reacting, without exploding? Your sister needs your help.

BRUNO: Yes, I can do it.

MRS. CABRINI: Are you sure?

BRUNO: Yes. It'll be okay, Mom.

With Rachel's support, Bruno reassured his mother that there would be no bloodshed, regardless of his stepfather's reaction. He explained that he felt less hatred toward Mr. Cabrini since he had heard him talk about the pain of his childhood, and that he felt he could talk with him calmly now. As Bruno spoke, his mother relaxed and agreed to let him pursue her husband. Fifteen minutes later, Bruno and Mr. Cabrini returned to the session.

MR. CABRINI: *(awkwardly, looking at his wife)* I want to apologize for running out. I'm sorry, I really am. We talked, no fighting. He listened, and then he told me to come back and talk.

RACHEL: Can you let your wife know what Bruno said to you, not all the details, just the heart of it?

MR. CABRINI: *(With tears in his eyes)* He told me he loved me—he wanted us to stop fighting; he wanted me to stop running away from my problems and the problems of the family. I'm sorry for what I've done to you and the family. *(Looking at Maria)* And I'm sorry, Maria, for letting you down. Bruno is right; we need to get Billy out of the house and get help for him.

RACHEL: *(To Bruno)* You did a good job. You really came through. *(To Mr. Cabrini)* He's a good kid. He cares a lot about you and the family. In the past half hour, he has been very helpful, don't you think so?

MR. CABRINI: Yes, he has.

At this point, wanting to leave everyone with a vivid picture of the changes that had occurred, Rachel recommended taking a break for several hours and then reconvening to plan how the parents would make the house safe.

SETTING THE REORGANIZATION

Rachel, Joan, and the family met two hours later and discussed how the parents could implement the practical steps needed to make their household safe: one, tell Uncle Billy about Maria's disclosure of the abuse; two, make it clear that he would have to leave their home within a few days; three, call the proper authorities to get information about appropriate facilities to deal with Billy's needs. The team was aware of the difficulties involved in finding a facility that worked with mentally retarded adult sexual offenders, but the pressing concern was that action be taken immediately. If necessary, a temporary shelter might have to do, until the family could explore more adequate arrangements in the community.

The fourth step, in anticipation of Maria's return home, would be to modify the sleeping arrangements in the house in order to build clearer boundaries and provide a greater sense of physical security. The family discussed the following arrangement: Maria would move from her attic room on the third floor to the second floor, where she would share a room with Anita; Bruno would occupy a room nearby on the second floor; and Mr. and Mrs. Cabrini would move into Maria's old room. The parents went home to take care of these matters.

In reviewing the two stages of crisis induction in this phase of treatment, we see that the first stage involved anchoring Maria in a supportive containment with her siblings and the siblings in a supportive containment with the team, in anticipation of the crisis that would ensue.

Following the disclosure of the secret of sexual abuse, the team emphasized the heightened need for vigilance and containment to prevent any further acts or threats of abuse or violence, exemplified by insisting that the parents inform Uncle Billy that the secret was now out, and by requiring that he leave the home for a protected and supervised setting where he could receive treatment.

The next stage, planning for the reorganization of the entire system, provides the grist for the final phase of treatment. Family members' struggles to come to grips with the secret were going to be exceedingly painful. Dealing with the pain in the context of the therapeutic system, however, would allow them to struggle with each other to reach a new resolution. The collapse of the wall between Bruno and Mr. Cabrini created a climate of relief, in which conflicts could be dealt with without the emergence of unbridled aggression and violence. Bruno and Anita appeared ready to protect their sister, and the redistribution of rooms spoke of a containment policy on the part of the parents. The team would need to support and monitor the family's plan in order to prevent the dismantlement of this protective network by the parents' abdicating once again and protecting Uncle Billy.

In cases of abuse and violence, the destructive patterns often recur despite dramatic rituals of penance and forgiveness and despite the selection of monitors and protectors from the extended family. Therefore, therapists should not put excessive faith in the family's ability to create its own protective system or in their own therapeutic prowess. External controls, not merely intrafamilial restraints, must be immediately accessible and active. Without these in place, the family's tendency to relax its vigilance and exonerate the abuser may return. Therapeutic biases toward keeping the family together at all costs are unwarranted in situations of repeated violence and abuse.

The Harmons

LAYING THE GROUNDWORK FOR CRISIS INDUCTION

In Paul's next session with the Harmon family, Barbara's opening statement signals that Paul's previous embrace of the runaway would need to be repeated. "I've been trying to work with Robert," she said, "but I just keep feeling that all he wants to do is punish Josh. He does that a lot. If he gets angry with me, he'll punish Josh. Like you said in the last session, the way he fights me through Josh is wrong." The indication that Paul had not yet fully harnessed the runaway between the parents was that Barbara was communicating distrust of her husband while inviting Paul to collude with her. Even though Barbara had previously expressed awareness that protecting Josh from his father encouraged both her son's immaturity and her husband's retreat, she remained on alert, prepared to step in at a moment's notice.

In working with severely symptomatic families, the therapist's initial attempt to embrace the runaway in the second phase of treatment is often insufficient. Repeated efforts, and stepping up the intensity of pursuit, may be necessary, for embracing the runaway is not merely a technique, it is a process of fortifying relationships. The challenge for the therapist is to redirect a distrusting parent in flight back toward the partner, so that he or she is embracing the partner, not the therapist.

Therefore, in the initial stage of precipitating a crisis, Paul first embraced Barbara's continued runaway by accepting and working with her view of the triangle comprised of herself, Robert, and Josh. He asked Barbara to explore what made her husband behave so harshly toward Josh. Paul assumed that there was some sort of emotional knot within Robert that mirrored his habitual impasse with his wife and children. If he could help Barbara identify this knot, it would point toward a path of disentanglement.

In the course of the ensuing conversation, Robert repeatedly castigated himself for being a failure as a father. When Barbara tried to reassure him, he responded by complaining that she didn't understand. When she tried to help by pointing out how he could change, he retreated even further into angry isolation.

In light of Paul's formulation that Robert's isolation was a central problem in the family, he decided to find a way of connecting even more strongly with Robert himself. Paul hoped to create a portal through which Barbara, Josh, and Suzanne could join him in a more solid relationship with Robert, much as Rachel did when Maria began talking about the devil. Paul anticipated that pursuing Robert would unleash a crisis.

PRECIPITATING A CRISIS OF GRIEF

Paul entered the conversation by sharing his own affective response to the symptomatic pattern in which Barbara persistently encountered emotional dead ends when trying to connect with her husband. To increase the intensity, he moved closer to them and injected his own feelings into the conversation, challenging Robert's avoidance of painful matters.

PAUL: *(Speaking slowly and softly to Barbara)* There's something that Robert has trouble swallowing. It makes me feel sad, so very sad when I'm around him, yet I don't know what it is. Is it his sister's illness, his father's death, his alienation from his mother? I'm not sure. But there's something that comes over him, something that leaves him feeling unhappy, overwhelmed, lost.

BARBARA: He won't talk to his mother. He tells me to call her for him, or sometimes he'll call just to hear the sound of her voice and then hang up. God, how it must hurt him. As for his father, well, we can't bring his father back. *(She hesitates, then continues.)* Sometimes, when I'm not angry at Robert, I wonder how he bears it all, but then I think, what else can he do? *(Her voice begins to crack, and Robert looks at her in surprise.)*

The room filled with sadness. When Barbara said, "As for his father, well, we can't bring his father back," she hinted at an understanding of what her husband might have been experiencing, but her manner of expressing it had the effect of curtailing further discussion. It was as if they had agreed that when events could not be controlled, discussion should be closed, and powerful feelings should not be explored. This arrangement, in which Barbara discounted her understanding of Robert's longing for his father, cut her off from him.

In this phase of treatment, the therapist's task is to use the new sense of competence family members have gained in the preceding phase to bring about a crisis through which they can discover new ways of relating to old problems and conflicts. One way of precipitating this crisis is for the therapist to find out what particular element of family members' emotional responses creates an intense personal response in her and to share that response with the family. The therapist's openness helps family members to free themselves from their habitual restrictions in regard to the issue at hand.

Paul did not simply want to prescribe a corrective emotional experience, namely, for Robert to express his feelings about his father's death. Paul chose to focus on the death of Robert's father because he sensed that Robert's emotional distance from his family was exacerbated by unresolved grief. Paul's choice also sprang from his empathic connection with Robert, since Paul's own father had died when he was a teenager. He felt that he stood a better chance of increasing his proximity to Robert if the connection between them was authentic. The therapist's choice of an issue to pursue is idiosyncratic to each family and each therapist; if one does not become the fulcrum for the struggle, another will.

As Paul and Barbara continued to talk, her speech became much slower and was filled with emotion. Robert listened intently with a sad expression.

PAUL: Maybe he misses his father.

BARBARA: He may. He may miss him very much.

PAUL: Maybe he's not over that.

BARBARA: He never cried when he died.

ROBERT: *(Shakes his head as if he still can't believe it)* No, I didn't.

PAUL: Do you think that there was something unfinished between him and his dad?

BARBARA: Maybe. I know his father was a very handy person, and we moved into our house right after he died, and Robert would say "Gee, if my father was alive he could help us with the painting and the papering." He wanted to continue with his father.

PAUL: That must hurt.

BARBARA: But his father was always correcting him, always showing him how to do things better. He never got over it. He never learned to overcome the criticism.

Paul felt tremendous compassion for Robert, for he sensed the dimness of the possibility of Robert's emerging from his father's shadow into the light. From Paul's own experience, he could appreciate the impasse created for Robert by such an unfulfilled legacy. His instant association to Barbara's last remark was, "That's exactly how Robert now relates to *his* son!" And with that thought, Paul saw an opportunity to induce a crisis out of Robert's longstanding impasse, a crisis that could be a turning point in Robert's relationships with his family. Perhaps Paul could activate and help channel the powerful feelings with which Robert was struggling to lead him closer to, rather than farther away from, his son.

COMPLETING THE CIRCLE: LINKING THE CRISIS TO THE PRESENTING SYMPTOM

The therapist must link the presenting symptom to the relationship structure she is challenging, since it is the symptom that is the family's calling card. The Harmons' desire for treatment came from their distress over Josh, not from concern about Robert's depression. To bolster Robert's motivation to go farther into uncharted and painful territory, Paul would need to show that the journey was connected to Josh's presenting symptoms.

Since Paul believed that the way to help Robert move out of his longstanding isolation and melancholy was through changing his relationship with Josh, Paul brought Josh into the dialogue. In the following sequence, Paul stays close to both Josh and his father, supporting Robert in his approach to Josh and helping Josh to be direct with Robert.

PAUL: *(To Robert, amplifying Barbara's previous statement)* Maybe that's why you get so caught up in this young man's stuff *(pointing to Josh)*. But then Josh gets mad, and you feel mad, and then Josh feels sad, and then both of you feel sad and powerless.

ROBERT: Yes.

PAUL: *(To Josh)* Did you know that your dad was as sensitive as you?

JOSH: No.

PAUL: Who do you think is having the hardest time with your growing up?

JOSH: My dad. He always treats me like I'm his two-year-old son.

PAUL: Unless you tell him not to.

JOSH: Even if I tell him, he'll still do it.

PAUL: Until he knows you really mean it.

JOSH: *(Getting upset)* I used to tell him, "Dad, I know how to do everything" . . . but he never believes me.

PAUL: Tell him how it makes you feel.

JOSH: It hurts.

ROBERT: You hate me?

JOSH: Sometimes.

PAUL: *(To Robert)* Where does that leave you? Cause he's got to know.

ROBERT: Well I don't want him to hate me, that's for sure.

JOSH: So stop treating me like a baby.

ROBERT: That's true. But every time I get into your life I get this attitude from you. Like I'm butting in, so I back off.

PAUL: He pulls you into his life about suicide or drugs or any other kind of stupid, impulsive behavior, and you call that butting in?

Paul's last statement was meant to reinvoke Josh's symptoms, using them to maintain proximity and create more intensity in Josh's relationship with his father. He wanted to remind Robert that retreat was irresponsible. To continue the discussion and mobilize a reorganization of the system, Paul would need to remain in proximity to each of them, encouraging them to stay in close contact with each other.

PAUL: *(To Josh)* You see the issue here—and maybe this is what's really difficult—it seems to me the issue has to do with respect. And it may be that your dad never helped you feel like he respected that you could take care of yourself. So maybe you haven't had that sense of respect from another man. And *(to Robert)* it seems to me that that's what this is all about. It's about learning how to respect yourself and how to help your son respect you and how you can respect him. Josh needs you to respect him so that he can talk to you about how lonely it feels to be in school and not have any friends, or how he sometimes feels left out by his sister. Cause I think he feels all of that. I think that you guys talk about his screwing up instead of talking about how he really feels.

ROBERT: He won't tell me how he really feels. He hasn't in the past.

PAUL: *(Emphatically)* He needs to. But he'll only tell you how he feels if he believes that you'll be able to listen without running scared.

ROBERT: I know.

In the long conversation that followed, Robert felt permission to reveal his ongoing, previously submerged inner torment related to his family of origin. He talked with Paul about the relationship he never had with his own father and the feelings of disconnectedness that had previously been expressed through violent outbursts or emotional withdrawal.

SETTING THE REORGANIZATION

Robert appeared to derive an intense sense of relief from Paul's ability to tolerate the intensity of his feelings. In the following dialogue, Paul crystallizes and expands this process of reaching out to Robert by talking about the death of his own father, which further allows Robert to plumb the depths of his feelings, yet still reach out to his son.

PAUL: You know, my father died when I was seventeen. He never saw my kids—never knew them. Never saw my house. Never saw me become a man. I don't know if that was your experience, too. It sounds like it was. You know, there's a torch that passes from father to son. And I don't think that ever happened to you.

ROBERT: *(Tears in his eyes)* No, it never did.

PAUL: And Josh is asking you to pass the torch to him. And you're saying, "I can't. Because I don't even have it to give." Robert, he loves you very much.

ROBERT: *(Crying)* I know he does. I know it.

PAUL: It hurts you.

ROBERT: Uh-huh. He has a lot of compassion, too.

PAUL: He's a very caring guy. I think sons can sell themselves short. I think they believe it's a miracle if somebody likes them. Josh is looking all the time for people not to like him.

ROBERT: *(Nodding slowly)* Like me.

PAUL: Yeah.

ROBERT: Terrible way to be.

PAUL: Yeah. Do you think that I like you, Robert?

ROBERT: Yeah. Maybe I'm letting you like me.

PAUL: I do like you, and I'm pleased you're sharing more of yourself with your family. I'm not interested in telling you how to love your son. But I am telling you he's asking for a torch. So you will have to light one. Maybe you have to go to your father's grave and talk to him. Maybe you have to get some pictures of him and just talk to him. Passing the torch to Josh will help you be free.

ROBERT: I never grew up.

PAUL: You know, Josh, I think you're going to have to invite your father to spend some time with you.

JOSH: Without my mom? *(Barbara smiles at Paul and pulls her chair back a little.)*

PAUL: Without your mom. Just you and your dad. Go to the gym, play some basketball. Where you're doing something together, instead of him telling you what to do, or you telling him to back off. Your dad looks at you, and it's like he's looking into a mirror. I think he gets scared. So, are you ready to invite him and not let him stand you up?

JOSH: *(Head down, mumbling)* Would you go with me to the . . .

PAUL: Wait, wait, wait! Don't speak so softly.

JOSH: *(In a clear voice)* Could you go with me to the gym today, Dad?

ROBERT: Sure.

PAUL: What do you want him to do with you?

JOSH: Just be a dad. *(Looking at Robert)* I just want you to be yourself.

ROBERT: You are going to help me do that, right?

JOSH: Yes, I'm going to try.

Recalling moments of nurturance through physical contact with his own father, Paul prompted Josh to ask Robert for a hug, giving Josh a concrete way of helping his father take the step of reaching out to him. As Paul watched Robert and Josh embrace each other, he sensed the awakening of a vitality that had been deadened for a long time. Paul saw the stirrings of a transformation in Robert, both individually and in his relationship with Josh, which Barbara endorsed and respected.

Paul precipitated a crisis in this phase of treatment by first reembracing the runaway represented by Barbara's persistent feelings of distrust for her husband. With his relationship with her on firmer ground, Paul tapped into his personal experience and allowed his feelings to guide him to intensify and deepen the relationship he had cultivated with Robert in the previous phase. Barbara supported this process by listening quietly and respecting the boundaries surrounding Josh's pursuit of his father.

Paul's empathic attunement to Robert's pain differed considerably in emotional tone from Donna's aggressive challenge to Carl in her first session with the Monroes, and from Rachel's pursuit of Maria's encounter with the devil. Nevertheless, all three situations illustrate how the therapist can use her own affective responses as leverage in creating therapeutic relationships and in transforming the relationships of the symptomatic cycle.

The Monroes

LAYING THE GROUNDWORK FOR CRISIS INDUCTION

The events of the two days following the initial session with the Monroes demonstrated that it was possible, at least temporarily, for the parents to work together to supervise Jennifer, and that in that context, she could behave in a nonsymptomatic manner. Then came the runaway, which could be seen as a response to the increased compression of the family created through the task of Carl and Nancy's monitoring Jennifer over a three-day period.

As a consequence of Brian and Donna's embracing the runaway, momentum had been generated toward several goals of the consultation. For instance, Brian had begun to change his role as Jennifer's primary caretaker, using the increasing strength and flexibility of his relationship with Donna as both an anchor and a catapult. After Donna helped him to recognize his previous overidentification with Nancy, he started to differentiate himself by challenging her to take greater responsibility for her daughter and to engage Carl in fulfilling his role as Jennifer's father. Because it occurred in a safe context, this struggle for differentiation allowed Brian and Nancy to reconnect on a more empathic level, one on which Nancy felt understood and accepted for the first time. The issue now was how to use their rapprochement as leverage to disrupt the symptomatic cycle.

The ingredients of a crisis come from the family. Often crises are induced by accentuating conflicts that emerge during the course of treatment. At times, random events in the family's life provide the focal point around which a crisis is precipitated. Here, Donna hears of an unexpected occurrence in the Monroe family that she and Brian will later use to help precipitate a crisis during this phase.

Early on the morning after the last session, Brian called to inform Donna that he had just received news from Nancy that her mother had been rushed to the hospital in the middle of the night. It seemed that she may have had a stroke, but no one was sure. Jennifer spent most of the night in the hospital with her mother and grandmother. Nancy said she and Jennifer would be attending the session as planned, unless her mother's condition worsened.

Later that day, at the start of the session, Donna asked Nancy what had happened.

NANCY: After our session yesterday, and after what happened last night between me and Jennifer, I wanted to talk to Mom, so I called her late last night. Her speech was all slurred, and she couldn't express herself well. I took Jennifer and went right over to Mom's apartment, and found that she was having trouble walking, too. We called Dr. Carmody, took her to the hospital, and they admitted her—they think she had some sort of stroke. They'll know more in a few days.

DONNA: I'm really sorry to hear about your mom, Nancy. How are you doing?

NANCY: Well, of course I'm upset, I just hope she'll be okay. *(Pauses to compose herself)* But I'm okay. Yesterday's session gave me strength.

DONNA: *(Looking at Jennifer)* How does your mother seem to you?

JENNIFER: She seems stronger. The way she talked to me last night was really different. . . . It was strange, but I felt like she could handle things better.

DONNA: Handle what better?

JENNIFER: My vomiting, Dad's drinking, even Grandma getting sick.

As they listen to what happened the previous evening, Donna and Brian encounter once again the symptomatic cycle—the family's triangular arrangement in which Jennifer enters a parental conflict and Carl winds up leaving the field.

DONNA: *(To Brian)* I think we ought to find out more about what happened between the two of them last night. It sounds like something has changed. *(Donna pulls her chair back to be less central.)*

NANCY: We went home after the session, and for a while nobody talked to anybody. Your comment *(looking at Brian)* about "maybe you don't need Carl's help after all" really got me thinking. *(Carl looks worriedly at Nancy.)* When we sat down to dinner, I told Jennifer what she needed to eat, and right away she started whining and fussing. She tried to get her father to back me off, but I told him to just sit there next to me and be quiet, and I'd let him know if I needed him to do anything. Instead, he got up and left the room.

CARL: *(To Brian)* Yesterday Nancy said that when I got involved I made things worse, so I figured maybe I should leave the table, so I wouldn't get in her way.

SOLIDIFYING THE FRAME

The pattern of conflict avoidance between the parents was as predictable as if it had been choreographed. Donna will use her relationship with Brian to challenge him to ignite a fire in the family. She will encourage him to push the conflict between Nancy and Carl beyond their usual threshold of tolerance, urging Nancy to challenge Carl's absence in a direct and unyielding way. Donna will define Nancy as the key to her daughter's growth by asserting a causal connection between Jennifer's developmental impasse and the lack of collaboration between her parents. Such a linear formulation, though an oversimplification, is an effective strategy for generating intensity and activating parents to take greater responsibility for their participation in the process of change.

DONNA: I'm beginning to think that Carl is finally hearing Nancy's message—that she would prefer him to move out, and let her deal with Jennifer alone.

BRIAN: But how could he leave now? He can't leave before he and

Nancy have worked out a viable way of parenting Jennifer. If I were Jennifer, and my dad walked out on me and my mother at this point, I'd see him as selfish and hate him for abandoning me.

DONNA: I see this as a crucial moment in Jennifer's life. A lot is at stake, and Nancy is pivotal. She has to take a clear position with Carl and find a way to engage him in sharing the parenting responsibilities. Her threats and back-and-forth pattern is destructive to Jennifer, to Carl, and to herself.

BRIAN: I agree, Donna. *(Turning to Nancy)* Well, what's it going to be, Nancy?

NANCY: I *do* want Carl to support me and get involved with Jennifer. *(To Carl)* I don't want you to make matters worse, Carl, but it doesn't help me when you disappear either, because Jennifer just takes that as implicit proof of your disapproval with whatever I'm doing. When Jennifer saw that you weren't going to rescue her last night, she started escalating. She began shrieking and crying, and threatened me with everything she could think of. When she started talking about killing herself, I got really anxious. I started thinking, Where the hell are you two *(gesturing at Donna and Brian)* when I need you? What am I supposed to do now? All of a sudden, I thought about being here yesterday afternoon and how horrible I felt about everything that had gone wrong in my life. And I remembered how much better I felt when you *(looks at Brian)* just stayed with me. You didn't try to do something to make me feel better, you were just *there . . .* you helped me just to sit with those feelings, and it wasn't so awful as long as we could face them together.

So I started to wonder if I could do the same thing with Jennifer. Instead of trying to make something happen, I could just *be* with her. Maybe if I found out about the terror and the loneliness that made her feel like committing suicide, instead of taking it as a threat or a personal attack, we could face it together at that moment.

Donna's position of staying close to Brian and accepting his dilemma, while simultaneously expecting him to be authentic and challenging with Nancy, was isomorphically replicated in Nancy's position with Jennifer. In effect, Nancy embraced Jennifer's participation in the dinner table runaway, much as Bruno and Anita pursued Maria after she revealed her secret and fled from the room. The family's ability to embrace its own runaway is one of the surest indications to the therapist that a therapeutic system has coalesced. Brian will now engage Jennifer to understand more about her experience of this event.

BRIAN: *(To Nancy)* That makes a lot of sense to me. I feel we're on the same track now. So Jennifer, what was it like for you?

JENNIFER: Mom told me that she didn't want me to die, but she said she knew she couldn't physically stop me. She said if I kept acting like that she would take me to the hospital, but it wasn't like an angry threat—she was really calm about it. She said she'd even commit me involuntarily if she had to, but if she did, she'd still stay with me and keep asking what was going on inside of me. She told me that she could accept that I felt like I wanted to die sometimes, but that she couldn't accept not understanding what it meant to me. And then *(beginning to cry)* she came over and put her arms around me, and she said she wanted to read a book to me.

DONNA: A book?

JENNIFER: *(Still crying)* Yeah, it was my favorite book when I was little. I used to sit in her lap and have her read it to me over and over again. But I had completely forgotten about it—I hadn't seen it for years. Maybe you know it—it's called *The Runaway Bunny.*

Donna knew that book well. It is an old children's picture book (Brown 1942) about a young bunny who issues a series of challenges to his mother. Each time he threatens her with an abrupt separation, she responds in a way that maintains a connection. In the end, the little bunny concludes: "I might just as well stay where I am and be your little bunny.' And so he did."

Jennifer recounted the gist of the story, and then went on to describe the tremendous relief she experienced when her mother read it to her. Her mother's closeness and nurturance, combined with the permission to be herself—even if that meant feeling suicidal—provided Jennifer with a feeling of peace. She mentioned that even after eating she had no impulse to vomit or flee to her room. She felt content and stayed close by her mother through the rest of the evening and night, including the vigil in her grandmother's hospital room.

To Donna, Jennifer's experience was clearly a response to her mother's unconditional acceptance. Nancy's determination to stay with Jennifer at the edge of the cliff, rather than responding to Jennifer's suicidal statements with either abandoning helplessness or angry efforts to control her, allowed her to approach Jennifer with more nurturance. A sense of new possibilities was emerging in their relationship.

Meanwhile, Carl was listening intently to Nancy's and Jennifer's comments. When they finished, he spoke up and asked whether his participation in treatment was still necessary, given his wife's new confidence in her ability to handle the situation on her own.

CONFRONTING THE PARENTAL IMPASSE

When the rigidity of a parent–child relationship begins to loosen, the therapist may be tempted to focus on consolidating that change, neglecting the need to confront the accompanying impasse in the relationship between the parents. In this case, Nancy's new sense of competence with Jennifer provoked Carl to start questioning whether his family needed him after all. Donna wondered how much isolation Carl could tolerate before he started to entertain thoughts of suicide himself.

Donna felt that the change between Jennifer and Nancy could be consolidated and sustained only if a complimentary change in Carl's participation with Nancy and Jennifer were achieved. It would not be sufficient for Nancy to find a way to stay with Jennifer on the cliff; Carl, too, would need to join his daughter there and not allow himself to back off or be sent away. The parental conflict would have to be pushed harder; the temperature would have to rise higher still to reach a crisis point.

Donna decided to use Jennifer's grandmother's stroke, an event that threatened several relationships in the family. Her stroke could serve as a triggering device for Nancy to engage more intensively with Carl. Donna began by addressing Carl's question about his participation, pointing out to him that the effectiveness of Nancy's increased competence, although beneficial and desirable, was at this point entirely contingent on her physical presence and availability.

To persuade Carl of the importance of his involvement and the dangers inherent in counting exclusively on one parent to provide support and connectedness to Jennifer, Brian and Donna made their concerns concrete. Jennifer might begin to worry, Donna said, that her mother might become suddenly ill from the stress of dealing with so many problems. Fearful that her own difficulties could add to Nancy's burden, Jennifer might shy away from contact with Nancy, despite her vital need for it. And what if Nancy's mother didn't recover from her illness? How would her incapacity or death affect Nancy's emotional availability? These questions shook Nancy, prompting her to talk about the dilemma she faced regarding these possibilities.

NANCY: Last night Mom told me how scared she is that she's going to die. With the hypertension and all, she's always had that fear in the back of her mind. She made me promise that I wouldn't let her die alone. But I don't know how I can keep that promise in the situation we're in now. Carl's no help—look at what he did at the dinner table last night when things got heated.

JENNIFER: *(Shivers, and mumbles something under her breath)*

BRIAN: What's that, Jennifer?

JENNIFER: I said if I wasn't around anymore, it would be a lot easier for everyone.

The chill of death had entered the room once again. In their first meeting Jennifer told Donna that without the protection of her symptoms she would die. The previous day the stark reality of Jennifer's overdose had pervaded the office. With her mother's hospitalization, Nancy was threatened by death from yet another direction.

USING THE SYMPTOM TO AMPLIFY INTENSITY

Brian's efforts to explore and empathize with Nancy's dilemma failed to generate the additional intensity he had hoped for. Here, Donna enters to lend her support by repetitively provoking and perturbing the system until she sees a dyad persisting in a conflict until a new and different outcome is reached. She begins by returning to Jennifer's last statement.

DONNA: Jennifer, do you think your family would be better off if you were dead?

JENNIFER: *(Begins to cry)* I just feel like I'm such a burden to them—a waste of time, a waste of money . . .

DONNA: Do you think you're keeping your parents together, or do you think you're keeping them apart?

JENNIFER: Well, I remember one time a year or so ago. Dad had left the house after a fight with Mom. And I told Mom—I said to her, maybe if things get really bad, if I have to go into the hospital, maybe then Dad will be more involved, maybe he'll be there for me.

It surprised me that I felt that way, because Dad and I never seem to talk, we were always at each other's throats. But we used to be so close. It just doesn't seem right—we hardly know each other anymore. *(She looks longingly at Carl through her tears, but he fidgets uncomfortably and looks down.)*

DONNA: Did you ever talk to your mother explicitly about why you haven't had the confidence in her to keep your father involved?

About why you've had to go to such deadly lengths to try to do it
yourself?

JENNIFER: No, I never did. I didn't think she cared.

DONNA: Brian, it's clear to me that the burden of trying to bring Carl
back into the family is literally killing Jennifer. I remember you told
me that shortly before you consulted me, you had a session with Carl
and Jennifer in which she said she was "dying for a relationship" with
him. It seems that that's exactly what's going to happen if all the
weight's on her. I think that you're going to have to help Nancy get
Carl to be more involved, and time's running out. It's got to happen
now, Brian.

Given the intransigence of the stalemate between Nancy and Carl,
applying gentle pressure wasn't going to stress the system sufficiently.
Donna felt that the intensity would have to come from an increase in
Nancy's proximity to Carl, and Nancy's willingness to push Carl would
hinge on her trusting Brian to support her. Following Donna's cue, Brian
began to insist that Nancy challenge Carl's evasiveness and abdication.
A new sequence developed, in which each time Nancy tried to blame
Carl for disappearing, Brian pointed out how she had invited him to
become invisible.

Months earlier, Nancy did not have the cushion of a relationship in
which she felt validated, but now she was open to acknowledging her
participation and collusion. Even when Jennifer interceded to defend
her mother, Nancy turned to Jennifer and said: "It's okay, Jennifer, you
don't need to protect me. Brian is just trying to help me see my part in
the problem. The important thing now is to change it."

As Brian continued to challenge Nancy, she gradually lapsed into a
troubled silence, and Brian's intensity faltered. Leery of letting go of the
momentum they had generated, Donna resurrected the theme of death.

DONNA: Do you have a burial plot picked out for your daughter, Nancy?
Have you thought about what to put on the gravestone? Think about
it. Think about what it will look like. Think about going there on
Sundays, bringing flowers. Think about how you'll feel.

NANCY: *(Her voice breaking)* I know how I'll feel! I've thought about it a
hundred million times in the last few weeks. *(Agonizedly)* What do you
want from me?

DONNA: What do *you* want, Nancy?

NANCY: I want her to live, goddamn it! I'm tired of this. I just don't know
what else to do! I don't know how to get her to be better.

DONNA: It's going to take a lot of work on Carl's part to help her get better. Not just on your part, Nancy. On *Carl's* part, and you're going to have to bring him in.

Nancy looked at Donna for a long moment. Then she sighed, and with that sigh something seemed to shift. There was an almost palpable loosening of tension between Nancy and Donna and between Nancy and Brian, a loosening that seemed to free Nancy from the last vestiges of her reluctance to challenge Carl.

THE STRUGGLE: NOW OR NEVER

In working with severely symptomatic families, the therapist must always remember that despite their pain and feeling of powerlessness, they can negotiate previously insurmountable obstacles when challenged to do so in the context of a trusting relationship. Nancy perceived the challenges that Brian and Donna had issued as calls to her competence, rather than as attacks and criticisms. Her new sense of confidence showed as she turned to Carl with an unfettered, yet controlled, fury and for the next thirty minutes pursued him from every possible angle. Sometimes she became enraged with him, sometimes she laughed, but always she monotonously persevered in her insistence that he find a way of becoming more connected to Jennifer. What was most important was her relentlessness.

Occasionally, Carl turned to Donna or Brian in exasperation, but they simply redirected him to Nancy, expressing their belief in his ability to work out something new with his wife if he hung in there with her long enough. As helpful to Carl as Brian and Donna's support was, more important was the way in which Nancy communicated to Carl her own confidence in his ability to help. Nancy's renewed belief in herself led her to view her relationship with Carl in a different light, which illuminated previously unseen possibilities. Some aspects of the change in the parents' interaction can be seen in the following segment of dialogue, which occurred near the end of the session.

NANCY: I really need you to be strong now, Carl, and to learn ways of handling Jennifer when she gets upset. I can't do it alone.
CARL: *(Angrily)* Sure, just like all the times when I've tried to do something and you told me to butt out, to get lost, because I made everything worse. That really made me feel great, you know, like I had a lot to offer. As if you were doing such a great job yourself.

NANCY: Okay, you're right—we've both made mistakes, and I've certainly made my share. But we've got to bury the hatchet, we really do. You simply have to get more involved with Jennifer, without throwing up the past, and without concocting a hundred and one excuses why it's not the right time. There's no other way.

CARL: *(Grudgingly)* Maybe, but you'd have to change too, Nancy.

NANCY: How?

CARL: By letting me find my own way. I'd have to get to know Jennifer again . . . it's been so long that we've practically become strangers. You'd have to give me some space.

NANCY: Can you tell me how I get in your way?

CARL: You try to control everything, that's how. Ever since she was a little girl. You'd ask me to fix her something to eat, and when I did, you'd tell me it was the wrong thing, that she didn't like that, and you'd say, "Isn't that right, Jennifer?" Then if I fixed her what you told me to, you'd tell me I wasn't feeding her the right way, that I was holding the spoon in the wrong hand. Didn't you think that if the kid didn't like something, she'd let me know that herself somehow? If it's so important that I have a relationship with her now, Nancy, you're going to have to let Jennifer and me work it out on our own, without trying to dictate what it's going to look like.

NANCY: Okay, Carl, I hear you. I really do. Let's try and see what we can work out.

To Donna and Brian, this exchange sounded like the beginning of an authentic process of negotiation. The future of this transformation in the parents' relationship was uncertain, but it was now anchored in a more substantial and sustaining nexus of relationships.

To summarize the steps in the process of crisis induction in this phase: after exploring and validating the change in Nancy's relationship with Jennifer, Donna directed Brian's energies to the parental conflict. She encouraged him to push Nancy to challenge Carl's abdication of his parental responsibilities in a direct and relentless fashion. The combination of Brian's pushing and Donna's intervening to maintain focus and intensity impelled Nancy to engage Carl. A crisis had been induced for Nancy, reflected in her conviction that the pattern had to be broken *then and there.* She relentlessly pushed for a commitment from Carl to change his relationship with Jennifer, a commitment she viewed as essential, nonnegotiable, and necessary *at that moment,* not at some vaguely promised future time.

By engaging with Carl and sticking to him like glue, Nancy induced a crisis in their relationship. As a result of the therapeutic system's ability to precipitate and contain conflicts and catalyze their resolution, Nancy's relentlessness in maintaining proximity did not lead to a violent outburst or rupture as in the past. The ensuing transformation in the parental relationship would open up new space in which renewed development of people and relationships could occur. The task for the next phase of the consultation would be to consolidate and expand on this transformation, which constituted a new foundation on which Brian's therapy with Jennifer, and Jennifer herself, could once again move forward.

CHAPTER 7

Transformation and Beyond: Consolidating and Expanding Change

It is a quality of the unknown to give us a sense of hope and
happiness. Man feels robust, exhilarated. Even the apprehension that it
arouses is very fulfilling. The new seers saw *that man is at his best*
in the face of the unknown.
— Carlos Castaneda, *The Fire from Within*

Freedom is not chaos, though there are similarities.
— Alan Dean Foster, *To the Vanishing Point*

The Symptomatic Cycle Disrupted

IN the fourth phase of treatment, the family finds itself free of the prison of the symptomatic cycle, with its rigid transactions, and can resume the development and maturation of its relationships. New forms of attachment and separation can be tried out, as the therapeutic system continues to be a context in which safe experimentation can occur. Increased differentiation among family members is encouraged, as is the family's confidence and competence in managing its life and relationships.

The goal of this phase is to help the family explore and consolidate the new patterns of interaction that have opened up through the disruption of the original symptomatic cycle. These changes inspire the family to be less dependent on the presence, input, and leadership of the therapist. However, caution is in order. The therapist must recognize that in families with severely symptomatic members, the problem is not simply that people are too close or too involved with one another, and the solution is not simply to foster greater separation. The family's symptomatic relationships oscillate between engulfment and abandonment, between blind loyalty and betrayal, between ultimatum and capitulation, without a middle ground where mutuality and negotiation prevail. The therapist must keep in mind that he is simultaneously working toward greater differentiation and greater integration, for an essential accompaniment of autonomy is the capacity to participate in more satisfying relationships. In other words, helping people to separate is a necessary step toward helping them to reconnect more effectively.

Helping the family to struggle with the process of individuation during this phase requires that the therapist assume a less directive and central role. He must recognize that problems and conflicts that surface in this phase do not necessarily represent a resurgence of the conflicts of the symptomatic cycle. They may be dilemmas of choice, which the family can now embrace and act on responsibly. The pitfall for the therapist is to be overly involved in directing the resolution of these conflicts, rather than allowing family members sufficient room to struggle with them on their own.

The experience of transformation is different for every family and for each family member. Nevertheless, a few themes occur with some regularity. Often the presenting symptom evaporates as the symptomatic cycle is disrupted and the developmental impasse is dissolved. At other times, the behavior that was previously construed as symptomatic persists but is viewed differently. For example, behavior that was considered involuntary may be relabeled willful and irresponsible. After Mr. Jepsen discovered that his daughter, Susan, had vomited and lied about it, he and his wife disciplined her for lying rather than taking her for immediate medical attention, thereby opening up new ways for the family to approach the symptom (chapter 2).

This example also illustrates two other effects of transformation on symptom perception. Rather than trying directly to control Susan's behavior, the parents decided to hold her accountable for the consequences of her acts. Recognizing the difference between trying to control the behavior of others and enacting consequences is a phenomenon often seen during this phase of therapy. Witness Nancy Monroe's response, in the third phase of treatment, to her recognition that she had no control over her daughter's behavior, that all of it, including Jennifer's very survival, was ultimately up to Jennifer. The liberation Nancy felt allowed her to approach Jennifer more closely and provide her with more support than she ever had before. Also, in the process of disentangling the symptom from the system there is a change in perceived ownership of the symptom, with the locus of responsibility shifting from a larger to a smaller system. For example, with the Jepsens the responsibility for managing Susan's vomiting moved from the medical system to the family, and then from the parents to Susan.

Transformation may also change family members' experience of differentiation and relatedness. Typically, individuals report a powerful realization that "it's up to me to solve the problems in my life; no one else is going to do it for me." Coupled with this insight comes the opportunity and the responsibility for making choices when previously external forces were blamed. Toward the end of treatment Jennifer Monroe remarks on the change she experienced: "Before, I just thought that I was destined to die. Now I know that I *can* survive, but I'm not always sure that I want to."

Whether a family member is reporting a change toward greater autonomy or toward greater connectedness, the frame of reference for the change is always the person's intimate relationships. As Martin Buber states in his classic work, *I and Thou,* "In the beginning is relation. Consider the speech of 'primitive' peoples, that is, of those that have a meagre stock of objects, and whose life is built up within a narrow circle of acts highly charged with presentness. The nuclei of this speech . . . mostly indicate the wholeness of a relation. We say 'far away'; the Zulu has for that a word which means, 'There where someone cries out: "O mother, I am lost"'" (1958, 18).

Anchoring the Family

During the final phase of treatment, as the therapist reduces the extent to which he directs the therapeutic process, his goal is to anchor the family in the changes it has made through the crisis induction. Tasks and rituals focused on integrating personal development with family-based goals are an effective means of consolidating and expanding these changes.

The therapist should avoid becoming overly invested in a particular outcome for an assigned task or ritual. The point is for family members to devise a solution reflecting their family's uniqueness and ingenuity. The therapist should assign a task or ritual, not to provide an answer for the family but to ask a question to which the family will discover its own answer.

Some tasks or rituals may have the goal of locking in a new pattern of interaction by prescribing that very pattern, as when Paul asks Mr. Harmon and Josh to play basketball together. Others may be designed to evaluate whether a current conflict in the family represents a throwback to the old patterns of the symptomatic cycle or is in fact a necessary step in the family's struggle to create something new. The therapeutic artistry lies in designing a task or ritual such that in performing it, the family experiences a reinforcement of its ability to make choices about perceiving and transacting relationships, especially in situations of conflict.

Severely symptomatic families are susceptible to rapid returns to the patterns of the symptomatic cycle, particularly at times of transition. The therapist needs to watch for slips during this final phase of treatment, being prepared to block symptomatic patterns when they start to surface. To help stabilize new patterns, the therapist must anchor family members in supportive and containing contexts outside the therapeutic system. His sphere of activity may have to extend beyond the family to larger social systems.

One way of anchoring the family outside the therapeutic system is to involve extended family members in treatment. For example, the parents of a ten-year-old boy with superlabile diabetes had become competent in managing their son's diabetes but were neglecting their own relationship and afraid of separating from their son because his illness was unpredictable. After requesting that the parents bring all four grandparents to the next session and asking the parents to teach them how to manage their grandson's diabetes, the therapist urged the parents to go away for an entire weekend, leaving the boy with his grandparents. On their return, the parents reported that the support now available from their parents had allowed them to begin to deal with the gulf that had existed between them as marital partners for the past nine years.

Another means of anchoring is to help the family cultivate resources in its community, as will be described in the case of the Cabrinis when Rachel connects Maria and her family with the staff of the partial hospitalization program prior to her discharge from the hospital. Families can seek respite care workers to care for a difficult child in their home, providing parents with temporary relief from the child's demands and allowing them to socialize with other adults. In addition, effective collaboration between families and schools can bolster a youngster's social and academic development as well as support parental competence, as seen in the case of the Harmons.

If an adolescent displays violent behavior, parents can turn to members of the community, such as police officials or counselors from neighborhood centers, who can supervise the adolescent and use their relationship with him or her to channel the child's energy and talents through structured activities, much as a mentor does with an apprentice. Members of the community can be invited to therapy sessions in the therapist's office, in the family's home, or in the neighborhood—for example, at the police station or at a neighborhood center. Bringing the community into the family's private life is a compression that helps strip terrorizing children of the power they hold over their parents and forces new paths of conflict resolution within the family.

Ending Treatment

At some point beyond transformation, the question arises whether treatment should be continued, and on what basis. How should the therapist handle the issue of termination? He needs to be alert to the possibility that the family may interpret his decreasing involvement as abandonment. He also needs to make sure that leaving treatment does not represent the family's recoil from the stresses of change. If perceptions of abandonment or indications of flight are present, the therapist should discuss them with the family openly and directly, because the process of diminishing involvement occurs most effectively when it is agreed upon between the family and the therapist.

With families who have had a long history of unproductive involvement with professionals, the therapist may recommend after the transformation that the family proceed on its own without further psychotherapy. Such a suggestion conveys his confidence in the family's ability to pull together and cultivate its own resources. If needed, the therapist can set a future date to meet with the family as a follow-up to obtain information about its experiences living without therapy and to evaluate whether reinitiating therapy would be of value; the therapist should emphasize that he would be willing to consider working with the family in treatment at that future time, as long as there is evidence that the family has continued to struggle successfully and to develop new patterns of relating.

Ultimately, of course, the decision about interrupting or ending treatment rests with the family, as Rachel will discover some months after Maria Cabrini leaves the hospital. Sometimes the family will decide to end formal contact with the therapist as a result of the changes consolidated during this fourth phase. At other times, a new contract for treatment may be negotiated, and the sequence of phases may begin anew. Even when the family and therapist agree to stop meeting for regular appointments, the therapeutic relationship terminates in an administrative sense only, as illustrated in the following vignette.

The Erickson family entered treatment when Ricky was fifteen, after he had been suspended from school for stealing money from the cafeteria and menacing his teacher with a knife. Father was on his third marriage, stepmother on her second, and their violent, alcohol-induced arguments threatened to derail everyone from considering Ricky's predicament.

The therapist surmised that the marriage was all but over and devoted her energy to helping Ricky get through high school and stay out of jail. She worked with him intensively, on an individual basis, for the next one and one-half years.

Following his successful graduation from high school, Ricky moved away and found a job in a distant city. He wrote an occasional postcard to the therapist, informing her of his father and stepmother's eventual separation, and his own series of increasingly responsible jobs. Five years after graduation the therapist received a call from Ricky; he was coming to town to visit his father and would like to meet with her.

Ricky arrived in a suit, twenty-two years old and a far cry from the fifteen-year-old delinquent. He stated sincerely to the therapist that he had benefited greatly from the preceding seven years of treatment with her (the past five of which had occurred without the knowledge or personal participation of the therapist).

However, he explained earnestly, he felt that he was doing very well now, and that therapy was no longer necessary. He hoped that the therapist would understand, and would agree to a termination of treatment. After careful consideration and discussion with Ricky, she assented.

The Cabrinis

REORGANIZATION: UPDATING THE THERAPEUTIC MAP

The Cabrini family's transformation in the previous phase of treatment was marked by the significant change in the relationship between

Mr. Cabrini and Bruno. Following Maria's revelation, they began to listen to each other, and the physical violence characterizing their previous attempts to resolve conflicts was absent. In addition, the siblings were forming a more cohesive support system for one another that crystallized when they challenged their parents to take a firm position with Uncle Billy. Mr. and Mrs. Cabrini had confronted Uncle Billy on his abuse of Maria and removed him from the house. Rachel had met separately with Anita and Bruno, who denied being molested by Uncle Billy or anyone else; the preschool staff had been alerted to Maria's disclosure, and evaluation so far had not unearthed evidence that Nicholas had been sexually abused.

The goal of the next phase of treatment would be to anchor these changes more firmly and to oversee the reorganization in the family. The disclosure of secrets, though dramatic, suffices neither to bring about nor to consolidate a change in the symptomatic cycle. Further efforts are required to help the family develop new patterns that are truly protective, given the power of old patterns to reassert themselves.

In their next meeting, team members discussed how best to reorient themselves on the therapeutic map. They recalled the core dynamic wherein Maria would become symptomatic and her parents would respond by disconnecting and turning to professionals to care for her. Now a new ingredient had to be taken into account—Maria's sexual abuse. The team speculated that Maria's only escape route to safety during her adolescence was through symptomatic behavior, after which her parents placed her first in a group home, then in hospitals. Institutions gradually became the only places where she could feel protected from violation. Mrs. Cabrini's loyalty to her brother and her unresolved conflicts regarding her own victimization, coupled with her husband's permissiveness and volatility, had contributed to the neglect and abandonment of Maria.

The team identified the specific arenas in which Maria's personal differentiation could be fostered and the reorganizational shifts in the family consolidated. The map would need to incorporate the revelation of the abuse, without being dominated by it.

SEEING MARIA IN INDIVIDUAL THERAPY

Rachel planned daily sessions with Maria to provide a private and protected arena for a dialogue that would allow Maria to define her needs and regain a sense of control over her life. Before this intensification of individual therapy, the team agreed that an anti-anxiety medication could help Maria tolerate the stress she would be encountering as she faced the trauma of her abuse. The treatment contract stipulated that medication could be used as an adjunct to the involvement Maria required from her parents, not as a substitute for it. Because Mr. and Mrs. Cabrini had become more engaged with Maria and the treatment team since the day of admission, medication could now be introduced.

Rachel and the psychiatrist agreed to present this intervention jointly to Maria and the family. They specified that the medication was targeted for use during the next several weeks only, but it could be used for longer if Maria and the team thought it worthwhile. The psychiatrist defined the medication as a means of helping Maria keep her anxiety at a tolerable level so that the anxiety could serve as a source of motivation to deal with the stresses of therapy rather than as a source of despair and helplessness.

In a session with Rachel on the day after her disclosure of the abuse, Maria spoke in a guarded fashion about her experiences. She reported being repeatedly abused by Uncle Billy from the ages of ten to thirteen, when she went into placement. He had threatened to hurt her if she did not cooperate with his desires, which consisted primarily of oral sex but had included rape on several occasions. Maria tearfully wondered if the encounter that had resulted in Nicholas's conception, with a young man she barely knew at the group home, had somehow been related to her desire to "get back at Uncle Billy. All I know is that when I came back home and he found out I was pregnant, he left me alone. He never bothered me after that."

Maria vividly recalled lying awake at night, trembling, in her room, waiting to hear his footsteps and the turning of the doorknob. Her sleep was filled with nightmares of terror and violence. "I was always scared, always looked over my shoulder," she said. "Whenever I was scared, I'd hear voices that said do something, do something. But I was too afraid to talk. I couldn't discuss it. I felt like I had no control over anything. Even as it was happening, I would just take a deep breath, and say, 'not again.' I pretended that I wasn't really there, that it was all in my imagination."

She acknowledged knowing that what was happening was wrong, but she was confused about what to do and afraid of her uncle's threat should she divulge the secret. Clearly, part of her waking nightmare was having no way to talk about the abuse. Maria expressed great fear of how Uncle Billy was going to react once he knew she had let the secret out. She was afraid to return home because she did not trust her parents to keep him away. She said that she felt secure in the hospital because she trusted that the team would not allow anyone to harm her. She was also afraid for Anita's safety.

In the course of their conversations, Rachel and Maria began to identify certain of her previously unexplained and seemingly bizarre experiences, including her auditory hallucinations, as possible flashbacks. As they recognized this, the flashbacks began to occur more often and more intensely, and Maria became increasingly consumed by raw emotional pain. The integrity of her relationship with Rachel gave her the security to relive the details of the abuse and to express her rage without fearing that her hatred and pain would send Rachel away. To help Maria regain a sense of control, Rachel encouraged her to keep a diary to record the flashbacks. By defining a delimited area in which Maria could *do* something with the memories and feelings about the abuse, a sense of control was reestablished. The diary became a symbolic home where the traumatic memories were stored; it could be accessed or buried, depending on Maria's needs.

Although flashbacks and nightmares are terrifying, they are also familiar, an intimate companion. Over time, as an individual becomes increasingly in charge of the demons and separates from them, it may become necessary to grieve—not only for the lost demons but for the lost opportunities resulting from their prolonged occupation of his or her spirit. This mourning process requires the leaving behind of the old patterns associated with the abuse and the cultivation of new ones. Rachel and the team worked with Maria over a period of two weeks to develop new skills, such as asking for what she needed, speaking honestly about her feelings, and making decisions for herself.

Rachel and Maria also discussed how to approach the legal and criminal aspects of the situation. Since Maria was now eighteen, and since the abuse had stopped several years earlier, the team was not legally obligated under local statutes to make a report, but Rachel felt it essential that the authorities be notified. If untreated, Uncle Billy's problems presented an ongoing risk to the other children in the family and the community at large. Rachel told Maria that although she was prepared to call the child protective services hotline herself, Maria's parents should be the ones to do the reporting. She also suggested that Maria investigate the possibility of consulting with a lawyer and pressing charges. At the moment, though, Maria felt overwhelmed at the prospect of facing the legal issues, and asked to table this issue until she felt more ready to pursue it.

CONSOLIDATING REORGANIZATION IN THE FAMILY

With respect to the family, the central challenge would be how to contend with the defensiveness and denial that family members had built up to protect themselves from the painful past, so that they could talk about the abuse. With most severely symptomatic families, particularly when the problem includes sexual abuse, talking about the abuse with the family is difficult because of the complexity of family loyalties and because of the mistrust, fear, and shame that develop over the years. Once a therapeutic conversation begins, the therapist must address a number of thorny issues: the family is often burdened with guilt; and if accusation and condemnation are reinforced, there can be further fragmentation within its ranks.

When the person who has been abused is ready to talk with the family, the therapist's role in maintaining order and monitoring and directing the flow of communication becomes critical. Maria and Rachel had agreed that Uncle Billy would not be invited to participate in sessions, until and unless Maria felt it would beneficial to her for him to come. Involving the offender in the therapeutic process is a delicate matter, the first issue being to provide the victim with a sense of protection. A rule of thumb is to keep the victim and the offender separate until the former indicates a readiness to be in the latter's presence, thus supporting her in defining the boundaries of her relationships. Even if the victim is prepared to include the offender, the therapist should agree only if he trusts the parents to actively assert constructive leadership as well.

In the first meeting of Maria and her parents following her disclosure of the abuse, Rachel would need to ensure that Maria was respectfully heard and not intimidated or blamed, while being careful to avoid distancing the rest of the family. She would do this by telling the parents at the outset of the session that she thought it essential for them to hear from Maria about her experiences of violation and betrayal while growing up, which she and Maria had been talking about in individual therapy. But the parents would first need to provide assurances that they would sit and listen. Both parents agreed, and Maria cautiously began to speak about her fears of continued violence and abandonment.

USING GUILT CONSTRUCTIVELY

A necessary, though not sufficient, step in repairing relationships damaged by violence or abuse is to require rites of penance. Stimulating feelings of guilt is an old-fashioned psychological means of persuasion that can be used to encourage this process. Motivating people through guilt is not a highly regarded tactic in the mental health field. However, in the treatment of families that engage in violence and abuse, the creative use of guilt can be an important aspect of the healing process.

There is therapeutic value in assigning responsibility not only to the abuser but also to the parents or caretakers of a child who was victimized while under their care, even if they were unaware of the abuse. Placing responsibility on the adults begins to counteract the child's experience of being alone. When parents can begin to take responsibility for protecting the abuser or failing to see the abuse, a context for healing is created. The child and his or her parents become engaged in grieving the past and in creating a different present and future.

Initially, Mr. and Mrs. Cabrini insisted that they had no responsibility because they had not "really" known about the abuse. After an intense discussion in which Rachel repeatedly defined them as participants *regardless* of the extent to which they were consciously aware of what was happening, the parents finally admitted their error in not acknowledging the problems Uncle Billy had, and, in a more general sense, in not being involved more actively in Maria's life as she was growing up. Mrs. Cabrini, in particular, seemed to beg Maria's forgiveness; she kept repeating, "He did it to me when I was young . . . I should have known better," over and over. The family, though still tense, seemed open to discussing these difficult and painful matters.

As a general principle, parental guilt can be used by the therapist in the treatment of severely symptomatic families as long as several conditions are met: (1) expiation of the guilt occurs not only verbally, but also through the medium of some constructive activity; (2) both the verbal expression and the concrete activity have demonstrable reparative benefit to the patient; (3) the therapeutic intervention is in the service of fostering greater connectedness between child and parents; and (4) the role of guilt in establishing such bonds is temporary and transitional, and becomes supplanted by other, more inherently affirming connections, as soon as possible.

BECOMING A PARENT: THE PRESCHOOL PROGRAM

As Maria was functioning more responsibly in her family and peer group, the therapeutic focus broadened to include her relationship with Nicholas in order to reduce the risk of his continuing to carry the familial legacy of intergenerational neglect and abuse. Nicholas had been attending the preschool program on a regular basis. The team planned for Maria to begin spending structured half days working with Nicholas there in her final week of hospitalization, rather than just visiting him on occasion as she had done so far. From this foundation, Maria would become involved more intensively in the preschool program on an outpatient basis.

The primary goals were for Maria to become more comfortable handling Nicholas's tantrums and oppositional behavior and to learn to play with him. Playing was a foreign activity to Maria, for she had been preoccupied through much of her life with protecting herself from danger. Nicholas's tantrums frightened Maria tremendously, for they conjured up images of her father and Bruno fighting, and of Uncle Billy's assaults. For Maria to be comfortable playing with Nicholas, she would first need to feel that she could handle him if he became out of control.

To prepare for this likelihood, the team taught Maria how to physically restrain Nicholas. The sessions helped Maria feel more in control of herself. They gave her a way to provide her son with physical contact that was containing and nurturing, rather than abusive. Teaching parents safe means of physical restraint helps desensitize them to the fear of hurting or being hurt by their tantruming children. However, such techniques—in which the child is held by an adult in a way that prevents harm to the child or others—are not meant to be used in every situation in which a child opposes adult authority or lashes out physically. Indications for physical restraint have to do with the seriousness of the immediate threat of physical danger. If the child responds to the adult's spoken word, then restraint is not indicated. If the child ignores the adult's verbal direction and persists in destructive behavior, then the adult should intervene to physically interrupt the child's actions. Only when the child will not stop hurting himself or herself or will not separate from whomever he or she is fighting does restraint become necessary.

Maria also learned developmentally appropriate ways of disciplining Nicholas that did not involve physical punishment or coercion. This balance of nurturance and limit setting was generalized to other contexts in which she and Nicholas were involved, including family sessions and trips with Nicholas to children's museums, parks in the community, and home.

The preschool program was a place where Maria could experiment with the creative and spontaneous parts of herself that she had forgotten. After she had become more adept in handling Nicholas herself, she would teach her parents what she had learned, with special emphasis on how they could support her competence by respecting the boundaries of her relationship with Nicholas.

RECONNECTING THE FAMILY WITH THE COMMUNITY

When families treated in an inpatient setting approach the time of discharge, anxiety in the patient, family, and team typically rises due to the uncertainty that lies ahead. An important tool in this task is the use of passes (Brendler 1987, 126). To activate the family's confidence and competence in handling problems on its own outside the hospital, the team recommended to the Cabrinis that Maria and her siblings spend several evenings at home during the final week of hospitalization, reacclimating themselves to that environment and to living again with their parents.

Because the reports from the team and the DHS worker's observations in the preschool indicated that Maria was discharging her parental responsibilities more competently, John Williams agreed to bring Nicholas to spend a few hours with Maria at her parents' home when she was on pass from the hospital. It was agreed that during the month after discharge, Nicholas would spend additional time with Maria and her family at home under DHS supervision. A SCOH worker (Services to Children in their Own Homes, a family-support program funded by DHS) would come regularly to the home to assist Maria in the management of Nicholas, thus freeing Maria from the position of having no one to lean on except her parents, with whom she still had many unresolved conflicts.

ARRANGING FOR OUTPATIENT THERAPY

One of the most important prerequisites for discharge from the hospital is the establishment of a viable arrangement for outpatient therapy, which facilitates separation between the inpatient team and the family as well as the family's reintegration into the community. The family had requested to continue working with Rachel, as she had traveled with the Cabrinis through much toil and travail, and each family member had developed a strong attachment to her. Rachel was agreeable to working with the family on an outpatient basis and with Maria in individual therapy, which Maria also wanted. After clearing this arrangement with Joyce, Rachel broached the potential complications, having to do with the mixed loyalties and issues of confidentiality that can arise when the therapist for one person is also the therapist for that person's family. She and the family agreed that any member of the system, including herself, who experienced any discomfort or conflict related to the therapeutic arrangement should bring this immediately to Rachel's attention. The entire group would then need to meet together to reach a resolution.

There were other components of the outpatient plan as well. Although Maria had begun to take more responsibility for herself as a young woman and parent, she did not feel ready to take on the responsibilities of a full-time job. In accordance with the treatment contract, a partial hospitalization program was recommended to provide a structure in which she could remain in contact with other young adults and receive guidance in developing vocational, social, and organizational skills, making strides toward her goal of eventually living in a place of her own with Nicholas. To facilitate Maria's transition to the partial program, the team developed a plan whereby she would spend time there during the last week of hospitalization.

Maria also joined an outpatient group for adult survivors of childhood sexual abuse. There she would have an opportunity to meet people whose traumatic backgrounds bore similarities to her own, thus enhancing a sense of connectedness and reducing feelings of alienation and shame. She would continue to attend the weekly group meetings following discharge.

SIX MONTHS LATER

Although Maria continued to attend the group for survivors of sexual abuse, her participation in the partial hospitalization program had declined and she was looking for a job. She was making friends and participating in social activities. Nicholas was developing better self-control and social skills. He had been living with the family for several months and attending the preschool program. Bruno and Anita were attending school regularly.

Uncle Billy was living in a therapeutic group home for mentally retarded adults. He spoke with Mrs. Cabrini several times a week on the phone, but was not permitted to visit the home or to be in public unchaperoned. These conditions had been judicially decreed following Maria's pressing formal charges against him and were criteria for his remaining out of jail while the legal system deliberated his fate.

The family was adhering to the plan of weekly meetings with Rachel for outpatient therapy, and Maria had reduced the frequency of her individual therapy from twice to once a week. Maria said that when she felt the anger building from the past, "I hear Rachel's voice, and friends from my therapy group, telling me my feelings are normal no matter how painful they are. They're only feelings, and feelings won't kill me. Rachel's voice is a source of strength inside me now. It keeps pushing me forward, telling me to be strong and value myself."

ONE YEAR LATER

Events took an untoward turn about ten months into outpatient therapy. One day after returning home from her job, Maria noticed Uncle Billy's hat on the table in the downstairs hall. Her mother told her that due to funding cuts in the city's budget, the community group home in which he had been living closed down suddenly, and she had agreed to take him in on a temporary basis. Criminal prosecution was still pending, but Mrs. Cabrini had promised the district attorney's office that Billy would be closely supervised in the home until a new placement could be found. Apparently the assistant district attorney had agreed, since there was no other immediate option except jail, and Uncle Billy's public defender had argued that there was no evidence his client had performed any "indecent acts" for almost five years.

At Bruno's suggestion, Maria called Rachel at home to inform her of the news. Rachel spoke with the parents and insisted on a family meeting that evening. In the meeting, Mrs. Cabrini said that she could not bear the guilt if she did not provide her now homeless brother with shelter. Prior to her making a decision, she had discussed her concerns about the childrens' possible reactions with her husband, and Mr. Cabrini saw no choice but to support his wife. Maria was furious with both parents and refused to go home. She said that this incident "wiped out my hope in my parents coming through for me. Now it's clearer than ever that I have to stop counting on them and take care of myself."

Maria's realization was perhaps the most significant transformation of the entire course of treatment. Though she experienced a repetition of the old pattern of betrayal and abandonment—in which Mrs. Cabrini yielded to her conflict avoidance with her brother, Mr. Cabrini did nothing, and Uncle Billy was rescued again at Maria's expense—Maria did not collapse. Instead, she called a friend from her sexual abuse group and asked permission for herself and Nicholas to stay with the friend and her husband until she could make other arrangements. Anita said she also was too frightened to stay in the house with Uncle Billy and wanted to go with Maria. Maria's friend agreed, and later picked up

Maria, Nicholas, and Anita at Rachel's office. Rachel said she planned to contact Uncle Billy's court-appointed attorney and the assistant district attorney to obtain more information and convey her alarm.

In the next family session, Rachel recounted her conversations with the lawyers. The public defender had predictably told her that Uncle Billy could not be incarcerated without due process. He was unresponsive to Rachel's argument that leaving his client in the Cabrini household was actually placing Uncle Billy at risk, giving him greater temptation and opportunity for improper behavior to recur without the presence of adequate controls. The district attorney was sympathetic to Rachel's concerns, but said that with all the recent publicity about overcrowding in the jails he couldn't possibly petition the court for immediate detention, and with the social service funding cuts, no other options existed.

"So it's up to you," Rachel concluded, looking at the parents. But the Cabrinis refused to budge from their position. Angela reiterated how she had promised her dying mother that she would look after Billy, and Joe backed her up. Rachel's exhortations were to no avail. Subsequently, Mr. and Mrs. Cabrini began missing sessions. After a few weeks of not returning Rachel's phone calls, the parents agreed to come to a final appointment. Though Rachel tried to persuade them to continue therapy until a mutual decision to end had been made, the parents said they had decided to stop coming. Following that session, the three siblings continued to meet with Rachel regularly, and Maria continued her individual sessions as usual.

THREE YEARS LATER

Bruno was now nineteen. He had graduated from high school, had started his first year of vocational training in electronics, and was still living at home. Although he had not had any more physical fights with his stepfather, their relationship was more distant. Anita, sixteen, had had a shaky sophomore year in high school, during which time she began living with a girlfriend and her family and then with a boyfriend. Nicholas was now six years old and had started kindergarten in the local public school.

Maria had stopped attending the sexual abuse group, stating that she no longer felt like a victim or a mental patient. Five months after Maria moved out of her parents' home, she met Frank, who was nine years older than she, and eight months after they first met, they married. A year and a half after her marriage, Maria gave birth to her second child, a daughter named Tanya. Maria saw Anita and Bruno frequently at her house. Periodically she brought her children to visit her parents.

In the last six months, after two and a half years of outpatient therapy, Maria had stopped meeting with Rachel on a regular basis. They agreed that Maria could call Rachel at any time and come in for a session if she felt it would be helpful.

Several weeks after Uncle Billy returned to the Cabrini home, a young girl in the neighborhood told her parents that he had come up to her, made suggestive remarks, and attempted to fondle her. This incident, combined with the charges already pending, led to his incarceration. A trial was held, and he was sentenced to three years in the county prison. Mrs. Cabrini visits him weekly.

The Harmons

CONSOLIDATING REORGANIZATION: THE THERAPIST BECOMES LESS CENTRAL

Since the last session, Robert had played basketball with Josh and had taken Barbara's suggestion to invite Suzanne to the movies. Though Robert was taking steps out of the fog, his tentativeness in his relationships with his wife and children was still evident to Paul, who was aware of how easily Robert could get lost again. In this phase of treatment, an important task is to assist each family member in using the relationship he or she has forged with the therapist to consolidate new relationships with each other. The therapist's focus shifts to facilitating relationships in which any two family members can resolve conflicts without the involvement of a third. To accomplish this, Paul sets up a series of dyadic interactions between Robert and each member of his family.

PAUL: Robert, I think you've been missing your whole family while you've been in the fog.
ROBERT: *(Nodding in agreement)* You're absolutely right. I think it had a lot to do with you pushing me to talk about my father. I can see how I'm doing a lot of the same things to my son and daughter that he did to me. You know, picking at them, but being too busy to help them.
PAUL: I think you should talk to each member of your family about

what they can do to help you from slipping back into that fog, because its pull is very strong and very familiar.

The conversations that followed were strained. Robert had great difficulty asking for what he needed from Barbara and the children without sounding critical and defensive. Over the next several sessions Paul helped all of them practice listening and talking directly with each other, and little by little, old patterns began to change. Paul became increasingly confident of Barbara's ability to enlist Robert's collaboration with her and facilitate his involvement with Josh and Suzanne. To emphasize his belief in the family's ability to maintain these changes on its own, Paul suggested decreasing the frequency of sessions to once a week. The Harmons continued to meet with Paul on a weekly basis for the next six months to consolidate changes in three primary areas: working with Josh's school, establishing rules at home, and helping Barbara and Robert to build a life of their own separate from their children.

COLLABORATING WITH THE SCHOOL

The situation at Josh's school had become a vicious cycle, in which the efforts of his parents and the school personnel to help seemed only to escalate the difficulties and add to everyone's frustration and disappointment. In such circumstances, it is common to find disputes between parents and school concerning the nature of the child's problems and how they should be addressed.

Discussions often focus on whether the child has a learning problem, or a behavioral problem, or an emotional problem, as if these are mutually exclusive. People become invested in advocating one of these positions at the expense of the others. As members of the system become ensconced in their particular point of view, their interest in collaborative exploration of new interventions to help the child diminishes. Blaming ensues; the school may accuse the parents of being too hard on the child while the parents find the school too easy, or vice versa. These conflicts mirror those between the parents.

The relevant questions to ask in such situations are: what are the child's needs, and how can the system be organized to help the child succeed in school? These questions encourage experimentation with various combinations of parental involvement and educational resources, a process that is most likely to occur when the relationship between the family and the school incorporates respect and mutual accountability.

At the Harmons' initiative, a meeting between Josh, his parents, several teachers, the guidance counselor, and the school principal was held to discuss Josh's difficulties and develop a way of working together to help him. In the next therapy session after the meeting, the parents reported to Paul their delight in Josh's speaking up for himself at the school meeting. Josh had announced that he was tired of being in special classes and wanted to resume a more normal school program. The school committee had responded with a litany of complaints about Josh's behavior. A couple of the teachers wanted to give him a chance, but the counselor recommended that he remain in special classes, except for math. Josh and his parents were angry and disappointed, and asked Paul how best to challenge the school's decision.

When the school and family are at odds, the therapist has several alternatives. He can work solely with the parents and the child to help them negotiate with the school, or he can become more directly involved with the school himself. For instance, the therapist can participate in a meeting with the family and school personnel, using the information he receives from direct observation to fine tune his input to the family about collaborating with the school. However, he should resist taking the role of intermediary between the family and school, because it is the parents' responsibility to negotiate with the school. At times the therapist may conclude that the family–school relationship is damaged beyond repair, in which case the best course of action is to advise the family to enroll the child in a different school.

Barbara and Robert were hoping Paul would intervene because they felt they lacked clout with the school. However, Paul preferred to empower them to negotiate directly with the school by helping them to arm themselves with a clear statement of Josh's current academic needs. He suggested that the parents ask whether the school would be willing to update its psychological evaluation of Josh to learn more about his abilities, strengths, and weaknesses. Alternatively, would the school accept an evaluation done by a psychologist retained by the family?

Robert called Paul before their next session to tell him that he and Barbara had decided to support Josh's request for mainstreaming only if he demonstrated better control of his behavior at school. The school principal had said that the school couldn't retest Josh in the next several months due to a backlog of requests for evaluations. However, he did agree to consider recommendations based on an evaluation done privately at the family's expense, as long as it was reviewed by the school psychologist. The principal also responded positively to Robert's request that the parents and the school develop a system of routine communication about Josh's behavior in school so that the parents could discipline Josh promptly when a problem arose. Relieved of the need to be preoccupied with meting out consequences for Josh's behavioral disruptions, school personnel could turn their attention to devising an appropriate educational curriculum for him.

Paul was pleased that Robert was working hard in collaboration with Barbara to establish a more constructive relationship with the school. He felt that it was reasonable for the time being that the parents assume responsibility for disciplining Josh when he exhibited behavioral problems in school. After the family and the school were more confident in their dealings with each other, the responsibility for dealing with Josh's behavior at school could be returned to the school, where it belonged.

Josh's psychological evaluation disclosed above average intelligence and an absence of noticeable learning disabilities. Impulsivity, distractibility, a reduced attention span, and a strong fear of failure were also noted. Among other recommendations, the psychologist suggested obtaining an opinion about the possibility of medication to help Josh channel his energy and focus his attention. In consultation with their pediatrician, Josh and his parents elected to proceed with a trial of Ritalin.

Over the next several months, with increased collaboration between the family and the school, increased parental monitoring of classroom performance, and stimulant medication, Josh began to complete homework assignments and improve his grades and behavior.

ESTABLISHING RULES OF THE HOUSE

Josh was thriving. He spoke more freely in sessions, accepted limits more readily, and challenged his parents more confidently and respectfully when he disagreed with them. Suzanne, however, had been increasingly abrupt; she was straining against the new rules. In one session, Robert reported that she had brought home a report card with several failures. The night following news of her grades, he and Barbara discovered an assortment of drug paraphernalia in Suzanne's room.

A heated confrontation broke out in the session as the parents expressed their upset at Suzanne's "relapse," and Suzanne expressed her fury at her parents' searching her room. Although tempers flared, no one left the session. At the height of the argument, Suzanne looked squarely at her father and said, "You can't stop me from using drugs. It's my life."

Something in Suzanne's statement, perhaps the intensity with which she voiced it, brought the conversation to a halt. Robert and Barbara looked at one another, then agreed with Suzanne that they could not control what she did out of their home. But they made it clear that using drugs in their house was not acceptable, and Suzanne would have to abide by that rule. Suzanne said if they stayed out of her business she would follow their rules. The parents agreed, and an uneasy truce prevailed for the next several weeks.

Suzanne refused to come to the next several sessions, arguing with her parents that she did not have to attend because she had been complying with the rules of the house. Three weeks later, Paul received a phone call from Janet, Suzanne's drug and alcohol counselor at school. Janet said that Suzanne was with her and had given permission for her to talk with Paul. After verifying this by speaking with Suzanne, Paul told Suzanne that he would need to have the discretion to discuss the call with her parents, but that his preference was for Suzanne to inform them herself of the call and what it was about. Suzanne agreed, and handed the phone back to Janet.

The counselor explained that she had worked with Suzanne on and off for several years. Recently Suzanne had joined a local chapter of Narcotics Anonymous (NA) and was seeing Janet regularly at school to help with her recovery. Janet said that Suzanne had a lot of hard work ahead. She was calling now because Suzanne wanted her support in requesting permission to drop out of family therapy while she addressed her problem with substance abuse. Paul suggested that Janet encourage Suzanne to ask her parents if both she and Janet could attend the next family session in order to discuss her request further.

In Paul's subsequent session with the family and Janet, Suzanne spoke directly to her parents. She said that she needed space to get herself together and that it was important for her to take responsibility for herself. Robert and Barbara were confused. Their daughter was working on her problems, but she was pushing them away at the same time. Suzanne made it clear that the network she was cultivating through NA and in her meetings with Janet had become her primary source of support.

Suzanne's request to drop out of family therapy could be viewed in various ways. It could be seen as a manifestation of Paul's failure to engage Suzanne in treatment, or of Suzanne's fear that Paul would collude with her parents against her. Paul chose to take Suzanne's request at face value, and supported it as an important step, both concretely and symbolically, in the process of managing her life. The challenge for Paul would be to help Robert and Barbara do the same by relinquishing their efforts to control her.

Two weeks later, the parents confirmed their increased competence in solving problems independently. Barbara reported that since the last session she and Robert had held a family meeting in which Suzanne confronted Josh about drugs, and he admitted to smoking marijuana in order to be more accepted by his peer group. The parents helped Josh to talk about his difficulty making friends and Suzanne offered to take Josh to one of her meetings for teens with drug problems, an idea that their parents supported. The parents had broken the symptomatic cycle. They had turned to one another, rather than to someone outside the family, to handle a problem with Josh.

PARENTS ARE PEOPLE, TOO

Therapy based primarily on guiding parents to develop, enforce, and follow rules constricts the family's experience, not to mention that of the therapist. It is also very boring. Therapy should foster an expansion of creativity, competence, and connectedness, allowing for family members to undergo differentiation and affiliation in a variety of contexts.

Paul had so far worked with the family on its collaboration with the school to create a system that would encourage the development of Josh's academic and social skills. It had also been necessary to connect Robert and Barbara with Suzanne's drug and alcohol counselor and to assist Suzanne in linking herself to a network of recovering adolescent drug users.

To promote further reorganization of the system, Paul suggested meeting with Barbara and Robert without the children to work on developing dimensions of themselves and their relationship not directly related to the parenting of their children. "Parents are people, too" was a phrase coined by Barbara one day when she and Paul were struggling to coax Robert to accept an invitation to sit in on a monthly poker game with some acquaintances at work. Once he grudgingly agreed to go, they tried to persuade him to give himself permission to enjoy it.

Five months into treatment, Robert asked Paul if he could bring his mother to a session. The question came as a surprise to Paul, who was unaware that Robert was even in communication with the elder Mrs. Harmon. Robert wanted his mother to attend a session because he hoped that Paul could help him talk more directly with her, as he had helped him to do with his wife and children.

The subsequent session, with Robert's mother, was tense and challenging. She went on at length about her despair over her daughter, whose behavior led to ongoing involvement with the mental health system, doctors, hospitals, and the courts. Robert became restless, and interrupted with his ideas of how to approach his sister. When his mother professed helplessness and an inability to change, he became frustrated and intrusive—an interaction that seemed to be just as Robert had previously described to Paul, and was reminiscent of Robert's behavior toward his wife at the start of therapy.

As a step toward disentangling Robert from his symptomatic relationship with his mother, Paul suggested that Robert could be more helpful by trying to understand the reasons for his mother's relationship with his sister instead of trying to change it. His mother nodded, and explained that she had promised her husband on his deathbed that she would always take care of their daughter. She talked about her sadness over losing her husband and about the overwhelming responsibility she had incurred. Paul spoke with Robert about the importance of respecting his mother's wishes and the arrogance of trying to discourage her from living her life as she chose, even if it meant living "in a nightmare" with her daughter. Robert listened thoughtfully, looked to his wife for support, and then spoke to his mother directly about how difficult it was for him to watch how his sister treated her. He told his mother that he missed her, but that he couldn't abide the situation with his sister.

Paul interjected that perhaps the presence of Robert's mother in the session presaged a change in their relationship, in which they could begin to have more contact with one another by arranging visits that would not include the sister. Paul's accent on alternatives, rather than on exploring past problems, allowed the session to end with a shift in the relationship between Robert and his mother. With the new acceptance and respect came an expression of mutual longing that had been long absent between them.

The following week, Robert called Paul and asked if they could stop bringing Josh to sessions. Josh had been reclassified as no longer in need of special education services and was very busy with homework, friends, and occasional NA meetings that he attended with Suzanne. Robert and Barbara wished to continue their meetings with Paul as a couple, though, and for the next eight months, they saw Paul once a month. Two months after the session with his mother, Robert mentioned that his sister had been hospitalized again, and his mother had refused to take her back home unless she participated in a day treatment program and took her medication properly. He and Barbara had even gone to visit her.

TWO YEARS LATER

Two years after ending treatment with the Harmons, Paul received the following letter:

Dear Paul,

Today Suzanne is celebrating her third year of being drug and alcohol free. This anniversary helps us realize that our family is going to make it, and we have you to thank for all your caring.

In the two years or so since our last session, we have stumbled but have not fallen. Suzanne graduated from high school and is working full-time. She continues to go to NA meetings. Josh has been doing okay in school in regular classes, and he occasionally goes to meetings with Suzanne. Four months after we stopped seeing you, we agreed that Josh would come off the Ritalin, and he has been doing well without it.

I talk to my mother on a weekly basis and see her every few months. I have a fairly good relationship with her now, though she drives me nuts sometimes. It helps to recall your telling me, "It's okay to feel this way, just accept your feelings for what they are." Barbara is doing okay, too. We try to go out either on our own or with friends once or twice a month. By the way, I won the other night in poker, not much, but it was fun.

Hope all is well with you and your family. Thanks again for all your help. We think of you often and know that you're only a phone call away if we need to talk.

Warmest Regards,
Robert and Barbara Harmon

The Monroes

REORGANIZATION: UPDATING THE THERAPEUTIC MAP

Donna began her fourth session with Brian Ross and the Monroes by outlining her understanding of the symptomatic cycle as it applied to the events so far in the consultation. Some therapists discourage the practice of providing the family with a cognitive explanation of its interactional patterns, saying that it is superfluous and even disrespectful to point out patterns of which the family members are aware on some level, and that insight does not produce change. However, providing a cognitive framework can solidify the experience of transformation and reduce the likelihood of relapse. Although intellectual understanding does not itself produce change, it can serve to anchor budding changes while more affective and experiential groundings develop over time.

To further consolidate change, Donna would need to go beyond her own version of the map to discover how Brian and the family perceived their journey and their current positions. Their feedback would contain clues about how best to proceed.

ANCHORING CHANGE: NANCY WAKES UP

As Brian reviewed his experience of the consultation thus far, he emphasized the shift in his relationship with Nancy. In the following sequence, as Brian talks with Nancy about that shift, Nancy describes the revelation that had come to her.

BRIAN: It's obvious to me, Nancy, that you have the capacity to make difficult things happen; namely, to bring Carl back into the family— so that he can give support to Jennifer.

NANCY: Yeah . . . I was just so confused before.

BRIAN: Confused about what?

NANCY: Well, it seemed to me that Donna was telling you to force me to deal with Carl, despite my having failed with him many times before, and despite the fact that I really didn't want to have anything to do with him.

And anytime you started to give me a break, to maybe realize that it wouldn't work any better this time than the last thousand times, you *(looking at Donna)* jumped in and started hammering away.

BRIAN: Sounds like you saw me as a marionette, with Donna pulling my strings.

NANCY: I kept thinking, surely you can see that I want to leave him. Why are you forcing me to keep trying to get through to him?

DONNA: It seemed to you that we were trying to keep the marriage together?

NANCY: Right. But then it clicked in my mind that what you were really saying was, even if *I* couldn't get any satisfaction from my relationship with Carl, that didn't necessarily mean that *Jennifer* couldn't. In fact, she desperately needs that connection. It sounds so obvious to say it now, but I just couldn't see it before. Anyway, it was simple after that.

DONNA: It must have been quite a shock to have your whole way of looking at the world change suddenly.

NANCY: Well, this is sure a better way to see it. Before, I reacted to any push in Carl's direction by accelerating in the opposite direction. And then I'd try to protect Jennifer from his influence, too.

BRIAN: And now?

NANCY: Now I feel that the best way for me to help Jennifer, in addition to continuing to work on my relationship with her as we've done recently, is to insist that she and her father cultivate a separate relationship, and then to give both of them the space to let that happen.

It is especially important during this phase to anchor behavioral changes with changes in relationships. Before withdrawing from active participation in sessions, the consultant should see evidence that each family member is grounded in a different relationship, not only with one another but also with the primary therapist. This grounding will permit a smoother separation between the consultant and the therapist as well as between the consultant and the family. *"A sign that a consultation has been effective is an absent consultant. . . .* A consultant-in-residence implies that the system cannot take care of itself" (Weber, Wynne, and McDaniel 1986, 50).

To start this process, Donna picked up and expanded on Nancy's last comment.

DONNA: *(Warmly)* Nancy, I want you to know how pleased and impressed I am with what you're saying. It makes a lot of sense to me, and I think that you're right on target about what needs to happen now.

NANCY: Thanks, Donna. These sessions haven't been very easy for me, but I'm really recognizing that things needed to be shaken up if anything was going to change. I feel like I've finally woken up after being asleep for a long, long time.

DONNA: Sometimes what happens in that situation, though, after the initial awakening, is that there's a tremendous pull to drift off back to sleep again. And in your situation, that could be catastrophic.

NANCY: *(Nods rapidly)* I know it would.

DONNA: So let's talk about what you can do to stay awake, and what the rest of the family and Brian can do to help.

As Brian and Nancy talked, it became clear that a warning sign of Nancy's having fallen asleep again would be her getting reentangled with Jennifer and Carl in symptomatic ways. As Nancy told Brian, "If I start talking like I have to cure Jennifer of suicide and control her bulimia, or that I have to deal with everything by myself because Carl won't get involved, please shake me and tell me to wake up."

ANCHORING CHANGE: CARL HAS A DREAM

Donna next asked Carl what effects the recent events had had on him. "When you started talking with Nancy about her 'waking up,'" Carl said, "all of a sudden I remembered a dream that I had last night. Do you want to hear it?"

Carl dreamed that he was a prisoner on a chain gang, supervised by shotgun-toting wardens. There were many other prisoners, including Donna, Brian, Nancy, Jennifer, and a baby. They were all depressed, starving to death, and constantly trying to escape. Then the scene changed, and everyone was free of the chains and running to freedom. Carl, however, had turned into one of the wardens, except that instead of holding a shotgun, he was holding the baby! He wanted to escape with the others, but the baby was crying and he felt an obligation to stay with it. There was some more that he couldn't remember, and then he woke up.

A dream is a marvelous vehicle for carrying the fears, wishes, and secret agendas not only of the dreamer, but of anyone who chooses to interpret the dream. Some schools of psychotherapy rely heavily on dream interpretation as a primary mode of understanding, but many family therapists do not spend much time on this nonverbal, unconscious mode of communication. Donna found Carl's dream to be of great interest and significance on several levels, especially in the context of the work she and Brian had done with the family over the preceding week. Donna recognized elements of the dream that spoke to her of despair, persistence, liberation, and rebirth. It seemed to portend major changes in Carl, in the family, and in the therapeutic system. The dream was not only about change; it contained change.

Here, Donna used Carl's dream as an opportunity to anchor Carl more firmly with Jennifer, by encouraging Brian to ask Jennifer to help her father explain his dream to her.

DONNA: I've always believed that dreams are like bedtime stories, except that we tell them to ourselves when we're already asleep. Brian, maybe you could help Jennifer to explore her father's dream in more detail with him. That way, the two of them can grapple with it together.

BRIAN: Good idea. So, Jennifer, what strikes you about your dad's dream?

JENNIFER: I guess the first thing is that baby. It sounded so pitiful, and so forlorn and out of place. I wondered if it could be me.

BRIAN: Why don't you ask your dad more about it, how it felt in the dream to turn into a warden with a baby.

JENNIFER: Dad, did you feel angry that everyone else ran off and left you with the baby, or were you glad that at least somebody was looking after it?

As Jennifer and her father talked to each other, a greater sense of comfort and familiarity grew between them. Carl's revelation of the dream reflected his readiness to participate in a more personal way in sessions than heretofore; similarly, Jennifer's interest in unearthing the dream's meaning connoted a readiness on her part to become more intimately involved with her father. She was curious to learn more about this man who dreamed of becoming a warden for abandoned children.

CONSOLIDATING THE REORGANIZATION: PLANNING FOR THE WEEKEND

The coming weekend provided an opportunity for the family to experiment further with the emerging possibilities. Donna returned to Nancy and asked what plans she had for the next few days. "My boss wants me to take a buying trip to the West Coast," Nancy replied. Donna recognized Nancy's need to attend to her career. But she felt that Nancy's pulling out before she had resolved her conflicts with Carl regarding separation, and before Carl and Jennifer had connected more solidly, might trigger an outbreak of the symptomatic cycle.

Donna therefore recommended that Nancy postpone her business trip until she and Carl made three important changes: first, that she move Jennifer and herself completely out of her mother's apartment and back in with Carl; second, that she and Carl decide together on the first step in a constructive process of separation; and third, that Carl demonstrate in concrete behavior, as well as in his dreams, his increased sense of responsibility toward his daughter.

These conditions may appear to confine Nancy in the very relationships from which she has sought to disentangle herself. But individuation occurs most naturally when the disengagement proceeds from within the relationship, not when it is unilaterally imposed by one member or accomplished artificially by an external hand, whether that of a therapist or a judge. By pushing family members together, the therapist helps them identify the points at which they remain fused. Disconnection can then be accomplished with enough precision to avoid the large-scale fractures, ruptures, and amputations that characterize the violent dislocations of the symptomatic cycle.

Carl and Nancy continued the discussion, talking over certain details of the coming weekend. The length of the discussion and the fact that it continued without input from Brian or Donna satisfied Donna that this new parental pattern was developing solidity. Then Carl and Jennifer began to make plans for the weekend:

CARL: *(To Jennifer)* I thought we could go on a picnic tomorrow.

JENNIFER: Sounds okay with me.

CARL: In the evening you could come with me to a party my old boss is having. It would give us a chance to get acquainted, like Brian and Donna have been saying, and—

JENNIFER: But what about your drinking? At parties you always get drunk, and bitter.

CARL: Look, Jennifer, the reason I drink at parties is because I feel awkward; I never know what to say to people. I just feel really uncomfortable, and the alcohol makes that feeling go away. The problem is, once I've had a few drinks, I start thinking how I don't really want to be around these people anyway, and then I drink even more, to get away from them.

JENNIFER: I didn't know that, Dad. You get so distant and cold when you're drinking, and it always scared me. It never occurred to me that you were scared, too. . . . I'm glad you told me that. But even though I understand that better now, I still don't want to go to any party with you.

CARL: But see, Jennifer, if you're there, you'd be somebody I could talk to. If you're there, I won't need to drink.

DONNA: Wait a minute, Carl. Something is really bothering me here. *(Turning to Brian)* I keep hearing Carl talk about the problems he has taking care of himself, and he seems to expect Jennifer to be there to rescue him. It's as if he expects his daughter to sacrifice herself for his sake, and the situation's only going to get worse once Nancy's gone. I think Jennifer needs your help in understanding her dilemma and freeing her from this bind.

Donna's statement prompted a shift in the relationship between Carl and Brian, as Brian began to challenge Carl to take care of his own life, including his drinking and his business failures, and not expect Jennifer to do it for him. Feeling supported by Brian, Jennifer spoke to her father more directly about her concerns for him and the burden they created for her.

Just before the end of the session, Donna suggested they meet again on the following Tuesday. After the Monroes left, Donna and Brian discussed the overall course and progression of the consultation. Considerable therapeutic momentum had been established in a number of crucial areas: Nancy's goals for herself individually; her relationships with Brian, Carl, and Jennifer; Brian's relationship with Carl; and Carl's relationship with Jennifer. There was only one major link that needed to form before Donna was comfortable defining the consultation as officially completed: Brian and Jennifer. Donna wanted to see Brian retake his role as Jennifer's individual therapist with greater freedom to challenge Jennifer. The changes in Carl's and Nancy's relationships with each other, with Brian, and with Jennifer would help Jennifer respond to Brian's challenges in nonsymptomatic ways.

CHALLENGING CHANGE: THE SYMPTOMATIC CYCLE TRANSFORMED

In Tuesday's session the parents reported that they had decided to put their house up for sale. Financially it made sense to do so, and it also symbolized their agreement to separate and leave the past behind. Carl also mentioned that Jennifer had not been eating much for a couple of days. She seemed upset about something, but so far she had not been willing to discuss it.

Therapists should expect to reencounter behaviors similar to those of the symptomatic cycle throughout the course of treatment. It is an error to assume that these behaviors necessarily have the same meaning during the fourth phase of treatment as they did earlier, before the therapeutic system was established. One way to distinguish the meaning of symptomatic behavior is by observing whether the system responds by organizing around this behavior in the same way as it did previously.

After deciding on a course of action, Carl and Nancy had begun to catalogue the contents of the house. Jennifer confirmed that this had upset her tremendously.

JENNIFER: I couldn't believe it! That house is the only place I've ever lived. I was born there, I grew up there, sometimes I thought I was going to die there. And they're just matter-of-factly walking from one room to the next, while I'm following them around, and they're saying to each other, "You can have this sofa, and I'll take this bureau." It felt like I was just another piece of furniture. I wonder who'll get me.

BRIAN: So you were upset, and—

JENNIFER: I decided I wasn't going to eat, that's all. I hate them both! *(She starts to cry.)*

Brian decided to take Jennifer's decision to stop eating as an opportunity to test a critical question: Had the family changed sufficiently to contain the effects of his challenging Jennifer's decision? If not, Brian would not feel comfortable working with the Monroes by himself yet, and he would want Donna to remain involved.

Brian first turned to Nancy and Carl and asked them what they thought about Jennifer's decision to stop eating. "We've been through this aggravation enough times for me to see that Jennifer's eating is totally within her own control," Nancy proclaimed, "even if she doesn't admit it. She'd better learn some other ways of dealing with her displeasure, unless she expects to spend a lot of time living in hospitals." Carl concurred. He said that he realized Jennifer was upset about his and Nancy's decision to close up the house. If Jennifer wanted to talk about how she could be involved in the process, rather than feeling victimized by it, he said he would be glad to talk with her.

The parents' responses conveyed much more of a realistic attitude toward Jennifer's symptomatic behavior than had been the case prior to the consultation, or in its early stages. Instead of seeing their daughter as frail and incompetent, they were more aware of the oppositional and rebellious aspects of her behavior. Their responses allowed Brian to feel more secure challenging Jennifer.

BRIAN: You know, Jennifer, your parents are right. You can't continue to deal with feeling upset, feeling angry, by lashing out at people and using your symptoms as weapons, and then expecting sympathy. Anorexia, bulimia, cutting yourself, suicide—they scare people away, they keep people at a distance. I know you feel scared, but you're doing this to yourself! You have to look at what you're doing, Jennifer, if we're going to work together.

JENNIFER: *(Angrily)* I don't have to stay here and listen to this. I thought you were on my side, but I guess I was wrong. *(She gets up as if to leave.)*

CARL: *(Stands up and puts his arm around Jennifer)* Hon, this isn't easy for any of us. I know you don't like what Brian is saying. A lot of times I've had an unresolved conflict with someone, and I walked away from it, too. Now I've learned that each time I do that, the situation just gets worse.

JENNIFER: *(Looks tearfully at Nancy)* Mom, can we leave now? Will you take me home?

NANCY: Jennifer, your father's right. Now, you're upset about what's happening about the house, and about what will happen to you. Maybe you're even more upset that we're splitting up for good this time, and who will take care of Dad, what will happen to Mom—all of that stuff.

But what you need is people to talk to about what's on your mind. That's what Brian is here for. Your father and I can help. We'll go all out for you if necessary, but it can't all come from us. You're going to have to demonstrate some effort on your own part. And that can happen right now, if you keep talking with Brian. *(Jennifer sighs and sits back down.)*

This interchange displays the potential of the transformed therapeutic system to contain its own conflicts and anxiety. The parents' support facilitated a containment of Jennifer's anxiety first within the family, then within her relationship to Brian. In effect, a transitional therapeutic context was created in which Brian could begin to sharpen his focus to the conflicts in a smaller subsystem, the dyad of himself and Jennifer. To be effective, this transitional context would still need to include the physical presence of Jennifer's parents, assuring Jennifer and Brian that the perimeters of the system were secure. Maintaining the parents' presence in therapy sessions would also allow the parents to hold on to the security of their connection with Brian while they developed more sustaining relationships outside the therapeutic system. For example, Carl was beginning to make friends and develop a support group for himself at AA, which he had recently begun to attend.

Brian, more confident in challenging Jennifer's symptomatic behavior because he was no longer working without a net, turned to Jennifer.

BRIAN: So, what's it going to be, Jennifer? Do you want to live, or to die? Staying alive, but living as an anorectic, or a bulimic, to me that's being sort of dead inside. Living means to face your feelings, to talk about all the loneliness and pain, to find reasons to survive—

JENNIFER: But that's just it. The thing that bothers me is that I know now that I can survive. I think maybe before I didn't know that; I thought maybe I was really meant to die.

BRIAN: Yes, I remember your having told me that before.

JENNIFER: But the thing is, even though I know that I *can* survive, I still don't know if I *want* to. That's still a big question. I mean every single day, and several times a day, I ask myself that.

BRIAN: Maybe for now it's enough to know that you *can* survive, and together we can look for reasons if you should, and why.

JENNIFER: I guess so. Isn't there an easier way to do it, though? Can't we sort of sneak up behind all of my problems, and my bad feelings, and surprise them when they aren't looking? It's so painful this other way. Sometimes I feel like I just can't do it.

BRIAN: Do you remember the story of Dr. Dolittle from Puddleby-on-the-Marsh, who could talk to animals [Lofting 1920]?

JENNIFER: Sure, I remember that book. He had a dog named Jip, and a duck called Dab-Dab.

BRIAN: On one of his voyages into deepest, darkest Africa, he found the rarest animal of all—the pushmi-pullyu. Instead of a tail, the pushmi-pullyu had a head on each end. Most of the wild animals, they got caught by the men sneaking up on them when they weren't looking, but you couldn't do that with the pushmi-pullyu. No matter which way you came towards him, he was always facing you. There wasn't any way to catch and bag a pushmi-pullyu. But he could be tamed, and that's what happened in the story.

Problems in life, the kind of really important problems you and I are talking about, Jennifer, they're like the pushmi-pullyu. You can't sneak up on them. You can't run around them. The only way is to confront them head on, to look them right in the face. Then you can get to know them, and you can talk them over with someone else who wants to understand, and eventually you can tame them.

JENNIFER: Well, I still feel like the only reason I can get out of bed every day is because I'm skinny. Somehow, the only reason I feel it's okay for me to talk to people is because I'm so thin. I feel that if I gained any substantial amount of weight I couldn't be with people.

BRIAN: Why not?

JENNIFER: I don't know. Because I would feel so bad about myself. That's the real problem, and I haven't solved that one yet. Part of me feels that I never will solve it, so I should just accept it and live with it as best I can. But part of me feels like that's too big a price to pay.

BRIAN: Maybe you don't need to pay that price, Jennifer. Why don't we see if there's another way? I'm willing to work together on this, if you are.

JENNIFER: I think I'm ready now.

DEATH AND REBIRTH

Following the dialogue between Jennifer and Brian, Donna felt that all of the component goals of the consultation contract had been accomplished. In a sense, they had come full circle, yet they had arrived at a very different place from where they had set out.

Donna discussed with the family and Brian their travels together over the past two weeks, and despite her strong sense of satisfaction about the changes that had occurred, she found herself feeling sad about saying goodbye. Although their encounter with one another had been relatively brief, its emotional intensity had generated bonds that could not be so easily set aside. The feeling of sadness grew, and Donna shared it with the group. "It feels as though I should be at a funeral," she said. "Well, at least it's not Jennifer's," Brian responded. "There were times when I had visions of that." "Or," added Nancy, "my mother's. It was touch and go there for a while."

Donna had an idea. "Perhaps there should be a funeral for the Monroe family," she said, "the old family. Although it was suffering a lot, and might not have survived much longer, it shouldn't be allowed to just disappear without having its passing marked in some way."

The Monroes were intrigued. Staging a funeral for the departed family would give them a unified sense of purpose. It was a signpost to which they could attach their bitterness and regret over the wounds and disappointments of the past, their present feelings of liberation and loss, and their hopes and uncertainties about the future.

Donna suggested that each family member select an item from the house that symbolized for him or her the worst of the family's past and another item that represented the birth of new opportunities. Each person was to write a brief eulogy describing the significance of the two items, and the items would then be buried in the yard of their house, as part of the ceremony. Final arrangements for the funeral were made, including the setting of a date two weeks hence, after Nancy had returned from her trip to California. Donna and Brian were both invited to attend.

Brian made an appointment to meet with Jennifer several days later, stressing that both Carl and Nancy would need to be present as well. The family members each shook hands with Donna, thanking her for her help, and the session ended.

FOUR YEARS LATER

Brian Ross continued to meet with Jennifer Monroe in twice-weekly therapy sessions following the consultation with Donna Jacobson. Carl and Nancy were at each session for the first few weeks; thereafter, Nancy stopped coming, and Carl attended sessions with Jennifer weekly for two more months, and sporadically thereafter. Donna and Brian occasionally had conversations about the family, from which Donna learned the following.

Jennifer joined an improvisational theater group where she made friends with several young women, and she began sharing an apartment with one of them. She enrolled in a local community college, graduated, and found a job as an artist in a small graphics design firm. She continued to see Brian in therapy twice a week for two years, then once weekly. Although still thin, she was not binging or vomiting and made no further suicide attempts. There were no further hospitalizations, medical or psychiatric, following the consultation.

Carl Monroe remarried two years after the consultation to a woman he met at an AA meeting. According to Jennifer, he is no longer drinking. He has a job as a manager in a local retailing and merchandising organization.

Nancy Monroe lives in a neighboring state and has a successful career as a buyer for a large chain of department stores. Her mother is in a nursing home, walks with assistance, and interacts actively with others. Jennifer says that Nancy is doing well and enjoys her life.

Jennifer sees her father and stepmother at least once a week and visits her mother one weekend a month. She says that her relationship with her parents is good. Brian has no reason to think otherwise.

CHAPTER 8

———

Epilogue

Established custom is not easily broken, till some great event shakes the whole system of things, and life seems to recommence upon new principles.
—Samuel Johnson, *A Journey to the Western Islands of Scotland*

The Nature and Context of Crisis Induction

THE CABRINIS, the Harmons, the Monroes, and many other severely symptomatic families have taught us not only about the process of change but also about the possibilities and perils of teaching, learning, and applying the model of crisis induction. Crisis induction is more than simply a treatment modality for intervening in social systems with life-threatening problems. It is a particular way of thinking about the process of change, a way of engaging and interacting with families in serious trouble.

Crisis induction can be easily misunderstood to be a discrete tool for achieving a particular result; for example, at the end of a workshop, we are often asked, "How can I apply the method of crisis induction in the setting where I work?" Though the process may be experienced as hammering, crisis induction is not like a hammer. The process is more akin to cultivating a crop, which requires interaction between the grower, the seed, and the growing conditions. The complexion of therapy based on crisis induction emerges from the therapist, the family, the principles of the model, and the work setting. Their interaction shapes and colors the therapeutic process. For example, in a long-term psychiatric institution the initial phase of treatment might take months, whereas in an acute-care hospital like that of the Philadelphia Child Guidance Clinic, where the length of stay for a hospitalized family averages three weeks, the initial phase is likely to last no longer than a few days. Therefore, a more useful question to ask is, "How can I use myself and the resources available in my work setting and its context to ignite and capitalize on crises to promote change in severely symptomatic families?"

There are three consequences of formulating the question in this way. First, the therapist must be prepared to use and change herself, as Paul used the experience of his own father's death to induce a crisis in Robert Harmon, and Brian had to recognize and change his unconscious collusion with Nancy Monroe before Donna could help him to induce a crisis in the Monroes' marriage. Second, the therapist's context—the supervisory and organizational resources of the work setting—needs to be enlisted, and at times changed, in the service of learning and applying crisis induction. Third, the therapist's role in relation to agents of larger systems, of which her own work setting is but a part, must be clearly negotiated and actively exploited, as Rachel did in her dealings with Nicholas Cabrini's DHS caseworker and Uncle Billy's prosecuting and defense attorneys. The rest of this chapter discusses implications of these three consequences regarding who should learn crisis induction, what type of training and supervisory format is most advantageous, considerations about the institution in which crisis induction is practiced, and thoughts about therapists as agents of social control.

Who Should Learn Crisis Induction?

Not all therapists should practice crisis induction. Responding to madness, chaos, and violence requires a high degree of activity, intentionality, and purpose on the therapist's part. To be effective with the model, the therapist has to feel competent to take charge of difficult situations, comfortable with conflict and confusion, and confident in directly confronting destructive behavior. Therapists who practice crisis induction with severely symptomatic families need a combination of physical stamina and emotional toughness and flexibility. They must also have the ability to laugh at themselves and at the absurdity of life. Therapists must be willing to get their hands dirty; crisis induction is not for therapists who prefer to work only in the comfort of their offices. They need to be prepared to mix it up with the family, not only by bringing extended family members and significant others from the community into the office, but by going into the community with the family, seeing the family several days a week, perhaps several hours at a time, and tackling middle-of-the-night emergencies.

Yet it is an error to respond (as therapists in training often do after viewing a particularly dramatic videotape of crisis induction) by saying, "I could never generate that level of intensity." The error lies in forgetting that the therapist does not act on the family from the outside, that crisis and transformation are induced by engendering and maintaining a high degree of intensity in a relationship that includes the therapist. Thus, the level of intensity needed to induce a crisis is not determined by measuring the strength of the symptomatic cycle and calculating what it will take to overcome it. It is determined by marking the limits of the holding capacity of the relationship the therapist establishes with the family, and then expecting everyone—including herself—to go beyond those limits. Although not every therapist is *suited* to practice crisis induction, any therapist *can;* she simply needs to be willing to stretch her limits.

Just as the context of the family is pivotal to the development of its members, so is the therapist's professional context pivotal to her own training and development. Disconnected from supportive, growth-enhancing relationships with colleagues, the therapist can easily find herself on the edge of the cliff, vulnerable to becoming symptomatic herself. Two important aspects of the therapist's context are her clinical supervision and the overall institutional context in which she works.

Training for Crisis Induction: The Format of Supervision

Learning the model of crisis induction is like learning a foreign language. Although attending workshops and seminars and reading books are helpful in becoming acquainted with theory and techniques, the real learning happens not cognitively but through the therapist's immersion in the therapy process. This immersion leads her to become disoriented at times, as if caught in surf where she is tossed about and turned upside down. It is therefore essential that she be engaged in a relationship with a supervisor whom she trusts to teach her how to ride rough waves and to navigate in a turbulent sea. The therapist's primary responsibility in the supervisory relationship is to help her supervisor understand the nature of her relationship with the family as it evolves—its strengths and points of conflict, the areas in which she feels confident she can help and those in which she feels at sea.

The supervisor's job is to nurture the therapist's competence, unleash her intuition and creative energy, and encourage her to feel secure in challenging her own limits and those of the family. A therapist will be willing to take risks and change her own behavior only if she trusts that the supervisor will remain engaged with her. The supervisor thus needs to create a climate of acceptance that allows both supervisor and therapist to challenge each other's thinking and behavior, and to understand each other's feelings, without threatening the relationship. Together, the therapist and the supervisor need to be free to struggle with each other, resolve conflicts effectively, share responsibility, and have fun in the process—the critical ingredients in any healthy relationship. Trying to learn crisis induction in the absence of this type of supervisory relationship leaves the therapist in danger of absorbing the family's stress and of retreating from it through having intellectual discussions with her supervisor and creating strategies to control or fix symptomatic behavior.

The supervisor, in turn, must be prepared to stay close to the therapist. The supervisor must be accessible to the therapist not only to discuss cases and observe the therapist's work on videotape, but to participate in the actual process of therapy. By being behind the one-way mirror or in the room with the therapist and the family, the supervisor can be involved with the moment-to-moment process of the session. Often the most useful format of supervision is for the supervisor to join the session and work with the family in the therapist's presence. In this way, the supervisor can accomplish two primary goals: to model a different way of approaching the family and to provide the therapist with a different experience of the family.

Teaching crisis induction is subject to the same caveats Richard Rabkin (1972) described when he referred to the training of therapists in crisis intervention.

There is no hope of teaching crisis intervention unless it is possible for people to see a competent crisis intervention team *at work*. . . . This means that crisis intervention can probably be taught only by example. . . . In the model I'm proposing, students spent their first year or two doing very little but watching experts. . . . It is one thing to take an individual patient who has relatively little wrong with him and have him meet three times a week with a student who is pretending to be a therapist, and another thing to do this with life-and-death issues—let us say, recent incest. (Pp. 585, 587)

Practicing Crisis Induction: The Ideology and Organization
of the Institution

Crisis induction requires the therapist to go against the grain of social systems and provoke change. Since most systems, from individuals to families to psychiatric institutions to societies, are invested in maintaining stability, crisis induction is fundamentally a disturbing and disruptive process. Again there is a striking parallel with Rabkin's comments about crisis intervention: "Crisis intervention is dissent. Dissent is personally hazardous and conceptually difficult. . . . Crisis intervention, then, is often incompatible with, or subversive to the goals of many institutions which ask that it be taught. . . . and students must be cautious in other courses about its application in other contexts" (1972, 587, 589). The institution in which the therapist practices crisis induction should espouse the belief that the family is the central healing context for the symptomatic person. Therapists should be actively encouraged to work with whole families in the institution as well as the community, because working intensively with families is the only way to get beyond the typical focus on their pathologic and noxious effects to discover their resilience and competencies. A therapeutic approach that divides up the family and assigns a different professional to each person or subsystem—for example, a psychiatrist for the symptomatic child and a social worker for the parents—risks exacerbating the fragmentation in the family and reinforcing the symptomatic cycle.

The institution's ideology about families is reflected in its physical structure. For example, in residential facilities there should be a place for family members to sleep overnight comfortably, with ready access to privacy, meals, staff, and bathrooms. When the patient is a child who is frightened of being alone or who is at risk of hurting himself or someone else, the institution should make it possible for the child's parents and other family members to stay in the child's room or on a cot in the hallway, available to supervise or comfort him through the night.

The emphasis in crisis induction on constructing and working with interpersonal networks is likely to require changes in the institution's treatment planning and programming. The focus begins to shift from the individual patient or groups of patients to the context, that is, to the family and its interactions with the symptomatic person, as well as to interactions of the family with other families, with the institution's staff, and with the community. For these new contexts to thrive, it is essential that the institution promote clear and open communication among people at different organizational levels and functions. Boundaries between the various components of the institution, and between the institution and the community, should be flexible and permeable. Administrative support services, such as utilization review, maintenance and housekeeping, quality assurance, and fiscal management, among others, need to be conversant with and supportive of the clinical model, so that institutional policy and priorities are informed by and synergistic with clinical considerations. In such contexts, a social worker can supervise a psychiatrist, a referring therapist can work with the inpatient team during a symptomatic person's hospitalization, and an inpatient therapist can continue to work with the family following the patient's discharge from the hospital. When institutions and agencies gauge performance primarily by caseload productivity and compliance with policies and procedures, they stifle creativity and promote helplessness and burnout in their staff.

No institutional context precisely fits the ideal we are depicting. However, therapists can work toward reform in institutions by employing the same principles of crisis induction as they use to promote transformation in families.

Crisis Induction: Therapeutic Conversation or Social Control?

Crisis induction is at heart an intimate conversation, just like all psychotherapy. As Thomas Szasz wrote, the therapist's "task is, first, *not to diagnose the patient, but to engage him in a meaningful dialogue. . . .* In actuality, there is no such thing as 'therapy'; there is only a particular therapist, a particular patient, and their communications, especially their promises, to each other" (1965, 89, 130). Crisis induction with severely symptomatic families, however, is a conversation characterized by intensity, repetition, and challenge, which are necessary to counteract the destructive processes that tend to persist in these families in spite of the therapist's best efforts. In some cases, societal agents external to the family must eavesdrop and sometimes intrude on the conversation. Often, powerful forces that influence the family beyond the therapist's domain, and over which neither she nor the family has any control, take over. This point is poignantly illustrated toward the end of therapy with the Cabrini family, where city funding cutbacks and the politics of the legal system allowed Maria's mother and stepfather to collude in permitting Uncle Billy to return home.

When madness, chaos, and violence are part of the family's conversation, the therapist must participate in the construction of a monitoring system that serves to protect herself, the family members, and the therapeutic process. The watchful eye and alerting voice of the therapist may need to extend beyond the therapy room. She may need to reach out to community agencies such as the police and the child protective services. The therapist may communicate observations and recommendations to societal agents who in turn can exert considerable influence over the family. In these situations the therapist can avoid acting as an instrument of social control vis-à-vis the family provided that (1) she intends to influence these societal agents in the family's behalf; (2) she continues to define and experience her primary affiliation and obligation as being to the family; and (3) she discusses these "extratherapeutic" conversations with the family, preferably before speaking with the external agents.

Actually, much of what is described as social control is an illusion. Social control may appear to operate when a person is involuntarily committed by a court to a mental hospital, or children are removed from their family by the Department of Human Services and placed in a foster home or residential facility. But these interventions do not control the family as much as they dislocate relationships and shift the locus of responsibility for the problem. Although these interventions may in fact provide the only means of preserving the last tattered shreds of connectedness in the family, when they masquerade as control they can blind participants to the need to create a larger system in which the responsibility for dealing with the problem is shared.

Because the boundaries of severely symptomatic systems generally extend beyond the family to include neighborhoods, community agencies, schools, medical institutions, mental health agencies, and legal systems, therapists must avoid the error of becoming overly focused on intrafamilial dynamics, despite the compelling pull to do so. It is necessary for the therapist to join the family in its world by becoming directly involved in the larger social networks with which the family is entangled. From this position of proximity, the therapist's integrity and credibility are greatly enhanced. She can then act strongly out of her own convictions and make recommendations authoritatively, knowing that the ultimate authority and responsibility always rest with the family.

Precepts for the Therapist

Working with families who live at the brink of disaster pulls the therapist to the brink as well. We have formulated ten precepts to help
therapists manage the stress of crisis induction without sacrificing their
flexibility, creativity, and sense of humor.

1. Be honest and clear with yourself and others about your needs and
   expectations, and do not abandon your principles under any circumstances.
2. Believe that families are more competent than they appear; they
   present themselves to therapists at their worst, not at their best.
3. Know your limits, and what you can and cannot control.
4. Take no responsibility for anyone else's behavior, and take complete responsibility for your own.
5. Take risks. Embrace your mistakes and forgive yourself for them,
   and encourage others to do the same.
6. Resolve interpersonal conflicts directly as they arise.
7. Have at least one close friend among your colleagues, someone with
   whom you can laugh easily and cry openly.
8. Maintain a clear sense of priorities in your relationships: personal
   relationships—family, friends, and colleagues—come first, and then
   the patient and the patient's family.
9. Accept the thoughts and feelings of others unconditionally, without
   trying to change them no matter how painful they are, and attend
   carefully to what others tell you through their behavior.
10. Feel free to challenge everything.

BIBLIOGRAPHY

Abroms, G. M., Fellner, C., & Whitaker, C. A. (1971). The family enters the hospital. *American Journal of Psychiatry, 127*(10), 99–105.

Anderson, C., Reiss, D., & Hogarty, G. (1986). *Schizophrenia and the Family: A Practitioner's Guide to Psychoeducation and Management.* New York: Guilford.

Anderson, H., & Goolishian, H. (1988). Human systems as linguistic systems: Preliminary and evolving ideas about the implications for clinical theory. *Family Process, 27,* 371–393.

Andolfi, M., Angelo, C., Menghi, P., & Nicol-Corigliano, A. M. (1983). *Behind the Family Mask.* New York: Brunner/Mazel.

Auerswald, E. H. (1972). Interdisciplinary versus ecological approach. In J. Sager & H. S. Kaplan (Eds.), *Progress in Group and Family Therapy* (pp. 309–321). New York: Brunner/Mazel.

Ausubel, N. (1980). Things could always be worse. In *A Treasury of Jewish Folklore* (pp. 63–65). New York: Bantam.

Bateson, G. (1972). *Steps to an Ecology of Mind.* New York: Ballantine.

Bateson, G. (1979). *Mind and Nature.* New York: Dutton.

Bateson, G., Jackson, D., Haley, J., & Weakland, J. H. (1956). Towards a Theory of Schizophrenia," *Behavioral Science, 1*:4

Bell, J. E. (1971). *The Family in the Hospital.* Washington, DC: Government Printing Office.

Berger, M. (1978). *Beyond the Double Bind.* New York: Brunner/Mazel.

Bergman, J. S. (1985). *Fishing for Barracuda: Pragmatics of Brief Systemic Therapy.* New York: Norton.

Bhatti, R. S., Janakiramaiah, N., & Channabasavanna, S. M. (1980). Family psychiatric ward treatment in India. *Family Process, 19,* 193–200.

Bogdan, J. (1984). Family organization as an ecology of ideas: An alternative to the reification of family systems. *Family Process, 23,* 375–388.

Bowen, M. (1961). Family psychotherapy. *American Journal of Orthopsychiatry, 31,* 40–60

Bowen, M. (1966). Family psychotherapy with schizophrenia in the hospital and in private practice. In I. Boszormenyi-Nagy & J. L. Framo (Eds.), *Intensive Family Therapy* (pp. 215–243). New York: Harper & Row.

Brendler, J. (1987). A perspective on the brief hospitalization of whole families. *Journal of Family Therapy, 9,* 113–130.

Brendler, J., & Combrinck-Graham, L. (1986). The treatment of hospitalized families of young children. In L. Combrinck-Graham (Ed.), *Treating Young Children in Family Therapy* (pp. 85–95). Rockville, MD: Aspen.

Brown, M. W. (1942). *The Runaway Bunny.* New York: Harper & Row.

Buber, M. (1958). *I and Thou.* New York: Scribner's.

Combrinck-Graham, Lee. (1985). A developmental model for family systems. *Family Process, 24,* 139–150.

Combrinck-Graham, L., Gursky, E., & Brendler, J. (1982). Hospitalization of single-parent families of disturbed children. *Family Process, 21,* 131–152.

Cooklin, A., Miller, A. C., & McHugh, B. (1983). An institution for change: Developing a family day unit. *Family Process, 22,* 453–468.

Cousteau, V. (1973, summer). How to swim with sharks: A primer. *Perspectives in Biology and Medicine,* 525–528.

Crum, T. (1987). *The Magic of Conflict.* New York: Simon & Schuster.

Davis, A. E., Dinitz, S., & Pasamanick, B. (1974). *Schizophrenics in the New Custodial Community.* Columbus: Ohio State University Press.

Dell, P. (1982). Beyond homeostasis: Toward a concept of coherence. *Family Process, 21,* 21–41.

Dell, P. (1985a). Review of *The Invented Reality,* by P. Watzlawick. *Family Process, 24,* 293.

Dell, P. (1985b). Understanding Bateson and Maturana: Toward a biological foundation for the social sciences. *Journal of Marital and Family Therapy, 11,* 1–20.

Elizur, J., & Minuchin, S. (1989). *Institutionalizing Madness: Families, Therapy, and Society.* New York: Basic Books.

Foss, L., & Rothenberg, K. (1987). *The Second Medical Revolution: From Biomedicine to Infomedicine.* Boston: New Science Library of Shambhala.

Foster, A. D. (1988). *To the Vanishing Point.* New York: Warner.

Fox, M. (1990, March). Empowering families facilitates effective hospital treatment. *Psychiatric Times,* 39.

Gharajedaghi, J. (1985). *Toward a Systems Theory of Organization.* Seaside, CA: Intersystems.

Glasscote, R. M., Cumming, E., Rutman, I. P., Sussex, J. N., & Glassman, S. M. (1971). *Rehabilitating the Mentally Ill in the Community.* Washington, DC: Joint Information Service of APA and National Association of Mental Health.

Gleick, J. (1987). *Chaos: Making a New Science.* New York: Viking.

Goldberg, E. M. (1966). Hospital work and family: A four-year study of young mental hospital patients. *British Journal of Psychiatry, 112,* 177–196.

Goldner, V. (1985). Feminism and family therapy. *Family Process, 24,* 31–47.

Goldner, V. (1987). Instrumentalism, feminism, and the limits of family therapy. *Journal of Family Psychology, 1*(1), 109–116.

Griffith, J., Griffith, M., & Slovik, L. (1990). Mind-body problems in family therapy: Contrasting first- and second-order cybernetics approaches. *Family Process, 29,* 13–28.

Gruenberg, E. (1967). The social breakdown syndrome: Some origins. *American Journal of Psychiatry, 123,* 1481–1489.

Grunebaum, H. U., & Weiss, J. L. (1963). Psychotic mothers and their children: Joint admission to an adult psychiatric hospital. *American Journal of Psychiatry, 119,* 927–933.

Haley, J. (1973). *Uncommon Therapy: The Psychiatric Techniques of Milton H. Erickson, M.D.* New York: Norton.

Haley, J. (1985). *Conversations with Milton H. Erickson, M.D.* (3 vols.). New York: Triangle Press.

Harbin, H. T. (1979). A family-oriented psychiatric inpatient unit. *Family Process, 18,* 281–291.

Hatfield, A., & Lefley, H. (1987). *Families of the Mentally Ill: Coping and Adaptation.* New York: Guilford.

Healey, J. (1989). The cybernetics of community responses to incest and child abuse. *Family Systems Medicine, 7*(3), 305.

Heiman, M. (1988). Untangling incestuous bonds: The treatment of sibling incest. In M. Kahn & K. Lewis (Eds.), *Siblings in Therapy: Life Span and Clinical Issues* (pp. 135–166). New York: Norton.

Henry, J. (1973). *Pathways to Madness.* New York: Vintage.

Herrigel, E. (1953). *Zen in the Art of Archery.* New York: Vintage.

Herz, M. I., Endicott, G., & Spitzer, R. L. (1977). "Brief hospitalization: A two-year follow-up." *American Journal of Psychiatry, 134,* 502–507.

Hochman, G. (1979, March 18). The apartment: Window on the troubled family. *Today Magazine, Philadelphia Inquirer.*

Hoff, B. (1982). *The Tao of Pooh.* New York: Penguin.

Hoffman, L. (1981). *Foundations of Family Therapy.* New York: Basic Books.

Hoffman, L. (1985). Beyond power and control: Toward a second order family systems therapy. *Family Systems Medicine, 3,* 381.

Hoffman, L. (1990). Constructing realities: An art of lenses. *Family Process, 29,* 1–12.

Hofstadter, D. R. (1979). *Gödel, Escher, Bach: An Eternal Golden Braid.* New York: Basic Books.

Kafka, F. (1946). *Metamorphosis.* New York: Vanguard.

Keeney, B. (1983). *The Aesthetics of Change.* New York: Guilford.

Keith, D. V., & Whitaker, C. A. (1981). Play therapy: A paradigm for work with families. *Journal of Marital and Family therapy, 7,* 243–254.

Langs, R. (1989, March). Psychotherapy and psychoanalysis defined by mathematical models. *Psychiatric Times, 14.*

Langsley, D. G., & Kaplan, D. M. (1968). *The Treatment of Families in Crisis.* New York: Grune & Stratton.

Lofting, H. (1920). *The Story of Doctor Dolittle.* Philadelphia: Lippincott.

Luepnitz, D. (1988). *The Family Interpreted: Feminist Theory in Clinical Practice.* New York: Basic Books.

Lynch, M., Steinberg, D., & Ounsted, C. (1975). Family unit in a children's psychiatric hospital. *British Medical Journal, 2,* 127–129.

Madanes, C. (1989, November/December). Madanes presents fifteen steps for dealing with sex abuse. *Family Therapy News, 19.*

Main, T. F. (1958). Mothers with children in psychiatric hospital. *Lancet, 2,* 845–847.

Maturana, H., & Varela, F. (1987). *The Tree of Knowledge.* Boston: Shambhala.

Miller, D. (1989). Family violence and the helping system. In L. Combrinck-Graham (Ed.), *Children in Family Contexts: Perspectives on Treatment.* (pp. 413–434). New York: Guilford.

Milne, A. (1926). *Winnie-the-Pooh.* New York: Dell.

Minuchin, S. (1974). *Families and Family Therapy.* Cambridge: Harvard University Press.

Minuchin. S., & Barcai, A. (1969). Therapeutically induced family crisis. *Science and Psychoanalysis* (Vol. 14, pp. 199–205). New York: Grune & Stratton.

Minuchin, S., & Fishman, H. C. (1981). *Family Therapy Techniques.* Cambridge: Harvard University Press.

Minuchin, S., Rosman, B., & Baker, L. (1978). *Psychosomatic Families.* Cambridge: Harvard University Press.

Musashi, M. (1974). *A Book of Five Rings.* New York: Overlook.

Nakhla, F., Flokart, L., & Webster, J. (1969). Treatment of families as inpatients. *Family Process, 8,* 79–96.

Neill, J. R., & Kniskern, D. P. (1982). *From Psyche to System: The Evolving Therapy of Carl Whitaker.* New York: Guilford.

Pittman, F. (1984). Wet cocker spaniel therapy: An essay on technique in family therapy. *Family Process, 23,* 1–11

Pittman, F. S. (1987). *Turning Points: Treating Families in Transition and Crisis.* New York: Norton.

Rabkin, R. (1972). Crisis intervention. In A. Ferber, M. Mendelsohn, & A.

Napier (Eds.), *The Book of Family Therapy* (pp. 582–596). Boston: Houghton Mifflin.

Ruesch, J. (1966). Hospitalization and social disability. *Journal of Nervous and Mental Disease, 142,* 203–214.

Ruesch, J., & Bateson, G. (1968). *Communication: The Social Matrix of Psychiatry.* New York: Norton.

Sabelli, H., & Carlson-Sabelli, L. (1989). Biological priority and psychological supremacy: A new integrative paradigm derived from process theory. *American Journal of Psychiatry, 146*(12), 1541–1551.

Satir, V. (1988). The tools of the therapist. In J. K. Zeig & S. R. Lankton (Eds.), *Developing Ericksonian Therapy: State of the Art.* New York: Brunner/Mazel.

Scharff, J. S. (Ed.). (1989). *Foundations of Object Relations Family Therapy.* Northvale, NJ: Jason Aronson.

Schwartz, M., & Wiggins, O. (1986). Systems and the structuring of meaning: Contributions to a biopsychosocial medicine. *American Journal of Psychiatry, 143*(10), 1213–1221.

Segal, L. (1986). *The Dream of Reality: Heinz von Foerster's Constructivism.* New York: Norton.

Selvini Palazzoli, M., Boscolo, L., Cecchin, G., & Prata, G. (1978). *Paradox and Counterparadox.* New York: Jason Aronson.

Selvini Palazzoli, M., Boscolo, L., Cecchin, G., & Prata, G. (1980). The problem of the referring person. *Journal of Marital and Family Therapy, 6,* 3–9.

Silverstein, M. (1968). *Psychiatric Aftercare.* Philadelphia: University of Pennsylvania Press.

Simon, H. (1969). *The Sciences of the Artificial.* Cambridge: MIT Press.

Snyder, G. (1983). *Axe Handles.* San Francisco: North Point.

Stern, S., Whitaker, C., Hagemann, N. J., Anderson, R. B., & Bargman, G. J. (1981). Anorexia nervosa: The hospital's role in family treatment. *Family Process, 20,* 395–408.

Stewart, I. (1989). *Does God Play Dice? The Mathematics of Chaos.* Oxford: Basil Blackwell.

Szasz, T. (1965). *The Ethics of Psychoanalysis: The Theory and Method of Autonomous Psychotherapy.* New York: Basic Books.

Test, M. A., & Stein, L. I. (1975). The clinical rationale for community treatment: A review of the literature. In L. I. Stein & M. A. Test (Eds.), *Alternatives to Mental Hospital Treatment.* New York: Plenum.

Varela, F. (1976, fall). Not one, not two. *Co-Evolution Quarterly, 62*–67.

Watzlawick, P. (1984). *The Invented Reality.* New York: Norton.

Watzlawick, P., Weakland, J., & Fisch, R. (1974). *Change: Principles of Problem Formation and Problem Resolution.* New York: Norton.

Weber, T. T., Wynne, L. C., & McDaniel, S. H. (1986). Losing your way as a consultant. In L. C. Wynne, S. H. McDaniel, & T. T. Weber (Eds.) *Systems Consultation: A New Perspective for Family Therapy* (pp. 35–50). New York: Guilford.

Whitaker, C. A., & Bumberry, W. M. (1988). *Dancing with the Family: A Symbolic-Experiential Approach.* New York: Brunner/Mazel.

Whitaker, C. A., & Olsen, E. (1971). The staff team and the family square off. In G. M. Abroms & N. S. Greenfield (Eds.), *The New Hospital Psychiatry* (pp. 67–81). New York: Academic.

Wiesel, E. (1972). *Souls on Fire.* New York: Summit Books.

Woodcock, A., & Davis, M. (1978). *Catastrophe Theory.* New York: Avon.

Zeig, J. (1980). *A Teaching Seminar with Milton H. Erickson.* New York: Brunner/Mazel.

INDEX